50 classic backcountry Ski and Snowboard Summits

in California

classic
backcountry
Ski and Snowboard Summits
in California

Mount Shasta to Mount Whitney

Paul Richins, Jr.

Foreword by John Moynier

THE
MOUNTAINEERS

Dedicated to my daughter, Sierra Nicole Richins,
and my parents, Beverly and Paul Richins, Sr.

Published by
The Mountaineers
1001 SW Klickitat Way, Suite 201
Seattle, WA 98134

Published simultaneously in Great Britain by Cordee, 3a DeMontfort Street, Leicester, England, LE1 7HD

Manufactured in Canada

Edited by Jane Crosen
Maps by Jerry Painter
All photographs by Paul Richins, Jr., except where noted otherwise
Cover and book design by Kristy L. Welch
Layout by Kristy L. Welch

Cover photograph: *Backcountry skiing west of Mount Lyell in Yosemite National Park.* Photo by Paul Richins, Jr.
Frontispiece: *Spring skiing in the Sierra Nevada.* Photo by John Moynier

Library of Congress Cataloging-in-Publication Data
Richins, Paul, 1949–
    50 classic backcountry ski and snowboard summits in California:
Mount Shasta to Mount Whitney / Paul Richins ; with foreword by
John Moynier.—1st ed.
        p. cm.
    "Published simultaneously in Great Britain by Cordee."
    Includes bibliographical references (p.) and index.
    ISBN 0-89886-656-1 (pbk.)
    1. Cross-country skiing—California—Guidebooks. 2. Cross-country
ski trails—California—Guidebooks. 3. Snowboarding—California—
Guidebooks. 4. California—Guidebooks. I. Title. II. Title: Fifty
classic backcountry ski and snowboard summits in California
    GV854.5.C2 R53 1999
    796.93'2'09794—dc21
                                                                99-6549
                                                                    CIP

CONTENTS

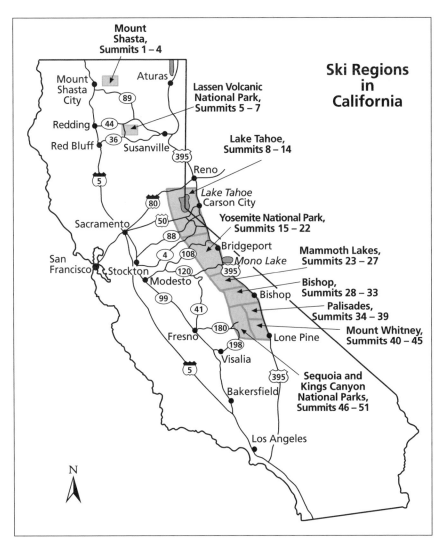

Ski Regions in California

Mount Shasta, Summits 1 – 4

Mount Shasta City

Aturas

Lassen Volcanic National Park, Summits 5 – 7

Redding

Red Bluff

Susanville

Lake Tahoe, Summits 8 – 14

Reno

Lake Tahoe
Carson City

Sacramento

Yosemite National Park, Summits 15 – 22

San Francisco

Stockton

Bridgeport

Mono Lake

Mammoth Lakes, Summits 23 – 27

Modesto

Bishop, Summits 28 – 33

Bishop

Palisades, Summits 34 – 39

Fresno

Lone Pine

Mount Whitney, Summits 40 – 45

Visalia

Bakersfield

Sequoia and Kings Canyon National Parks, Summits 46 – 51

Los Angeles

N

Map legend

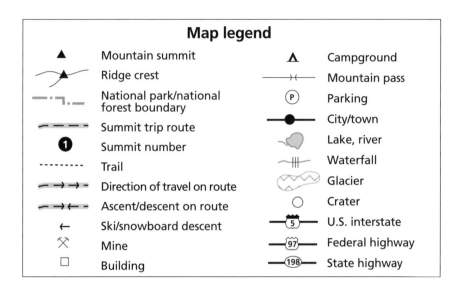

▲	Mountain summit	Λ	Campground
	Ridge crest	⊢⊣	Mountain pass
	National park/national forest boundary	ⓟ	Parking
	Summit trip route	●	City/town
❶	Summit number		Lake, river
- - - - - - -	Trail	‖‖	Waterfall
→ → →	Direction of travel on route		Glacier
→ ←	Ascent/descent on route	○	Crater
←	Ski/snowboard descent	⑤	U.S. interstate
⚒	Mine	㉗	Federal highway
☐	Building	⑲⑧	State highway

Acknowledgments

Growing up in Weaverville, a small rural town in northern California, I was naturally drawn to the mountains and the beauty and solitude of high places. I began learning the ropes of backcountry travel in my early teens, tagging along with Dick Everest on some amazing hikes and winter ski trips into the Trinity Alps.

Another major influence in my ski mountaineering life has been Gene Leach, who in addition to teaching me statistics and probability at Shasta Community College in Redding, California, shared my interest in hiking, climbing, kayaking, and cross-country skiing. Over the past thirty years our adventures have included countless ski crossings of Lassen Volcanic National Park, climbs of Mount Shasta, and trips into the Sierra Nevada wilderness.

Many of the summits in this book have been skied with Bob Carlson of Auburn, California, and Colin and Robin Fuller of Reno, Nevada. Their assistance with this project has been invaluable, as we have explored hundreds of backcountry summits, from Mount Shasta to Mount Whitney, in search of the finest powder and the best spring corn snow.

I also want to thank John Moynier for the suggestions, guidance, and assistance he willingly provided, as well as supplying photos and writing the preface, the backcountry snowboarding material, and the avalanche awareness section for this book.

I also want to recognize those authors who have broken trail for subsequent generations of backcountry skiers, snowboarders, and climbers. Those of special note include David Brower (*The Sierra Club Manual of Ski Mountaineering*, 1969), Hans Joachim Burhenne (*Sierra Spring Ski-Touring*, 1971), Steve Roper (*The Climber's Guide to the High Sierra*, 1976), David Beck (*Ski Touring in California*, 1980), R. J. Secor (*The High Sierra: Peaks, Passes and Trails*, 1992), and John Moynier (*Backcountry Skiing in the High Sierra*, 1992).

Above all, I thank my parents, Beverly and Paul Richins, Sr., for instilling in me the belief that with hard work, self-discipline, courage, and passion, no goal is unattainable—and for providing me with that insatiable "Lewis and Clark" desire to explore regions beyond.

Preface

I was just a teenager in 1967 when I set out with my friend Dick Everest on my first overnight winter ski mountaineering excursion. After reading a short description of how to build an igloo in Gaston Rebuffat's *Between Heaven and Earth*, Dick and I—showshoes strapped to our feet, leather lace-up ski boots and alpine skis on our backs—charged into the depths of the Trinity Alps for four days. We knew the area well from summer hikes, but this was the first time for either of us in the winter. After a strenuous climb with heavy packs, we arrived at Bowerman Meadows by late afternoon. This left us little time to build our first igloo, as it would be dark in a couple of hours and a storm was fast approaching. There was no margin for error, as we had no tent, no Gore-Tex parkas, no bivy sack, no protective storm gear. It was nearly dark and snowing lightly when I finally climbed up the side of the igloo to place the top snow block. That night it snowed 18 inches.

A few years later, an igloo that my friend Gene Leach and I constructed on the summit of Lassen Peak saved our lives and those of two others as the gale-force winds of a fierce winter storm flattened the tent in which our climbing partners were sleeping. Winter ascents of Mount Shasta, Mount Whitney, Pyramid Peak, Price Peak, and Ralston Peak were soon to follow. Looking back on these and other early climbs, I realize how little I knew then of ski mountaineering techniques, but those first experiences galvanized my desire to explore the wilderness and climb high places. These early experiences were the beginning of my fondness for the mountains in winter. Ski mountaineering tests your skills, taxes your stamina, and challenges your resourcefulness, yet the mountains' incomparable wonders, beauty, and solitude are spiritually uplifting.

Today an additional joy is to ski and climb with my daughter, Sierra Nicole, and to share her enthusiasm for the mountains. At age ten she set a goal of climbing all the 14,000-footers in California, and by age thirteen she had accomplished her goal. By the time she was fifteen she had added Mount Rainier and many of Colorado's fourteeners to her list of summit climbs.

My daughter can attest to the fact that a successful mountaineer is not necessarily the strongest climber or the best skier, but the one with a full measure of mental strength, self-discipline, and persistence. For the backcountry skier, the joy of reaching that seldom-visited summit, followed by an exquisite ski or snowboard descent, is satisfaction enough, far exceeding the demands of the climb.

What I have enjoyed most in writing *Fifty Classic Backcountry Ski and Snowboard Summits* has been completing the research that obligated me to climb every peak and ski nearly every descent route detailed in the guide. These trips took me through some of the most beautiful terrain conceivable, to the top of

Powder skiing near Lassen Peak (Chapter 3)

some of the finest summits imaginable, and down slopes of powder and spring corn that were both challenging and exhilarating.

I hope you enjoy the book and California's many excellent ski and snowboard summits. Please send your feedback and comments to my e-mail address, prichins@energy.state.ca.us, or view my website http://pweb.jps.net/~prichins/backcountry_ resource_center.htm.

Paul Richins, Jr.

foreword

There was a time when I was a bit insecure about the quality of skiing here in the Sierra Nevada. I'd heard the boasts about the "Greatest Snow on Earth" elsewhere, and I'd cringed at the ridicule brought by "Sierra Cement." Everywhere I went, skiers whom I respected held nothing back in their insults of my beloved range. According to them, the snow was junk, the peaks were nothing; in their opinion, the whole place wasn't even worth a trip. I couldn't decide if they knew what they were talking about, or were just jealous.

At the time, I really didn't know any better. Having grown up in the big city, I was just in constant awe of the vastness of the Sierra Nevada, the seemingly unending wildness. What was I missing, I wondered? The Sierra offers an incredibly broad range of terrain, a ski and snowboard season lasting nine months or more, peak descents with 6,000 feet of vertical and more. Why did the Sierra get such a bad rap?

One evening I was sitting around a campfire with a group of mountain guides from other areas, keeping my thoughts to myself as they argued over whose home range was the best place to ski. Finally, I'd had enough. The Sierra Nevada has just as many good powder days, I asserted, and we have unquestionably the best wind-pack and spring-corn skiing, bar none—especially when you consider that we can ski and snowboard good snow almost all year long.

The silence was deafening. They may have argued about the powder, but wind-pack and corn? Skiing in the late spring and summer? Most of these guys would have traded in their skis for chalk bags and mountain bikes months before. I challenged them to come to the Sierra Nevada when their areas were dry dirt, to see if I spoke the truth. Sure enough, come spring I got a few calls and to the crest we went. Topping out on one of the big peaks, these guys would survey the endless summits marching off in all directions and invariably ask, "What range is that over there?" Deferring to the master, I would quote the late, great Allan Bard, and say, "We ain't got but one—that's just the Sierra."

Over the years, I finally came to understand old-timers who came to roost in the Sierra Nevada. These graybeards had climbed the world over, skied from here to there and back again, and chose this little pile of hills to make their home. As young bucks, we would press them about this climb or that tour and after skimming over the rough details, they would pause and look us in the eye, saying, "You know, traveling to other ranges is an exercise in appreciation for the Sierra."

I found out that they were right. Sure, it's fun to travel, but this wonderful range offers just about everything you could ever want for climbing, skiing, or living. For me, the best of the best is the unlimited potential for ski descents off countless peaks. For more than a hundred years, better men and women than I have been enjoying the mountains of California on skis, and who am I to argue with my elders? I believe that the Sierra Nevada offers ski mountaineering challenges that are at least the equal of any other range in North America. *Fifty Classic Ski and Snowboard Summits of California* offers the proof. Get out, try some of these fabulous trips, and I think you'll agree. In the process, I hope you come to enjoy ski mountaineering in the Sierra Nevada as much as I have. Happy skiing!

John Moynier

Risks of Ski Mountaineering

Ski mountaineering is one of the finest sports imaginable, but to practice it without technique is a form of more or less deliberate suicide. Technique encourages prudence; it also obviates fatigue and useless or dangerous halts and, far from excluding it, permits meditation. It is not an end in itself but the means of promoting safety.
—Gaston Rebuffat, On Snow and Rock

There are inherent risks in glacier travel, backcountry snowboarding, and ski mountaineering. Many of the routes described in this book will, at times, be unsafe due to potential snow and ice avalanches, rock falls, or weakly bridged crevasses. While the author and publisher have done their best to provide accurate information and to point out potential hazards, conditions change from year to year and from day to day due to weather and other factors. It is up to the users of this guide to learn the necessary mountaineering skills for safe climbing and skiing and to exercise caution at all times, especially on glaciers and ice, and on terrain prone to rock falls, snow slides, and avalanches.

Many of the peaks described in this guide require strong ski and snowboard mountaineering skills. It is presumed that the user of this guide possesses the skiing and snowboarding ability for a safe descent and is skilled in the use of compass and map, route finding, navigation in whiteout conditions, snow stability evaluation methods, avalanche rescue techniques, and crevasse rescue procedures. Many summits may also require the use of an ice axe and crampons, and some may require a climbing rope for protection in the ascent and descent.

Getting down and dirty in the deep powder near Tryon Peak (Summit 14)

Skiers, snowboarders, snowshoers, and others using this book do so entirely at their own risk, and the author and publisher disclaim any liability for injury or other damage by anyone ski touring, ski mountaineering, snowboarding, telemarking, randonnée skiing, alpine skiing, snowshoeing, or any other methods of travel and descent in the areas described in this guide.

A NOTE ABOUT SAFETY

Safety is an important concern in all outdoor activities. No guidebook can alert you to every hazard or anticipate the limitations of every reader. Therefore, the descriptions of roads, trails, routes, and natural features in this book are not representations that a particular place or excursion will be safe for your party. When you follow any of the routes described in this book, you assume responsibility for your own safety. Under normal conditions, such excursions require the usual attention to traffic, road and trail conditions, weather, terrain, the capabilities of your party, and other factors. Keeping informed on current conditions and exercising common sense are the keys to a safe, enjoyable outing.

—*The Mountaineers*

Chapter 1
THE FIRST RUN

Some of the finest skiing and snowboarding can be found in the mountains of California. The temperate winter climate, along with the fabulous spring weather and abundant snowfall, combine with splendid scenery to create a skier's paradise stretching nearly the length of the state. California's superb ski conditions—a deep snow pack, winter powder, and some of the best spring corn snow found anywhere—create an ideal environment in which to explore the untracked summits of the Sierra Nevada and the Cascade Range.

Skiing or snowboarding California's backcountry summits is a unique and unforgettable experience providing all manner of adventure and enjoyment. From the 14,000-foot glaciated summit of Mount Shasta in the north to Mount Whitney in the south, this unbroken chain of mountains, spanning more than 550 miles, offers an endless variety of skiing and snowboarding opportunities. Gigantic volcanoes, splendid summits, elegant arêtes, sheer granite faces, precipitous couloirs, immense glacial cirques, high open bowls, hanging valleys, lofty mountain passes, and deep canyons inspire the dauntless backcountry traveler to action.

Crossing the Ionion Basin, heading towards Evolution Basin (Bishop region)

This guide concentrates on the chain of mountains comprising the southern end of the Cascade Range and the Sierra Nevada. The Cascade Range occupies the northern fourth of the state and is dominated by Mount Shasta and Lassen Peak. The Sierra Nevada begins where the Cascade Range ends, a short distance south of Lassen Peak, and stretches nearly 400 miles to Tehachapi Pass (Highway 58, southeast of Bakersfield). For geographic perspective, consider that the Sierra Nevada easily exceeds the size of the entire European Alps— the French, Swiss, Austrian, and Italian Alps combined.

In general, the peaks in the Sierra Nevada gradually increase in elevation from north to south. The highest peaks in the north near Lake Tahoe barely reach 10,000 feet. Moving south along the crest of the range, 11,000-foot peaks emerge, followed by 12,000-footers and then 13,000-footers. All of the Sierra Nevada's 14,000-foot peaks are in the Palisade and Mount Whitney regions, culminating in the highest summit in the lower forty-eight United States, Mount Whitney. Six miles to the south is Mount Langley, the last 14,000-footer. From this point, the peaks rapidly decrease in elevation, and the Sierra Nevada ends, near Death Valley.

The mountains of California offer an excellent combination of summits that can be completed in less than a day (see the list of "Single-Day Gems" in Appendix 1), along with remote wilderness peaks requiring a week-long mini-expedition through some of the finest backcountry ski and snowboard terrain anywhere. Those unfamiliar with the skiing possibilities in California will be pleased to learn that many of the summits described in this guide are remote; on these trips you will encounter few other backcountry travelers. Due to the remoteness of many of these summits and the possibility of an unexpected winter storm, the ski mountaineer must be self-reliant and prepared to deal with any eventuality (see "What to Expect," later in this chapter).

Much has been written about California's landscapes and the Sierra Nevada, but Clarence King (*Mountaineering in the Sierra Nevada*, 1872) said it best:

> *By far the grandest of all the ranges is the Sierra Nevada, a long and massive uplift lying between the arid deserts of the Great Basin and the Californian exuberance of grainfield and orchard; its eastern slope, a defiant wall of rock plunging abruptly down to the plain; the western, a long, grand sweep, well watered and overgrown with cool, stately forests; its crest a line of sharp, snowy peaks springing into the sky and catching the alpenglow long after the sun has set for all the rest of America.*

HOW TO USE THIS BOOK

This guide includes fifty of the best snowboard and ski summit descents in California (plus a bonus peak, Mount Rose, located just across the border in Nevada north of Lake Tahoe). Some of these classics are well-known and popular destinations such as Mount Shasta, Lassen Peak, Mount Tallac, Matterhorn Peak, Mount Tom, and Mount Whitney. Others are not as familiar but provide

The Sabrina Lake basin and the approach to Echo Col; Echo Col is in the left background (Bishop Region).

exceptional skiing opportunities for those willing to explore California's remarkable backcountry wildernesses. The trips range in length from a half day to seven days, with the level of difficulty ranging from intermediate to advanced to expert; there are no beginner descents, and only a few are rated extreme.

Of the thirteen peaks in California over 14,000 feet, I have included six: Mount Shasta (the Whitney Glacier is perhaps the longest single run in California, with a descent of 8,600 feet), North Palisade and Thunderbolt Peak, Mount Sill's Glacier Creek Cirque, Mount Williamson, and Mount Whitney. I have also included snowboard and ski descents of twenty-five of the one hundred highest peaks in California, some of the most notable being Mount Darwin, Mount Brewer, Mount Goddard, Mount Dade, Mount Ritter, Mount Lyell, Mount Tom, Mount Kaweah, University Peak, The Thumb, and Birch Mountain.

The fifty-one ski and snowboard summits are grouped into nine geographic regions and are organized from north to south—Mount Shasta, Lassen Volcanic National Park, the Lake Tahoe region, Yosemite National Park, the Mammoth Lakes region, the Bishop region, the Palisades region, the Mount Whitney region, and Sequoia and Kings Canyon National Parks.

Each chapter contains a regional map showing towns and access roads in sufficient detail to guide the backcountry skier to the trailhead of each featured trip. Each trip writeup includes a summary of the route, 7.5-minute USGS topo(s) needed, trip duration, level of difficulty, mileage, elevation gain, effort factor, a snowboard recommendation, snow conditions, and the best time to go. Also included are directions to the trailhead, a detailed description of the ascent and descent routes, and camping recommendations. Many of the trip descriptions include alternate ascent routes and various descent routes, and some suggest nearby summits with their approach routes.

The terms "skiing," "ski summit," and "ski mountaineering" are used throughout the book. These terms are not meant to be exclusive but rather inclusive of all methods of descent—whether using skis or snowboards. All summit descents in this guide can be completed on traditional backcountry telemark skis, the new shorter and wider tele-skis, randonnée skis, or snowboards. However, summits with short, direct approaches may be more enjoyable for snowboarders, and this is noted in the trip description. (See also the list of the best snowboard summits, "The Snowboard Challenge," in Appendix 1.) Some summits are not recommended for snowboarding due to a long approach and/or descent terrain that is not continuous, requiring a significant amount of traversing or uphill travel. (See "Backcountry Snowboarding," later in this chapter.)

The routes detailed in this guide are approximate. Numerous ascent and descent variations exist. Some portions of many of the routes may be unsafe during, or immediately after, a storm or when avalanche conditions are present, either in winter or spring. Deep powder, breakable crust, icy snow, avalanches, cornices, and crevasses should influence the route selected and the difficulty of the ascent and descent. The backcountry skier and snowboarder must select the best and safest route and know when to turn back or re-route the trip when unsafe conditions persist. (See "Avalanche Awareness," later in this chapter.)

Summit Selection Criteria

From the hundreds of summits that were considered for this guide, determining which peaks to include was no simple task. To minimize the subjectivity, the following criteria were used.

Quality of the Skiing. The peak should offer excellent skiing opportunities, varied terrain, and an interesting approach and climb. Quality means variety—open bowls, steep chutes, headwalls, glaciers, cirques, high ridges, nicely spaced tree skiing.

Length of the Ski Descent. The descent must exceed 2,000 feet. Also, for a peak to be included in the guide, one must be able to ski from the summit or from near the summit. An exception was made in a couple of cases (Mount Sill's Northwest and L-Shaped Couloirs, and North Palisade and Thunderbolt Peak) where the skiing was just too good to overlook.

Aesthetics. The peak should look striking from afar and be aesthetically pleasing. Fascinating geography, exceptional summit views, exquisite scenery,

A spectacular view of the Palisades Glacier and Amphitheater: Mount Sill (left) and North Palisade (right) with the U-Notch in the center (Summits 34 and 35)

large glacial cirques, headwalls, arêtes, and an alpine environment add to the peak's status as a classic.

Access. Peaks were selected based on their difficulty of access. A balance was sought between the number of peaks easily accessible in a single day and those more remote, requiring two or more days.

Geographic Balance. Providing a sampling of the best ski summits from each of the nine regions set an arbitrary limit of only five or six peaks per region; unfortunately, this meant that many deserving summits were excluded.

Level of Difficulty. The fifty-one classics are a mix of intermediate, advanced (Black Diamond), and expert (Double Black Diamond) ski and snowboard descents. Although there are hundreds of extreme chutes in California, only a couple of routes requiring extreme skiing skills were included. For a ski descent to be considered a classic, it must have a certain level of repeatability and popularity not characterized by most extreme descents.

Skiing and Climbing History. The peak's mountaineering history was a consideration. A few of the summits with a rich skiing and climbing history include Mount Shasta, Castle Peak, Red Lake Peak, Mount Ritter, Mount Goddard, Mount Brewer, and Mount Lamarck.

Using these criteria, an original list of well over a hundred summits was pared back to what I believe are the fifty-one finest summits and ski and snowboard descents in the various regions of the state, all differing in length, level of difficulty, terrain, and geographic setting. (Since few peaks meet all the criteria, personal judgment and preference played a role.) Of these, I have made a selection of twenty summits I consider the "crème de la crème," designated Ski Mountaineers' Peaks and noted throughout the book with the symbol ★. (You'll find a listing of them in Appendix 1 under "Ski Mountaineer's Peaks.")

Approach and Descent Ratings

The guide provides two ratings: "effort factor" for the approach, and "level of difficulty" for the descent. "Effort factor" defines the magnitude of the overall undertaking required to reach the summit. "Level of difficulty" identifies the skiing or snowboarding skills required for the descent.

Many of the peaks require strong ski mountaineering skills—not just the skiing or snowboarding ability for a safe descent, but experience in the use of compass and map, route finding, navigation in whiteout conditions, snow stability evaluation, and avalanche rescue (see "What to Expect," later in this chapter). Many summits also require the use of an ice axe and crampons, and some may require a climbing rope for protection in the ascent and descent.

In writing this guide, I did not rely on the experiences of others to rate each peak. Instead, I climbed every summit and skied nearly every route to ensure the consistency and reliability of the ratings.

The Approach. The approach and climb for each peak has been rated based on the overall effort or strenuousness of the climb. This rating provides a way of determining whether the peak is a half-day endeavor or a multiday mini-expedition. A simple calculation for the "effort factor," based on a formula developed by Scottish climber W. W. Naismith, takes into account both the distance to be traveled (in miles) and the elevation to be climbed (in feet) for estimating the total amount of time required to gain the summit.

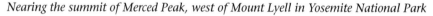

Nearing the summit of Merced Peak, west of Mount Lyell in Yosemite National Park

Naismith's formula assumes that one can hike at 3 miles per hour and gain 2,000 feet an hour; however, in snow, over rough terrain with a heavy pack at the much higher elevations of the Sierra Nevada, his formula is not particularly useful. The effort factor formula used in this guide, adjusted for some of these differences, is as follows:

Time in hours = (distance hiked in miles/2 mph) + (elevation gain in feet/1,000 feet per hour)

The formula assumes that, over the course of a day, a hiker or skier in good shape carrying a 35- to 40-pound pack can average about 2 miles an hour on level terrain and climb at a rate of 1,000 feet per hour. For example, if the summit of Mount Tallac is 4 miles and a climb of 3,300 feet, then the effort factor is (4 miles/2 miles per hour) + (3,300 feet/1,000 feet per hour) = 2 + 3.3 = 5.3 hours. It will take about 5 hours to climb to the summit of Mount Tallac. Of course, the snow conditions, the elevation of the peak, the weight of one's pack, as well as the condition and strength of each skier are major factors not reflected in this equation.

On shorter trips, such as Mount Tallac, a skier in good condition may easily beat the predicted time. On longer and more difficult trips, the same skier may take longer than the predicted time to reach the summit as the rate of progress slows over the course of an exhausting day. This rule can be easily adjusted to suit your pace by either assuming a slower or faster hiking rate or adjusting the climbing rate. To adjust for a strong and fast climber, one might assume 2.5 miles per hour and 1,200 feet of elevation gain per hour. To adjust for a slower traveler, one might assume 2 miles per hour and reduce the rate of ascent to 750 feet per hour.

The Descent. Each ski descent is also rated for the level of difficulty and the skiing or snowboarding skills required, based on a system similar to that used by alpine ski resorts. The familiar "Intermediate—Advanced—Expert" rating system is used to indicate the terrain's steepness:

Intermediate— Terrain includes slopes to 24 degrees in steepness

Black Diamond—Advanced terrain, includes slopes of 25–34 degrees

Double Black Diamond—Expert terrain, includes slopes of 35–44 degrees

Extreme—Slopes of more than 45 degrees, where a fall is likely to result in serious injury or death

Each summit in this guide has been skied with traditional metal-edged backcountry skis such as the Fischer Europa 99™ or Chouinard™ (Black Diamond) backcountry telemark skis with leather boots, or with the shorter (170–180 cm) and wider backcountry skis with plastic telemark boots. However, rating the difficulty of a route's ski terrain is inexact and subjective at best. A summit ski descent with a rating of intermediate terrain under normal snow conditions could become advanced, or even expert, terrain under "breakable crust" or "icy" conditions.

Also, the steepness of a route can be significantly overstated. For example, one publication states that a particular couloir offers 900 feet of 45-degree skiing. In researching the route for possible inclusion in this book, I found the couloir to be 900 feet as stated, but it only approached 45 degrees for a couple of hundred feet near the top, with lower-angle slopes prevailing below. Examining a route straight-on can be misleading because the view is foreshortened; as a result, the slope is not as steep as it appears. The only way to get a good reading on the steepness of a slope is to actually climb the route and measure the slope. Hopefully, mistakes of overstating or, conversely, understating the difficulty and steepness of a particular route have been avoided in this guide.

Terrain identified as intermediate is about the same steepness as comparable alpine ski resort terrain but without the added benefit of grooming. If you are able to ski or snowboard the most difficult *ungroomed* intermediate terrain at an alpine ski resort in complete confidence with your backcountry gear and a *pack*, you should be able to handle the trips in this guide with an intermediate rating. Likewise, if you are able to ski the more difficult *ungroomed* slopes—advanced (Black Diamond) and expert (Double Black Diamond)—at an alpine ski resort in total confidence, you should be able to negotiate the descents in this guide similarly rated.

SNOW AND WEATHER CONDITIONS

California's renowned weather is a major attraction for the backcountry skier and snowboarder. The Cascade Range and the Sierra Nevada tend to get snow deposits in a series of consecutive storms. It is not unusual for the weather to remain stable for weeks at a time, then be followed by a series of intense storms. In Spanish, Sierra Nevada literally means "sawtooth mountain range capped in snow"—an appropriate name given that the high mountain summits of California are covered with snow much of the year.

Normally, the jet stream's continental crossing place is to the north of California, over Oregon and Washington. Occasionally, the jet stream is diverted southward. When the high-pressure system that normally prevails over California's weather is pushed out and the jet stream becomes focused on California, the entire state can be wracked by storm after storm in quick succession. In the heavy snow years of 1951–52, 1968–69, 1977–78, 1981–82, 1982–83, and 1997–98, the Sierra Nevada (Norden, near Donner Pass) received more than 50 feet of snow over the course of the snow season. In 1969, 1975, 1981, 1982, 1996, and 1997, single storms dumped upwards of 12 feet of snow near Donner Pass. The largest single storm snowfall recorded by the University of California Central Sierra Snow Laboratory in Norden occurred on March 27, 1982, when a huge storm deposited 470 centimeters (185 inches or 15.4 feet) of snow at the 7,000-foot level.

Sierra Nevada spring snow Photo by John Moynier

Following normal weather patterns, the mountains receive large amounts of snow even in average snow years. At the higher elevations, the snow may accumulate to 20 feet, with snow drifts much deeper. These ample snow depths provide for a ski season stretching from November/December through May/June.

WHEN TO GO

In the Sierra Nevada, nighttime temperatures rarely drop below zero in the winter months. Lassen Peak and especially the higher elevations of Mount Shasta are somewhat colder. By late February and March the temperatures gradually increase, with nighttime lows in the teens. Even when the temperature drops to near zero at night, the sun warms the day quickly.

The ski season begins with the first substantial snows in November/December. In a good year one can expect to be skiing by Thanksgiving. Early in the season, November through February, the snowpack is usually shallow and unconsolidated. Trail breaking can be slow and discouraging immediately after a storm. The days are short and the nights long. Those 14-hour nights in a tent can get old in a hurry. However, good powder can be found early in the season, and it is worth the added effort to seek it out. Single-day and short 2- to 3-day tours, which keep one within a day's travel of the car, are best during this unstable season.

Near Lassen Volcanic National Park with Mount Shasta in the background. The Hotlum-Wintun route on Mount Shasta (Summit 3) is on the right skyline.

Most of the snow falls during January, February, and March. Toward the end of February, the days lengthen noticeably and the weather warms considerably. The snow is still unconsolidated but the base is now much deeper. Keep an eye on the weather reports if considering any extended trip that may take you over the crest of the Sierra Nevada. If caught on the opposite side of the crest, you may be unable to cross back over to your car, as extreme high winds, zero visibility, blowing and drifting snow, and potential avalanche danger can prevent all travel. In these situations the backcountry skier and snowboarder must be resigned to wait it out, whether it takes one or two days or longer. Waiting 24 hours usually makes a big difference. Generally there is a 12- to 24-hour break between storms that will allow you to get out, if you hurry.

In late March and April the snow consolidates, and spring corn snow starts to form; skiing is in its prime in April and May, when the days are long and warm, the nights short and cold. The backcountry skiing and snowboarding in the California mountains are at their best in the velvety-smooth corn snow of spring when the daytime temperatures dictate short sleeves and a sun hat. Under ideal spring-corn conditions, backcountry skiing and snowboarding can be superior to, and perhaps easier than, comparable groomed slopes of an alpine ski resort.

The springtime daily cycle finds the snow freezing during the night. In the early morning, the snow remains hard for several hours. By mid-morning the top half inch has softened, providing for near-ideal ski conditions. These conditions continue throughout the morning. Plan to begin your descent by 12:00 or 1:00 P.M. for the best corn snow. A descent too late in the afternoon may be less than ideal, because on a warm spring day the snow softens and turns to "mashed potatoes."

WHAT TO EXPECT

Many of these backcountry tours are remote, and in many cases, the remoteness of the trip adds greatly to its appeal. It continually amazes me that in the most populous state in the nation, backcountry skiers can ski for less than an hour and find themselves all alone in the midst of hundreds of square miles.

The backcountry traveler must be prepared to deal with all situations that may arise. A storm can quickly turn a genteel tour into a serious matter with little warning. Conditions can change rapidly and become harsh and unforgiving. High winds, heavy snowfall, whiteout conditions with zero visibility, increased avalanche danger, and the remoteness of location conspire against you. The backcountry skier and snowboarder must be self-reliant, capable of handling all eventualities—a tent destroyed by high winds, a broken tent pole, a malfunctioning stove, a broken ski, or even a broken leg.

In addition to being able to make emergency repairs to skis, tents, stoves, and other equipment, it is absolutely necessary that you be able to use map and compass in whiteout conditions. I cannot overemphasize route finding and orienting the map to the terrain. Caught in a storm with little visibility, you can easily become disoriented. In such cases, trust your compass, even if

Muir Hut on the top of 12,000-foot Muir Pass (Bishop region) provides shelter for winter skiers.

you do not believe it. Questioning your compass is a losing proposition; you will be wrong every time. The correct use of a GPS (Global Positioning System) receiver can also be helpful for route finding and orienteering in both storms and good weather conditions.

Mountaineering and Survival Skills

Winter camping and survival skills—especially building an igloo, snow cave, or other emergency shelter—are critical. If you are not experienced in these areas, take an on-the-snow seminar, then practice on your own. A blizzard is not the time to experiment with construction techniques; your life may depend on your success. Your first attempt to construct a snow cave or igloo should be done on a day tour when you do not plan to spend the night—or bring a tent along on an overnight trip, as a backup in the event that your snow shelter is less than successful.

Before setting out, you should also have a thorough understanding of basic mountaineering skills, avalanche hazard detection, and first aid. If you have limited experience, take courses to improve your knowledge and skills. Going on guided tours such as those organized by the Sierra Club or other groups can help build your confidence and experience. Many professional ski mountaineering guides offer courses on various aspects of mountaineering, including in-the-field practice. Although there are many outstanding books on mountaineering, there is no substitute for on-the-snow experience. Mountain guides and schools, mountaineering clubs, and books are listed in Appendix 5 and Appendix 8.

Wilderness First Aid

Mountaineering first aid begins with the understanding that it is the responsibility of every backcountry skier and snowboarder to have complete knowledge of basic first-aid practices and the ability to properly care for an injured partner in the wilderness. All skiers and snowboarders should take basic first-aid training, offered by the Red Cross, and mountaineering first aid, offered by many mountain guides. A first-aid kit should be carried by each person. The kit should be small, compact, sturdy, and waterproof. Dr. Colin Fuller's suggested checklist for a wilderness first-aid kit is included in Appendix 7.

AVALANCHE AWARENESS
by John Moynier

Although we don't always like to admit it, much of backcountry skiing and snowboarding is a game of "Avalanche Roulette." Every time we head into the snowy hills, we place ourselves at risk. That is because, by definition, prime backcountry ski terrain is often prime avalanche terrain. Everyone skiing in the backcountry must recognize the risks. Although some areas may be consistently more hazardous than others, serious avalanche hazard is likely at some point wherever steep slopes and snow are found together. In order to become confident in our ability to determine hazard, to recognize and avoid danger, we need to educate ourselves, practice our techniques, and use the proper equipment.

Learn all you can about avalanche hazard by reading and taking field avalanche courses that focus on hazard evaluation and self-rescue techniques. A number of good reference books are listed in Appendix 8, including Tony Daffern's *Avalanche Safety for Skiers and Climbers*, *The Avalanche Handbook* by David McClung and Peter Schaerer, and my book *Avalanche Aware: Safe Travel in the Avalanche Country*. Professionals offering avalanche training are listed in Appendix 5 under "Mountain Guides and Schools." Avalanche awareness is developed through education as well as practical experience and observation. It is the responsibility of all members of a group to evaluate their own risk when traveling through mountainous terrain and to communicate their concerns to the rest of the group.

Avalanche hazard evaluation boils down to four components: terrain (slope angle, slope aspect, cornices, and routefinding); weather (local weather, precipitation, and wind); snowpack (physical evidence, layers, faceted crystal and other crystal processes); and human judgment.

Understanding and evaluating the first three factors are what make it possible for us to control the fourth factor—using good judgment to decide when and where we're going. What we do with our evaluation can make the difference between a fun day out with friends and an unnecessary tragedy. Good judgment and safe travel depend upon the following elements.

Preparation. You should form an opinion about stability before you even leave the trailhead and be prepared to change your opinion as conditions change. Gather all the information you can beforehand by calling the National Weather Service or accessing their website (see Appendix 5, "Weather and Avalanche Conditions"). Get a local avalanche forecast if one is available, or call someone in the area to ask for any local observations. You can also check out the CyberSpace Avalanche Center's (CSAC) local forecast on the Internet (see Appendix 5). Make sure everyone in your group carries a beacon, shovel, and avalanche probes and knows how to use them.

Avalanche transceivers, or "beacons," are your best insurance policy if you are completely buried in a slide. If your partners follow good protocol and have practiced search techniques, they should be able to find you within a short period of time. Remember, time is critical. In order to dig through heavy avalanche debris, each person will also need a sturdy shovel. A set of avalanche probe poles will also make their efforts more efficient as they can pinpoint your location without wasting effort digging a foot or two to the side.

Observation. On the mountain, keep your eyes and mind open as you travel. Be prepared to augment or even completely overhaul your assessment along the way. Nature generally provides obvious clues to stability if you know how and where to look. Listen to the snow, feel it with your poles and skis, and constantly evaluate each step or turn.

Communication. Always make sure everyone understands and approves of the group's objectives and that alternate routes have been taken into account. Listen to your intuition. If your gut tells you things are amiss, the time to act is now. Don't let the idea that "I don't want to spoil it for the group" lead to tragedy. It is much better to err on the safe side and come back another day than to have to dig a buddy out of a pile of debris. Communicate your plans constantly and make sure everyone understands.

Safe Travel. Beacons should be turned on "transmit" at the start of the day, checked, and left on until everyone is safe in camp. If you must travel in a hazardous area, limit your exposure. Cross one at a time with all eyes on the person crossing. Take advantage of safer areas like dense timber, rock outcrops, ridges, and wide valley bottoms. If you must ascend or descend a dangerous slope, stay close to the edge and choose as vertical a line as possible. Kicking steps straight up or down is much safer than cutting the slope with traverses, turns, or sitzmarks. Don't assume that a slope is safe just because someone else has skied or snowboarded through the area. Remember that traveling on a lower-angled slope can trigger steeper slopes above or sympathetically release a slope some distance away when things are really hazardous.

BACKCOUNTRY SNOWBOARDING
by John Moynier

Although they are designed for descents in all kinds of snow conditions, snowboards are not particularly well suited for touring. Leaving aside the idea of "split boards" for a moment, getting your board to the top of a peak can take a lot of fun out of the backcountry experience.

Until recently, the choices for uphill travel with a snowboard were limited to hiking, post-holing, snowshoeing, or skiing. Hiking is fine for short distances on firm snow, but when the going gets deep it can be a real drag. Snowshoes are marginally better, but are of limited value for long distances. In addition, snowshoes pose some problems when the uphill route involves traverses, especially on hard snow. In really deep snow, snowshoes may become more trouble than they are worth as the weight of the snow on the deck drags you down.

Backcountry snowboarding in the Sierra Nevada Photo by John Moynier

The only really viable alternative for trips involving much of an approach are skis. These can range from lightweight racing or skating skis (good for spring corn) or regular "telemark" skis. Also popular are short approach skis, similar to the old "Firn gliders" of the 1960s. Bindings are now available to accept soft-shell snowboarding boots for these skis. Otherwise, you will need to bring a separate pair of boots for the approach.

Recently, "split" boards have become a popular alternative for uphill travel. Although the first versions were Frankenstein hack jobs done in people's garages, split boards are now of a high quality and offer good performance. These hybrid boards break apart in the middle to form a rudimentary pair of skis for the approach, and then bolt back together for the descent. Although they may not offer quite the same performance as your regular board, they save the weight and hassle of carrying extra gear.

Most backcountry board riders prefer a soft boot and strap-type binding system. They like the soft boots for comfort and the simplicity of the strap system. Step-in systems are growing in popularity, and offer obvious advantages in certain conditions, including added safety in the event of a avalanche. Hard boots perform much like typical alpine climbing boots, accepting crampons and offering excellent protection against wet and cold. Kicking steps is also easier with hard boots, and this can be significant on frosty morning ascents in spring.

One other consideration is the use of ski poles. Backcountry skiers and snowshoers would feel lost without their ski poles, especially on the ascent. Many snowboarders, however, have no interest in the use of poles. This may be shortsighted. Not only is it easier to climb with the help of poles, but they can be used for self-arrest in the event of a fall. Using the poles on the descent allows the rider to push themselves across short flat sections, saving the rider from having to do the one-legged skate. Poles can also help the rider balance at the end of a run, instead of sitting in the snow. Finally, ski poles can be a major help when getting up from a fall in deep snow. Holding the poles in a big X in one hand will often provide enough surface area to allow you to stand up.

Safe travel in the wintry Sierra on a snowboard requires special considerations. There's no better tool for the backcountry when the route is straightforward, but a snowboard can be a real disadvantage when things get "interesting." The trips listed in this book fall into the realm of ski mountaineering and require care on both the climb and descent. Proper trip planning will tell you whether snowboards are a viable tool, or whether you should opt for skis instead.

BEFORE SETTING OUT

You should always have at least an informal plan in mind, even for the most casual day trip. For multiday trips, a more detailed plan is necessary. Below are some suggestions for planning any backcountry ski trip.

▲ Let someone know exactly where you are going, the name of the trailhead, the type and color of your vehicle, the license plate number, where the vehicle will be parked, and when you plan to return.

▲ Establish a trip itinerary. Leave plenty of time in your schedule for the unforeseen; bad weather, deep snow, or equipment failure will slow your progress. Your itinerary should include starting and ending points, planned campsites, the planned route, and prominent peaks and passes you will be ascending. Write down your trip itinerary and leave it with a responsible person.

Skiing toward Black Giant and the Ionian Basin (Summit 33)

▲ Secure a wilderness permit from the appropriate National Park Service or the National Forest District Office (see Appendix 4).

▲ If you are planning an overnight stay at a backcountry ski lodge or hut, you'll need to make reservations in advance (for information and addresses, see Appendix 5).

▲ Study the map. Make sure all members of the party are familiar with the route, route options, and potential escape routes along the way.

▲ Make sure everyone is aware of the overall level of difficulty of the trip. The terrain should not be too difficult for any member of the group. If so, an alternate route or a less difficult trip should be selected. Your party is only as strong as the weakest member.

▲ If taking a GPS (Global Positioning System) unit, set the various coordinates of your route—starting point and end point, camps, passes, summits—before starting the trip.

▲ Run through an equipment check (see the following section, along with Appendix 6, "Equipment Checklist") before departing. Ensure that all group equipment is accounted for and arrives at the trailhead.

▲ Check the compatibility of avalanche transceivers before leaving home. Bring extra batteries.

▲ Obtain the latest weather forecast. Check on avalanche hazard and snow stability before making the final decision on your route.

▲ Don't go alone; ski with at least one other person.

WHAT TO TAKE

In the early 1960s I purchased what I thought were among the first bindings to be called safety-release bindings, made in Germany. I skied for a couple of seasons and never came out of the bindings, so I really wondered about them. One day the Shasta College Ski Club was skiing at the old Mount Shasta Ski Bowl. We constructed a run and added a small jump for excitement. Late in the day the run fell into the shadows, and the snow became icy and very fast. I came down the approach much too fast, and taking the jump, I really became airborne. When I hit, I cartwheeled across the hard snow. I was surprised to see that my bindings had released. For certain, the safety bindings must have worked. When I walked over to put my skis back on, I was shocked to see the soles of my boots still attached to the skis with hundreds of little nails sticking up. I may not have had safety bindings, but I had safety boots.
—Gene Leach on the "high-tech" equipment of the 1960s

To maximize your enjoyment, go light. Many backcountry skiers, even the experienced, take too much with them. You can get by with a lot less than you think, without sacrificing safety, especially in the Sierra Nevada where the winter climate is relatively mild compared with other mountain ranges. In the mountains, speed equals safety and enjoyment. It is difficult to move through the mountains quickly with an oversized pack weighing 40 or 50 pounds, stuffed to the brim with the latest gadgets from your favorite mountaineering store. When considering purchasing an item—whether skis, boots, a Gore-Tex parka or pants, a pack, sleeping bag, or tent—think function and weight. Is the item really worth its weight? If a week's supplies will not fit inside a 4,000-cubic-inch (60–70 liter) internal-frame pack, you are taking too much. The "Equipment Checklist" in Appendix 6 provides guidelines for the equipment and clothing to take on a multiday ski-mountaineering trip.

Freedom of the hills is undoubtedly the goal of every ski mountaineer and backcountry snowboarder. Since backcountry travelers must be able to cope with every situation using only what can be carried in their packs, having the right equipment, both lightweight and durable, is critical. But freedom also means keeping gear to a minimum. Below are some recommendations for selecting snowboards, skis, tents, sleeping bags, backpacks, clothing, and food to take on your backcountry tour.

Skis

The ski industry is just now figuring out what the snowboard industry has known for years: Go fat! The wider the ski, the better. The new light, wide, short designs allow much greater mobility and enjoyment than their longer, narrower predecessors. Shorter, lighter skis reduce the weight and awkwardness of your backpack on steep ascents. During the descent, the lightness reduces swing weight so you can make jump turns quickly and effortlessly. Skis should be stiff torsionally for maximum edge control on steep, wind-packed slopes. Waist widths of 70–80 millimeters are optimal, with the shovel 100–110 millimeters wide. A 6-foot-tall skier can ski boards in the 170- to 180-centimeter range; shorter and lighter skiers need correspondingly shorter skis.

Snowboards

(See the discussion on backcountry snowboarding earlier in this chapter.)

Tents

Choose a high-quality three- or four-pole free-standing tent. The importance of a sturdy tent in the face of 40-mile-an-hour winds can not be overstated, but balancing weight, function, and size is difficult. Expedition-grade and four-season tents provide bomb-proof protection but tend to be too heavy. Three-season tents are lighter and may provide adequate protection, depending on the construction and quality of the tent. Look for tents in the 5- to 6-pound range. Unfortunately, many two-person tents are small and cramped for two, especially for winter camping. If you don't mind being shoulder-to-shoulder with your tent partner, your outside shoulder pressed against the frost-coated tent wall, you will find many acceptable two-person tents. A three-person tent may be more acceptable for the winter requirements of two backcountry skiers/snowboarders.

Base camp near Treasure Lakes in the Bishop region

Sleeping Bags

A down sleeping bag rated to 0–10 degrees Fahrenheit with a Dryloft® shell from Gore-Tex® is an excellent choice. The Dryloft® fabric makes the bag expensive, but you can leave the bivy sack at home and save a pound and a half. Without a Dryloft® shell, take a bivy sack to protect the bag from condensation in the tent and wet snow. Synthetic-filled bags are also a good choice but are heavier and bulkier.

Backpacks

An internal-frame pack is preferable, because it holds the load close to your back, reducing the tendency of the pack to shift on uneven or steep terrain, throwing you off balance. Try to find a pack that holds 4,000 to 5,000 cubic inches and weighs 5 pounds or less. Keeping the dry weight of your pack to a minimum is a challenge, as many packs produced today are heavy to begin with, weighing 7 to 8 pounds.

Clothing

Despite the heavy snowfall, the mountains of California are relatively mild: winter temperatures rarely drop below 0 degrees Fahrenheit, with mild temperatures, rain, sleet, and wet snow common at the lower elevations. Consequently, a weathertight outer Gore-Tex® parka is essential. For inner layers, choose synthetic fibers such as Polartec® fleece, Polartec® powerstretch, thermal polyester/Lycra® wear, and Capilene®.

For an overnight winter trip into the California backcountry, you might wear a midweight, long-sleeved thermal turtleneck next to your skin, topped by a short-sleeved thermal tee-shirt, then a light powerstretch or 100-weight micro-fleece vest. In colder weather, add a light nylon windbreaker over these layers, followed by a 200-weight Polartec® fleece jacket with a hood, and finally a Gore-Tex® parka with a hood.

For the bottom half, two layers are usually adequate. Make the first layer powerstretch tights (60 percent polyester, 30 percent nylon, and 10 percent Lycra®), and wear baggy nylon shorts over the tights. In the spring, shift to lighter, midweight thermal bottoms in place of the powerstretch tights. With gaiters covering to the knees and the baggy nylon shorts covering to mid-thigh, you should be comfortable in most weather conditions. When the weather turns cold or the wind picks up, add the second layer, a pair of Gore-Tex® pants with full-length zippers. For added warmth, some skiers will bring a pair of 200-weight fleece pants with full zipper. (See the "Equipment Checklist," Appendix 6.)

Alpine Cuisine

Good food gives a festive touch to summit celebrations and lifts the spirits during stormy days. Good food improves the scenery and keeps the spirits high. Bad food makes the nights colder, the approaches more difficult, and the weather unbearable. At altitude, finding cuisine that you like and look forward to eating is not always an easy assignment.

The key is to plan meals that are simple to prepare, inexpensive, lightweight, and tasty. Using ingredients found at your local grocery store, you can generally create meals superior to the freeze-dried meals sold in backpacking stores. A number of good outdoor cookbooks are available, such as *Backcountry Cooking: From Pack to Plate in 10 Minutes*, by Dorcus S. Miller, and *Gorp, Glop & Glue Stew: Favorite Foods from 165 Outdoor Experts*, by Yvonne Prater and Ruth Dyar Mendenhall.

As for cooking equipment, a hanging stove that is safe to use inside your tent (such as that made by Bibler) is a big improvement over the traditional white-gas stove for winter camping. Attempting to cook with a white-gas stove outside the tent in the face of high winds and a snowstorm is no one's idea of fun. With a hanging stove, you can prepare your breakfast and dinner in the warm confines of your tent while the storm brews outside. Make sure your tent is well ventilated, and be careful when lighting the stove.

Many backcountry skiers may experience a lack of appetite when going to higher elevations. Others may be just too tired at the end of a hard day to be interested in food. Resist the temptation to skip a meal. Eating is essential for the sustained level of output required in the backcountry.

As a general rule, plan on 2 pounds of food per person per day. And drink plenty of fluids. Throughout the day, keep hydrated by regularly drinking water, the sports drink of your choice, and hot drinks and soups.

HOW TO GET THERE

The Cascade Range and the Sierra Nevada occupy the east side of California, running roughly north to south. At the north end of the state, access to the Mount Shasta area is from Interstate 5 and Highway 97 or 89. For Lassen Volcanic National Park, take Interstate 5 to Redding or Red Bluff and proceed east on Highway 44 or 36. From the east, take Highway 395 to Susanville and then either Highway 44 or 36 to the park.

To this day, this skier refuses to admit that he was lost.

For the peaks in the Lake Tahoe region, access is gained from the three trans-Sierra highways that remain open in the winter—Interstate 80 over Donner Pass, Highway 50 over Echo Summit, and Highway 88 over Carson Pass.

The Sierra Nevada peaks to the south of Lake Tahoe are reached from Highway 395, which lies to the east of the range. The trans-Sierra highways in this part of the state (Highway 4, Ebbetts Pass; Highway 108, Sonora Pass; and Highway 120, Tioga Pass) are closed through the winter and into the spring. For seven months or more each year, there are no east–west roads crossing the Sierra Nevada for almost 250 miles. From Highway 395, numerous east–west arterials provide access to the trailheads on the east side of the Sierra.

Sequoia and Kings Canyon National Parks, at the southern end of the Sierra Nevada, are approached from the west via Highway 99 and then east on Highway 180 or 198.

Most approach roads in this guide are passable by car. In some cases a high-clearance vehicle or four-wheel-drive vehicle is necessary; if so, this is noted in the trip description.

Chapter 2
MOUNT SHASTA

Mount Shasta, rising to 14,162 feet, is one of the largest stratovolcanoes in the world. Its enormous bulk has been estimated at 80–84 cubic miles in volume. Not only is its sheer size overwhelming, it dominates the region for miles. Towering 10,000 feet above the Sacramento River and the towns of Dunsmuir, Mount Shasta, Weed, and McCloud, the peak can be seen for 80–100 miles in all directions. John Muir, after climbing to the summit of Mount Shasta, claimed to have seen the Pacific Ocean more than 100 miles away. When covered with snow, the mountain is truly a beautiful and picturesque sight.

A chain of towering volcanoes stretches from southwestern Canada through Washington, Oregon, and into northern California. These fire-born, ice-carved giants dominate the Cascade Range. Nowhere else in the forty-eight contiguous states has nature so dramatically linked these two great forces—volcanic fire and glacial ice. Mount Shasta and Lassen Peak anchor the southern end of the Cascade Range. Mount Shasta, the second highest peak in the Cascades, is only slightly lower than Mount Rainier (14,410 feet). Mount Shasta has seven named glaciers, the largest being the Wintun, Hotlum, Bolam, and Whitney Glaciers, which are perched on the north and east slopes of the peak. Although

On the summit of Mount Shasta. The summit rocks being covered with wind-driven snow gave us an unusual opportunity to start our ski descent from the top of the summit block.

Mount Shasta has the largest glaciers in California, they pale in comparison with the glaciers on other peaks in the Cascade Range such as Mount Baker, Mount Rainier, Glacier Peak, and Mount Adams.

Winter storms dump abundant amounts of snow on the slopes of Mount Shasta. Twenty- to thirty-foot drifts at the 7,000- to 8,000-foot level are common. In the winter, the weather on Mount Shasta can be abominable, especially above treeline. During major storms, which hit with regularity, gale-force winds blast the peak relentlessly, bringing storm clouds laden with wet Pacific Ocean moisture in the form of snow.

Summits like Mount Shasta or Mount Rainier that are significantly higher than their neighbors can create their own weather. These peaks thrust up into the mainline air, causing lenticular clouds to form under certain atmospheric conditions. The weather can be clear for hundreds of miles, yet a lenticular cloud cap may form over the summit when expansive marine air comes into contact with the dense, cold mountain air. These lenticular summit cloud caps look ugly from below, and indeed may be accompanied by high winds and much moisture. They may sometimes engulf the summit, depositing significant amounts of snow or sleet. A lenticular summit cloud cap does not necessarily signal a storm brewing above, but it is a sure sign of instability and a change in the weather.

The combination of ample snow lasting into the summer months, the great vertical relief of the peak, and the usually good weather in the spring combine to make Mount Shasta arguably the best ski summit in all of California, if not the United States. Where else can one find a ski or snowboard descent over 8,000 feet without the added danger of crevasses, as found on Mount Rainier or Mount Baker? Yes, you can ski from the summit of Mount Rainier, descending 10,000 vertical feet, but crevasses are a risk for the top 4,500 feet. By comparison, Mount Shasta is a fair-weather peak, with superior skiing. On a good day the skiing on Mount Shasta rivals that of the best ski resorts anywhere in the world, without the hassle of lift lines, crowded slopes, and rude skiers.

This guide features Mount Shasta's Whitney Glacier route (Summit 1), as well as two other routes on Shasta's north and east sides—the ridge dividing the Bolam and Hotlum Glaciers (Summit 2) and the ridge separating the Hotlum and Wintun Glaciers (Summit 3). On the west side of the mountain, a fourth route descends Cascade Gulch (Summit 4) from the top of Shastina, a 12,330-foot subpeak of Mount Shasta. The standard climbing route up Avalanche Gulch was not included, as it is greatly overused, with sixty to a hundred climbers attempting the peak on a given weekend. Avalanche Gulch is also far inferior as a ski descent, becoming heavily sun-cupped early in the spring ski season. Also, as you may surmise from the name, Avalanche Gulch is not the safest of routes; its steep sides avalanche regularly in winter and spring.

Before you begin your climb, register your trip with the U.S. Forest Service in Mount Shasta City or at the various trailheads. A fee is required to park and climb above 10,000 feet. If you plan more than one trip a year, it may be cost-effective to purchase an annual use permit, which covers parking. The annual pass can be purchased at the District Ranger Office in Mount Shasta City. The Forest Service's website (www.r5.fs.us/shastatrinity) contains valuable information on climbing Mount Shasta, including road descriptions.

How to get there: Mount Shasta is located about 50 miles south of the California–Oregon border and about the same distance north of Redding. The mountain is northeast of the town of Mount Shasta (Mount Shasta City), just off Interstate 5. Mount Shasta City, located at the base of the mountain, is a clean and charming community of about 5,000. Each route description explains how to get to the mountain from Mount Shasta City.

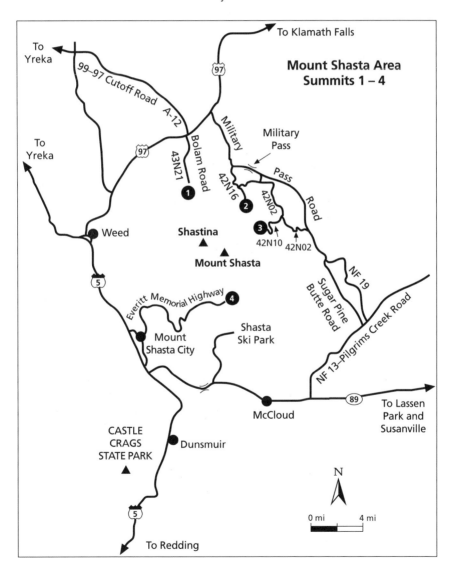

A Perilous Night on Mount Shasta

Mount Shasta, situated near the northern extremity of the Sierra Nevada, rises in solitary grandeur from a lightly sculptured lava plain, and maintains a far more impressive and commanding individuality than any other mountain within the limits of California.

We rose [April 30, 1875] at 2 A.M., warmed a tin-cupful of coffee, broiled a slice of frozen venison on the coals, and started for the summit at 3:20 A.M. The crisp icy sky was without a cloud, and the stars lighted us on our way. Deep silence brooded the mountain, broken only by the night wind and an occasional rock falling from crumbling buttresses to the snow slopes below. The wild beauty of the morning stirred our pulses in glad exhilaration, and we strode rapidly onward, seldom stopping to take a breath—over the broad red apron of lava that descends from the west side of the smaller of the two cone summits, across the gorge that divides them, up the majestic snow curves sweeping to the top of the ancient crater, around the broad icy fountains of the Whitney glacier, past the hissing fumaroles—and at 7:30 A.M. we attained the utmost summit.

Clouds the mean while were growing down in Shasta Valley—massive swelling cumuli, colored gray and purple and close pearly white. These, constantly extending around southward on both sides of Mount Shasta, at length united with the older field lying toward Lassen's Peak, thus circling the mountain in one continuous cloud zone. . . .

Presently a vigorous thunder-bolt crashes through the crisp sunny air, ringing like steel on steel, its startling detonation breaking into a spray of echoes among the rocky cañons below. Jerome peered at short intervals over the jagged ridge on which we stood, making anxious gestures in the rough wind, and becoming more and more emphatic in his remarks upon the weather, declaring that if we did not make a speedy escape, we should be compelled to pass the night on the summit. Anxiety, however, to complete my [barometric] observations fixed me to the ridge. No inexperienced person was depending upon me, and I told Jerome that we two mountaineers could break down through any storm likely to fall. The sky speedily darkened, and just after I had completed my observations and boxed the instruments, the storm broke in full vigor. The cliffs were covered with a remarkable net-work of hail rills that poured and rolled adown the gray and red lava slopes like cascades of rock-beaten water. These hail-stones seemed to belong to an entirely distinct species from any I had before observed. They resembled small mushrooms both in texture and general form, their six straight sides widening upward from a narrow base to a wide dome-like crown.

A few minutes after 3 P.M. we began to force our way down the eastern ridge, past the group of hissing fumaroles. The storm at once became inconceivably violent, with scarce a preliminary scowl. The thermometer fell twenty-two degrees, and soon sank below zero. Hail gave place to snow, and darkness came on like night. The wind, rising to the highest pitch of violence, boomed and surged like breakers on a rocky coast. The lightning flashed amid the desolate crags in terrible accord, their tremendous muffled detonations unrelieved by a single echo, and seeming to come thudding passionately forth from out the very heart of the storm.

After passing the "Hot Springs," I halted in the shelter of a lava block to let Jerome, who had fallen a little behind, come up. Here he opened a council, in which, amid circumstances sufficiently exciting, but without evincing any bewilderment, he maintained, in opposition to my views, that it was impossible to proceed: the ridge was too dangerous, the snow was blinding, and the frost too intense to be borne; and finally, that, even supposing it possible for us to grope our way through the darkness, the wind was sufficiently violent to hurl us bodily over the cliffs, and that our only hope was in wearing away the afternoon and night among the fumaroles, where we should at least avoid freezing.

Our discussions ended, Jerome made a dash from behind the lava block, and began forcing his way back some twenty or thirty yards to the Hot Springs against the wind flood, wavering and struggling as if caught in a torrent of water; and after watching in vain for any flaw in the storm that might be urged as a new argument for attempting the descent, I was compelled to follow. "Here," said Jerome. The patch of volcanic climate to which we committed ourselves has an area of about one-forth of an acre, but it was only about an eighth of an inch in thickness, because the scalding gas jets were shorn off close to the ground by the oversweeping flood of frost wind.

The marvelous lavishness of the snow can be conceived only by mountaineers. The crystal flowers seemed to touch one another and fairly to thicken the blast. This was the bloom-time, the summer of the storm, and never before have I seen mountain cloud flowering so profusely. . . .

I was in my shirt sleeves, and in less than half an hour was wet to the skin; Jerome fortunately had on a close-fitting coat, and his life was more deeply imbedded in flesh than mine. Yet we both trembled and shivered in a weak, nervous way, as much, I suppose, from exhaustion brought on by want of food and sleep as from sifting of the icy wind through our wet clothing. The snow fell with unabated lavishness until an hour or two after the coming on of what appeared to be the natural darkness of night. The whole quantity would probably measure about two feet.

We lay flat on our backs, so as to present as little surface as possible to the wind. The mealy snow gathered on our breasts, and I did not rise again to my feet for seventeen hours. We were glad at first to see the snow drifting into the hollows of our clothing, hoping it would serve to deaden the force of the ice wind; but, though soft at first, it soon froze into a stiff, crusty heap, rather augmenting our novel misery.

The night wind rushed in wild uproar across the shattered cliffs, piercing us through and through, and causing violent convulsive shivering, while those portions of our bodies in contact with the hot lava were being broiled. When the heat became unendurable, we scraped snow and bits of trachyte beneath us, or shifted from place to place by shoving an inch or two at a time with heels and elbows; for to stand erect in blank exposure to the wind seemed like certain death.

The acrid encrustations sublimed from the escaping gases frequently gave way, opening new vents, over which we were scalded; and fearing that if at any time the wind should fall, carbonic acid, which usually forms so considerable a portion of the gaseous exhalations of volcanoes, might collect in sufficient quantities to cause sleep and death, I warned Jerome against forgetting himself for a single moment, even should his sufferings admit of such a thing. Accordingly, when, during the long dreary watches of the night, we roused suddenly from a state of half consciousness, we called each other excitedly by name, each fearing the other was benumbed or dead. The ordinary sensations of cold give but faint conceptions of that which comes on after hard exercise, with want of food and sleep, combined with wetness in a high frost wind. Life is then seen to be a mere fire, that now smoulders, now brightens, showing how easily it may be quenched.

"Muir," Jerome would inquire, with pitiful faintness, "are you suffering much?"

"Yes," I would reply, straining to keep my voice brave, "the pains of a Scandinavian hell, at once frozen and burned. But never mind, Jerome; the night will wear away at last, and to-morrow we go a-Maying, and what camp fires we will make, and what sun baths we will take!"

The frost became more and more intense, and we were covered with frozen snow and icicles, as if we had lain castaway beneath all the storms of winter. In about thirteen hours day began to dawn, but it was long ere the highest points of the cone were touched by the sun. No clouds were visible from where we lay, yet the morning was dull and blue and bitterly frosty, and never did the sun move so slowly to strip the shadows from the peaks. We watched the pale heatless light stealing toward us down the sparkling snow, but hour after hour passed by without a trace of that warm flushing sunrise splendor we were so eager to welcome. The extinction of a life seemed a simple thing after being so gradually drained of vitality, and as the time to make an effort to reach camp drew near, we became concerned to know what quantity of strength remained.

In our soaked and steamed condition we dared not attempt the descent until the temperature was somewhat mitigated. At length, about eight o'clock on this rare 1st of May, we rose to our feet, some seventeen hours after lying down, and began to struggle homeward. Our frozen trousers could scarce be made to bend; we therefore waded the snow with difficulty. After making a descent of 3,000 feet, we felt the warm sun on our backs, and at once began to revive; and at 10 o'clock A.M. we reached camp and were safe.

—John Muir, condensed from an article originally published
in *Harper's New Monthly Magazine*, September 1877

Mount Shasta, Whitney Glacier ★

Height: 14,162 feet

Route: Whitney Glacier

Best time to go: February and March

Trip duration: 2 to 3 days

Mileage: About 8 miles to the summit

Elevation gain: 8,662 feet

Effort factor: 12.7

Level of difficulty: Intermediate terrain below 11,200 feet; advanced (Black Diamond) from 13,000 to 11,200 feet; expert (Double Black Diamond) from 13,800 to 13,000 feet

Snowboards: Not recommended; the icefall presents unique problems and the approach is longer than other routes on Mount Shasta

Map: Mount Shasta

The Whitney Glacier is the longest glacier in California. It is an active glacier with séracs, crevasses, and an icefall. The crevasses open up in April and May,

The 8,000-plus-foot ski descent of the Whitney Glacier as seen from near Highway 97. The main summit of Shasta is on the left and Shastina is on the far right. The Whitney Glacier lies to the left of Shastina and continues almost to the main summit of Mount Shasta.

so it is advisable to make this ski descent earlier than the other routes on Mount Shasta. I have experienced good skiing on the Whitney Glacier in March. February and March are perhaps the best time to ski this route.

Since this is an active glacier with an icefall and many large crevasses, the ascent and descent should be roped. Descending roped is a bit tricky, and it is important to ski with a partner who has skiing skills similar to yours. Early in the season it may be safe to travel on the glacier without being roped, but you take a considerable risk. Carry a rope and crevasse rescue equipment in the event of a crevasse fall.

From the town of Mount Shasta, proceed north on Interstate 5 to Weed. From the intersection of Weed's main street and Highway 97, drive about 12 miles on Highway 97 and turn right onto Bolam Road (43N21). The road, passable by car, is unmarked and intersects the highway just west of the 4,000-foot elevation marker and the 99–97 Cutoff Road (A-12). Follow Bolam Road for about 1.7 miles, cross the railroad tracks, and continue another 2.4 miles to the parking area near 5,500 feet.

The road ends at Bolam Creek wash. Cross the first wash and hike up the far side of the far wash. In about 0.6 mile, near a large boulder in the wash, turn sharply to your right, leaving the ravine by following an old logging road. Near 6,300 feet the road splits; take the right fork, which will take you toward Whitney Creek. Follow Whitney Creek to the snout of the Whitney Glacier.

The path of the Whitney Glacier is impressive as it snakes its way along the glacier-carved valley between Shastina and the main summit of Mount Shasta. At an elevation of 11,200 feet you will encounter the Whitney Glacier icefall. Early in the season with normal snowfall, the icefall may go completely unnoticed except for a steepening of the route for about 400 feet. The icefall may only appear as a ramp leading the skier to the next level as the winter snow completely fills in the voids between the ice and snow blocks. Hopefully, this is the case for your trip. If not, routefinding through the séracs in the icefall will add a measure of difficulty to your ascent and descent. Above the icefall, the glacier has gouged out of the mountainside a hidden and remote valley seldom visited by climbers or skiers. Even today, while thousands climb Mount Shasta via the standard Avalanche Gulch route each year, few visit this inspiring and beautiful part of the mountain.

If planning a multiday trip, you may want to camp below the icefall. When selecting a campsite, check for crevasses and stay away from any steep slopes that could avalanche from above or where rockfall could be a problem. The glacier swings up against the steep sides of Shastina where rockfalls and avalanches may originate. In the past, I have safely camped below the icefall near some séracs on the left side of the glacier.

At the 13,000-foot level you can angle to the left up a steep snow face to about 13,800 feet where the route joins the standard route across the summit "ballfield." The summit pyramid is visible a short distance away. An alternative route that avoids the steep slopes above 13,000 feet continues in a southeasterly direction, joining the standard route at the base of Misery Hill (13,400 feet).

From the summit, the ski or snowboard descent is extraordinary. This route is perhaps the longest single summit descent in California—over 8,000 feet! The upper slopes between 13,800 and 13,000 feet are exceptionally steep; use caution on both the ascent and descent, as a fall here would be difficult to arrest.

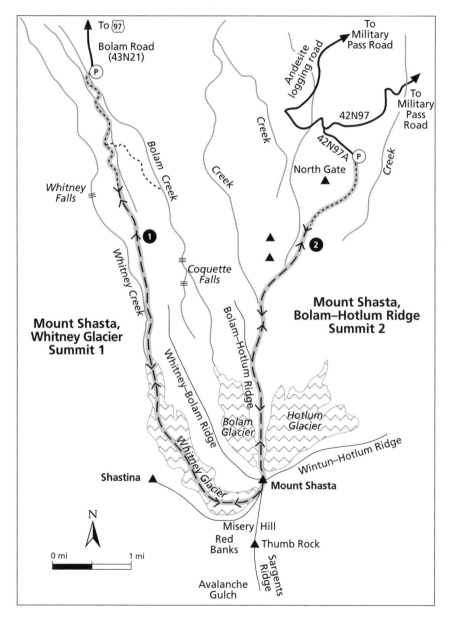

Mount Shasta, Bolam-Hotlum Ridge ★

Height: 14,162 feet
Route: Bolam–Hotlum Ridge
Best time to go: May through mid-June
Trip duration: 2 to 3 days
Mileage: About 6 miles to the summit
Elevation gain: 7,162 feet
Effort factor: 10.2
Level of difficulty: Intermediate terrain below 10,400 feet; advanced (Black Diamond) from the summit
Snowboards: Recommended; a short, direct approach and descent
Map: Mount Shasta

The view of Mount Shasta's north- and east-side glaciers from the intersection of Highway 97 and Military Pass Road is truly magnificent. The Bolam–Hotlum Ridge route ascends the obvious nose between the two glaciers. The route, although impressive, is not nearly as steep as it appears from this angle, as it does not exceed 35 degrees.

From the town of Mount Shasta, drive north on Interstate 5 to Weed. From the intersection of Weed's main street and Highway 97, drive about 15 miles on Highway 97 and turn right onto Military Pass Road (NF 19), which is well signed from Highway 97 and passable by car. Follow the road for about 1.8 miles and cross under the railroad tracks. In another 3.1 miles, turn right on the Andesite logging road. Follow this road to the North Gate parking area and trailhead. (Alternatively, travel a total of about 7 miles on Military Pass Road. Turn right at the North Gate turnoff, road 42N76. In 0.8 mile turn right on Road 42N16. Continue 1.6 miles and turn left up a hill onto road 42N16D. In 0.3 mile continue straight through an intersection, rejoining road 42N16. After 0.7 mile turn left onto road 42N97. Curve to the left and follow road 42N97A to the North Gate parking area.)

From the North Gate parking area (7,000 feet), follow the route of the summer hiking trail as it skirts to the left of the base of North Gate. Beyond North Gate are two prominent volcanic buttes about 1,000 feet higher. Continue up along their easterly (left) base to 8,600 feet, where there is a minor saddle to the south of the second butte. Follow the obvious valley above this saddle to a plateau at 10,800 feet. On the way up you will pass an ideal place to camp to the left and out of the main gully near the 9,500-foot level. This area is relatively flat and provides excellent views of the route, the Hotlum Glacier headwall, and the summit.

Get started early, so you can reach the summit by noon. (Descending too late in the day will result in less-than-ideal snow conditions, as the snow softens considerably throughout the day.) The climb from base camp entails 4,700 feet of elevation gain. Allow plenty of time (5 to 7 hours), keeping in mind that your pace will slow in the thinning air as you ascend the mountain. Plan to use crampons early in the morning.

From base camp, continue up the main gully to the 10,800-foot plateau. Up ahead is the prominent rock face of the Hotlum headwall, near 13,200 feet. Aim for the headwall, passing to the right by ascending the dividing ridge between the Bolam and Hotlum Glaciers. Above the headwall, bear slightly right, angling away from the headwall, and climb through the notch between two of the lesser summits of Shasta. Pass the fumaroles where on April 30, 1875, John Muir spent a bitter night in a full-scale blizzard without the benefit of a blanket or overcoat (see sidebar). The summit is but a hundred meters away. Normally the summit block is exposed volcanic rock with some snow and ice plastered to the exposed rock.

The ski descent from the top is superb. Ski through the gap in the two lesser summits, and descend your ascent route. Another option is to ski down the Bolam Glacier. If you plan to ski the glacier, you should first ascend the route to check the conditions and for crevasses before descending on skis. This is an excellent route but includes a greater risk of crevasses. Make sure you do not ski too far down the glacier, as you will need to make your way back to the right and the 10,800-foot plateau to reach your base camp.

The Bolam Glacier is on the right and the Hotlum Glacier on the left. Ascend the nose/ridge dividing the two glaciers. Pass to the left of the rocks forming an inverted V while staying to the right of the Hotlum Glacier headwall. The Hotlum headwall is just below and left of the summit.

Mount Shasta, Hotlum–Wintun Ridge ⋆

Height: 14,162 feet

Route: Hotlum–Wintun Ridge

Best time to go: mid-May through mid-June

Trip duration: 2 to 3 days

Mileage: About 6 miles to the summit

Elevation gain: Almost 7,000 feet

Effort factor: 10.0

Level of difficulty: Intermediate skiing below 11,000 feet; advanced (Black Diamond) from the summit

Snowboards: Recommended; great run for all whether fixed-heel, free-heel, or snowboards

Map: Mount Shasta

Mount Shasta's Hotlum–Wintun Ridge is simply one of the best descents in California. It is rare to find a descent of any considerable length, let alone one that drops 7,000 feet, with uniformly excellent snow from top to bottom, as you will here. This route has something for everyone—easy access, moderate terrain for intermediate skiers, and steeper terrain for experts.

The summit can be attained in a long single day or with a base camp established after a short 3- to 4-hour approach. A base camp will afford the luxury of exploratory day trips as well as a trip to the summit. Nearby is the Hotlum Glacier, a good place to practice ice climbing and crevasse rescue techniques.

From Mount Shasta City, proceed east on Highway 89 to McCloud. Continue east for about 3.5 miles and turn left on a paved road, Pilgrims Creek Road (NF 13). Proceed 7.5 miles to Military Pass Road and turn left. From this point the

Hotlum–Wintun Ridge lies on the left skyline. The 7,000-foot ski/snowboard descent is behind the Hotlum Glacier headwall, which can be seen just below the summit.

dirt roads, all passable by car, are well marked with signs to the Brewer Creek trailhead. Proceed along this road as it becomes Military Pass Road (NF 19), turn left on road 42N02, and then make another left on road 42N10 (Brewer Creek Road) and proceed to the Brewer Creek parking area at 7,200 feet. The road to the trailhead usually opens in late May—later in heavy snow years.

This trip is best from mid-May through mid-June. However, in May you will have to ski the last couple of miles up the road to the trailhead.

The trail runs south-southwest for the first 2-plus miles, then turns due west. After signing in at the trailhead, follow the Brewer Creek trail. If you plan a single-day ascent, set out early (pre-dawn), to reach the summit in time for a

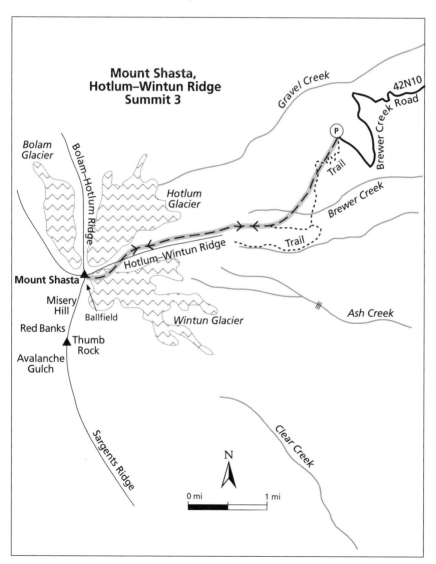

descent no later than noon or 1:00 P.M. Allow 7–10 hours to make the climb. Your reward will be optimum snow conditions on the descent (the snow turns to "mashed potatoes" in the afternoon). The trail switches back and forth up the timbered slopes, gradually gaining elevation from the 7,200-foot trailhead. After about 2.5 miles and 1,000 feet elevation gain, the trail fades.

There are numerous spots to camp from this point on up to 9,600 feet, with low-growing trees on the rounded ridges for protection. Higher up, the saddle between the Wintun and Hotlum Glaciers provides excellent views of the summit, the Hotlum headwall, and the crevasses of the Hotlum Glacier.

The route from the end of the trail to the summit is straightforward: Follow the ridge between the Wintun and Holtum Glaciers. Around 12,000 feet the ridge becomes more distinctive and steepens considerably. At this point climb the steep section, or traverse left out onto the Wintun Glacier. The summit is still 2,000 feet above; keep on keeping on.

The 7,000-foot ski descent from the summit back to the car or camp is worth every ounce of effort it takes to make the climb. On top, the climbers coming up the standard Avalanche Gulch route will be surprised to see you standing there with your skis or board. The views are great from the top, but you will not be able to see the Pacific Ocean, as did John Muir; the visibility and air quality have deteriorated in the last hundred years, denying us that privilege.

4
Shastina, Cascade Gulch

Height: 12,330 feet

Route: Cascade Gulch

Best time to go: March through early May

Trip duration: 1 to 3 days

Mileage: About 6 miles to the summit

Elevation gain: 5,470 feet

Effort factor: 8.5

Level of difficulty: Intermediate terrain below 10,000 feet; advanced (Black Diamond) above

Snowboards: Recommended, although this route has a slightly longer approach than those to Mount Shasta (Summits 2 and 3)

Map: Mount Shasta

Shastina is the 12,330-foot subpeak due west of Mount Shasta's main summit. Shastina contains an impressive crater with three separate lakes. The south, east, and north rims of the crater provide great vantage points for viewing the crater below or the Whitney Glacier and the main summit above. March, April, and early May are the best times to ski/snowboard from Shastina's unique summit.

From the town of Mount Shasta, drive up Everitt Memorial Highway (paved)

for about 11 miles to Bunny Flat at 6,860 feet. From the parking area, follow the trail to the Sierra Club Hut at Horse Camp, a hike or ski of about 2 miles. Horse Camp is located at the treeline around 7,900 feet in Avalanche Gulch. Due to the large number of skiers and climbers passing through this area, overnight stays are not permissible at the hut, but spring water and sanitation facilities are available. Avalanche Gulch is the standard route to the summit of Mount Shasta and is used by 95 percent of the summiteers. You will quickly leave the hordes behind as you traverse into Cascade Gulch.

From Horse Camp traverse north-northwest for a mile or so, slowly gaining elevation. Gradually turn northeast up Cascade Gulch and into Hidden Valley. The terrain levels off around 9,200 feet, providing a great place to camp. If you do not plan to camp here, continue up Cascade Gulch for an additional 3,000 feet to the col between Shastina and Mount Shasta, an elevation of 11,900 feet.

From the col it is a short climb to the top of Shastina and its crater containing three small "lakes"; these have been covered with snow and frozen every time I have been there. Camping near the crater affords not only views of the sunset over the Trinity Alps and the night lights of Weed, Mount Shasta City, and Dunsmuir, but a side trip to the summit of Mount Shasta. If you plan a climb of the main summit of Mount Shasta, skirt the Whitney Glacier and its upper crevasses. With snow covering the route, it may be difficult to determine where the glacier ends, so use caution. Stay to the far right as you ascend the ridge. You'll need an ice axe, crampons, and a climbing rope.

From the Shastina col, Cascade Gulch drops 4,000 feet to the treeline. The gulch's wide-open spaces offer excellent bowl skiing and snowboarding. To extend the length of the run, continue down Cascade Gulch to Everitt Highway, a descent of about 7,000 feet. Hitchhike to your car parked at Bunny Flat.

In addition to the ski descent of Shastina, other ski opportunities abound. A descent off the lower slopes of Casaval Ridge or from Lake Helen at 10,400

Mount Shasta and Shastina as seen from above the town of Mount Shasta. The Cascade Gulch route is left of center and tops out on the saddle between Shastina (left) and Mount Shasta's summit.

feet in Avalanche Gulch can be excellent. Go before the sun cups form. Due to the westerly exposure, they form early in the spring ski season.

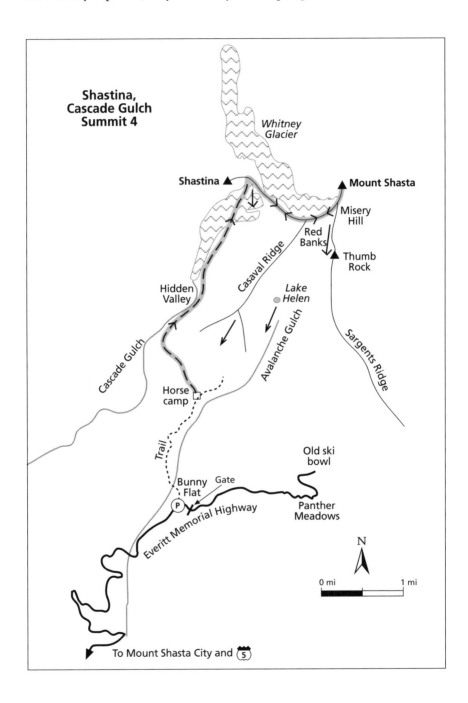

Shastina, Cascade Gulch Summit 4

Whitney Glacier

Shastina ▲

▲ **Mount Shasta**

Misery Hill

Red Banks

Casaval Ridge

▲ Thumb Rock

Hidden Valley

Lake Helen

Cascade Gulch

Avalanche Gulch

Sargents Ridge

Horse camp

Trail

Old ski bowl

Bunny Flat Gate

Panther Meadows

Everitt Memorial Highway

N

0 mi   1 mi

To Mount Shasta City and ⑤

Chapter 3
LASSEN VOLCANIC NATIONAL PARK

Lassen Peak is the southernmost Cascade Range volcano and the largest plug-domed volcano in the world. Its eruption in May 1914 began a seven-year period of sporadic volcanic activity; in 1915 the peak blew an enormous mushroom cloud some 7 miles skyward. The following year, Lassen Volcanic National Park was established.

Unlike Mount Shasta, its neighbor to the north, there are no glaciers on Lassen Peak, as its summit is not high enough to support permanent snowfields. However, it receives copious amounts of snow each year. Lassen Peak may receive more snow than any other place in California, as the path of the wet Pacific storms heading this way is unobstructed. Above 8,000 feet, drifts exceeding 30 feet are not uncommon.

Snow measurements have been taken in the vicinity of Lake Helen (8,000 feet) since 1930. In those early years, the snow surveyors started from Highway 36, a distance of about 10 miles. More recently, the ski route into Lake Helen has been cut in half, as Highway 89 is now plowed from Highway 36 to just beyond the Lassen Park boundary. The maximum depth recorded at the Lake Helen snow survey marker was 331 inches (27.6 feet) in 1983.

Backcountry skiing north of Lassen Volcanic National Park. The north ridge of Lassen Peak can be seen in the distance.

Both the Manzanita Lake entrance on the north and the Mineral entrance to the south are favorite winter areas for families. Many can be seen making their way along the unplowed roads in the park for a mile or two. However, after traveling a short distance you'll leave the majority of the skiers and snowshoers behind. Lassen Peak is one of my favorite summits because the snow is always plentiful and, due to a climate that is colder than the Sierra Nevada's, usually in great condition above 7,000 feet.

How to get there: Lassen Volcanic National Park is located about 160 miles north of Sacramento and about 50 miles east of Redding and Red Bluff. The park has two entrances, north (Manzanita Lake) and south (Mineral). In the

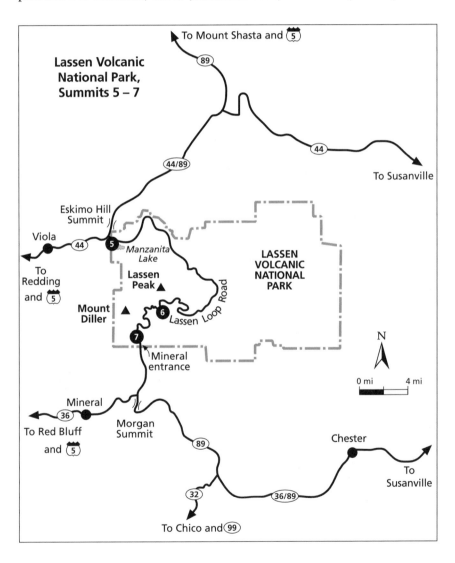

summer, these two entrances are connected by the Lassen Loop Road, which passes to the east of the main peak. The Lassen Loop Road is closed at the two entrances after the first winter snow. Depending on the amount of snow accumulation each season, the road is usually opened by May or June. See the trip writeup for Lassen Peak's Northeast Face (Summit 6) for a further explanation of the road opening dates.

From the south or north take Interstate 5 to either Red Bluff or Redding. To reach the north entrance of the park, take Highway 44 from Redding and drive east to Manzanita Lake. To reach the south entrance, drive east on Highway 36 from Red Bluff and turn north on Highway 89. To reach the park from the east, take Highway 395 to Susanville and proceed west on Highway 44 to the north entrance; or proceed west on Highway 36 and then north on Highway 89 to the south entrance.

Beginner's Luck—1954 Ski Traverse of Lassen Peak

As part of my responsibility as advisor to the Shasta College Ski Club, I would take the club over to Lassen Ski Park, which at the time consisted of a single T-bar surface lift near the south entrance. There I met the chief ranger of Lassen Volcanic National Park, Les Bodine, who taught me to ski. It was Les who told us about the cross-country trip across Lassen Peak over to Manzanita Lake on the north side. Some of my club members were all for the idea.

I am not certain how, or why, I attempted to make that first trip [i.e., first recorded trip: the first crossing may have been in the 1930s or 1940s] across Lassen Volcanic National Park in 1954, much less lead it. I really was a city boy from San Francisco, with no wilderness experience to speak of. I had a map, but no compass—nor even any idea how to use a compass.

As the eight of us left the safety of the Ski Park (elevation 6,800 feet), Les's parting words were, "Be sure to stay to the right of the Crescent Cliffs, and, for certain, do not miss the bridge across Manzanita Creek." What cliffs, and what bridge, I had no idea, but the image of cliffs stood out in my mind as some obstacle over which I might accidentally lead the group.

Until 1970 there were no lightweight cross-country skis as we know them today. We used our heavy alpine skis, Head Standards. The concept of quick-release safety bindings was unheard of back then. Cable bindings were the high-tech standard of the day for alpine skiers. For skiing uphill, we would remove the cables from the rear guides to allow some heel movement. On the descent, we would run the cables back through the rear guides to hold the heels down. The skis, of course, had no traction for climbing, but we were able to buy heavy mohair climbers from war surplus, which we attached to the bottom of the skis. The weight of the skis and mohair climbers was considerable.

Our route from the Sulphur Works on the south side of Lassen Peak followed the park road. Les had also told us about the cutoff around Diamond Peak. It does save 2 miles, but back then, with our makeshift equipment, it was a serious challenge.

Maybe the rest of the group had some false trust in me, but I felt as if we were headed for the moon. It would be many years before I would ever come across another person heading up toward Lassen Peak from the ski area.

We struggled on up to the pass between Lassen Peak and Eagle Peak. I can recall going 10 or 20 feet at a time, resting and gasping for breath. On this crossing, it took us 6 hours to reach the pass, and we felt it was a huge struggle. By contrast, now, with the advent of lightweight, waxless cross-country skis, I hardly ever stop until I am at the top of the pass, taking less than half the time it took on the original trip.

It is hard to imagine the feeling I had at the pass (elevation 9,000 feet), looking down, down to Manzanita Lake (elevation 5,600 feet), wondering how I was going to get the group down—and through all that country—successfully. I think I was blessed with what you could call "beginner's luck." This has been true so many times for me, and this was no exception. Everything went about perfect. We had great skiing all the way down, and by luck I seemed to have picked the best route, for in all the years since [making an annual crossing] I have hardly varied from this same route. We hit the bridge on upper Manzanita Creek right on—didn't even have to search for it. To this day, after over sixty crossings, I still marvel at our good fortune.

—Gene Leach

Lassen Peak, Summit Traverse ★

Height: 10,457 feet

Route: Ascend North Ridge, descend Southwest Face

Best time to go: February through April

Trip duration: 1 long day

Mileage: About 7 miles to the summit, a total of 14 miles

Elevation gain/loss: 4,600-foot climb with a 3,600-foot descent

Effort factor: 8.1

Level of difficulty: Advanced (Black Diamond) from summit to about 9,000 feet; intermediate terrain below 9,000 feet

Snowboards: Not recommended; long approach over varied terrain

Maps: Lassen Peak, Reading Peak, West Prospect Peak, Manzanita Lake

The traverse of Lassen Peak is a rewarding trip. The scenery is exceptional, the terrain is excellent for telemark skiing, and the snow is always superb. This traverse is seldom done, perhaps because of the extra planning and coordination required, but is truly a classic. The single traverse requires placing a second car and driver at the finish below the Sulphur Works, near the Mineral entrance on the Lassen Loop Road. For a double traverse, you could arrange a ride from here to Chester to spend the night. Camping is allowed in the park, but it cannot be recommended for this tour; carrying a full pack would prevent one from completing the 14-mile traverse in a single day.

From Redding on Interstate 5, or Susanville on Highway 395, take Highway 44 to the north (Manzanita Lake) entrance of the Lassen Volcanic National Park (5,800 feet). The traverse will terminate at the south (Mineral) entrance of the park.

Ski up the Lassen Loop Road past Manzanita Lake and the park entrance station. After about 1.5 miles, turn right off the road in an open, sparsely treed area near the 6,100-foot level. Proceed east, gaining elevation to around 6,600 feet. Turn south into the trees and cross a small ridge. Keep angling toward the base of Chaos Crags, gradually gaining elevation. You will soon come to a picturesque valley at the base of the Crags. Continue around the south side of the Crags to the saddle at the base of Lassen Peak's North Ridge.

Follow the North Ridge to the summit, a strenuous climb of about 2,400 feet. Bring your crampons; you will probably need them. From the summit you will be able to see 14,162-foot Mount Shasta to the north, the many summits in Lassen Volcanic National Park, and the snow-covered Lassen Loop Road far below. To the southwest is a ridge connecting Lassen Peak with a series of peaks—Eagle Peak, Ski Heil Peak, Pilot Pinnacle, Mount Diller, and Brokeoff Mountain. (The Mount Diller writeup, Summit 7, describes the tour of this beautiful ridge and its various summits.) Make your way across the summit crater to either the south or southwest face and descend to Lake Helen and the Lassen Loop Road below.

Follow the road to the Sulphur Works and the south entrance parking lot. You can eliminate about 2 miles of road skiing by taking a shortcut that passes Diamond Peak to the west and rejoins the Lassen Loop Road at the Sulphur Works (1 mile from the parking area). If you have planned to retrace your route the following day to retrieve your car and have arranged for a car to meet you, drive

Lassen Peak from Manzanita Lake. The traverse of Lassen Peak begins at Manzanita Lake and ascends the north ridge (left skyline).

into Chester for dinner and get a room for the night. You may be able to hitchhike into Chester, but the roads are not heavily traveled in this remote area. Return the next morning and ski back across the park to Manzanita Lake and your car.

There are many variations to this traverse. Starting from the north, instead of traversing over the summit, ski around the east side of the peak near the 8,000-foot level, joining the Lassen Loop Road to the south of the peak, and follow the road out to the south entrance. On the return trip the following day, starting from the south entrance, ski up the road and over the pass between Eagle Peak and Lassen Peak and back down to Manzanita Lake.

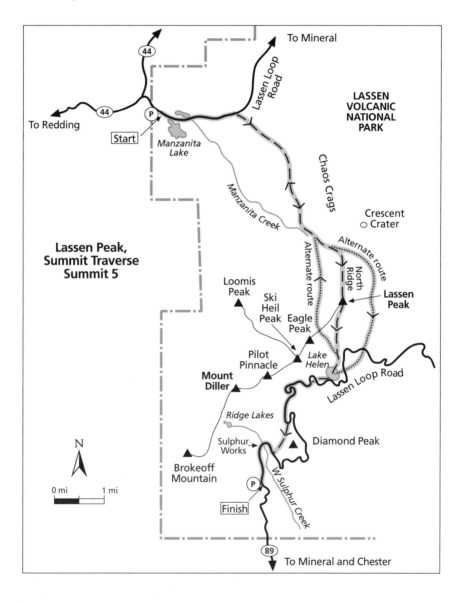

Lassen Peak, Northeast Face

Height: 10,457 feet	
Route: Ascend Lassen Peak's south side, descend Northeast Face	
Best time to go: April through early June	
Trip duration: Half day	
Mileage: 2 miles to the summit, 5 miles down	
Elevation gain/loss: 2,000-foot climb, 4,000-foot descent	
Effort factor: 3.0	
Level of difficulty: Top half of descent is advanced (Black Diamond)	
Snowboards: Recommended; climb 2,000 feet, board 4,000 feet	
Maps: Lassen Peak, Reading Peak, West Prospect Peak, Manzanita Lake	

This is a great spring trip. Ascend 2,000 feet, following the route of the summer hiking trail on the south side of the peak to the summit, then descend 4,000 feet to the Devastated Area to the east. Can't beat that for efficiency! Boarders will enjoy this trip immensely.

In the spring, many skiers and boarders can be seen carrying their skis up the south side of Lassen Peak for a great run down the South Face. After the Lassen Loop Road is opened, skiers enjoy easy access to the peak from the summit trail parking area, located just beyond Lake Helen at the 8,500-foot pass. The South Face is an excellent ski descent; however, our focus here is on both the Northeast and Southeast Faces. These descent routes allow a finish at the Devastated Area on the east side of the peak.

Lassen Peak's Northeast Face from the Devastated Area. Ski or snowboard the minor rib in the center of the gullies from the very top. Lassen's North Ridge is on the right skyline. Photo by Gene Leach

In late spring the Park Service begins plowing the Lassen Loop Road, attempting to open the area by Easter or early April. Crews begin to plow from Manzanita Lake in the north to the Devastated Area, then transport their equipment to the south entrance, where they plow up over the summit south of Mount Lassen and down to the Devastated Area. The road is usually open by Memorial Day, although in heavy snow years when the snowdrifts exceed depths of 30 feet the road is not opened until much later, sometimes into July.

To ascend the summer trail and descend the Northeast Face in a half-day tour, you'll need to leave a car on the east side of the mountain at the Devastated Area parking lot, then drive to the start of the summer trail above Lake Helen (8,500 feet). To reach the south (Mineral) entrance, drive east on Highway 36 from the town of Red Bluff on Interstate 5. After about 5 miles, turn north onto Highway 89 into Lassen Volcanic National Park and continue on the Lassen Loop Road to the summit parking area or continue to the Devastated Area located on the east side of Lassen Peak.

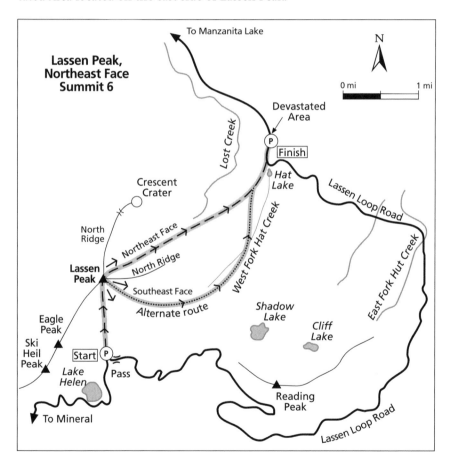

From the summit parking area, climb the south side of Lassen Peak, following the route of the summer trail to the summit. The route is straightforward and ascends directly up the south side of the peak immediately above the parking area.

Lassen Peak's Northeast Face is seldom skied, as it offers a greater challenge than the South Face. The Northeast Face is steeper, longer, and requires a greater level of commitment. Use caution, as the face avalanches regularly both in the winter and in the spring. The face is divided by several gullies, with a minor ridge in the center of the face. The safest descent route is down this rib, which is easily identified from the summit by two large boulders straddling the divide.

The following example illustrates the avalanche danger that can be expected on the Northeast Face. It was 1:30 P.M. when we arrived on the summit, and the fresh snow from the previous week had not completely consolidated. We suspected that the upper slopes of the northeast gullies just below the summit were unstable, as it was a warm day in June. From the summit we made a couple of quick jump turns to test the slope's stability; this activated a surface avalanche that ran for 2,000 feet (from the summit near 10,400 feet to 8,400 feet) down the main gully. A short traverse across the break point of the upper slopes just to the north of the summit also triggered several more wet-snow avalanches. We considered skiing down the North Ridge, but finally decided that the Northeast Face was stable enough to ski the avalanched slopes. After the avalanches had stopped moving, we carefully skied down the avalanche-cleared slopes with a wary eye on the slopes above.

An alternate route to the Northeast Face is to descend the Southeast Face, slowly angling east and then northeast down to Hat Lake and the Devastated Area at an elevation of 6,400 feet. As you approach 9,000 feet, begin to head in a more easterly direction and then northeast. Either remain on the ridge on the south side of the West Fork of Hat Creek, or drop down into the creek. The higher up and the earlier you turn from a southwesterly to a northeasterly direction, the steeper the terrain; conversely, a longer descent on the Southeast Face and a more gradual counterclockwise turn to the northeast will lead to more gradual terrain.

The skiing on the east side of the mountain is even better early in the season before the Lassen Loop Road is completely opened through the park. Drive to the Devastated Area parking lot via the north entrance at Manzanita Lake. Ski up Lost Creek to the saddle at 8,200 feet between the North Ridge and Crescent Crater. Climb the North Ridge to the summit, gaining 2,200 feet, and descend the northeast gullies as described above.

For best snow conditions, start your descent by 11:00 A.M., as the snow softens early at these elevations. An early descent time is also safer, since the top layer of snow will not yet be saturated with water, which can overload the slope and trigger an avalanche.

Mount Diller

Height: 9,087 feet
Route: Ridge Lakes
Best time to go: December through April
Trip duration: 1 day
Mileage: 3 miles to the summit
Elevation gain: 2,287 feet
Effort factor: 3.8
Level of difficulty: Intermediate
Snowboards: Recommended
Map: Lassen Peak

This is a wonderful tour in exquisite terrain—a good trip for an intermediate skier. This route can be completed easily in a single day or made into a relaxing overnight trip. The Ridge Lakes, just 2 miles and a 1,200-foot climb from your car, are a great place to camp, if you choose to spend the night. Although the south entrance to the park is a popular starting point for cross-country skiers and snowshoers, once you leave the road the crowds will disappear.

From the town of Red Bluff on Interstate 5, drive east on Highway 36 to Mineral. After about 5 miles, turn north onto Highway 89 into Lassen Volcanic National Park. In the winter, the road is only plowed to the old ski area and lodge. Park here (6,800 feet) and ski up the unplowed Lassen Loop Road for about a mile. Pass the Sulphur Works and ski across the bridge. After crossing

On the ridge between Lassen Peak and Brokeoff Mountain. Brokeoff is in the center and Mount Diller is on the right.

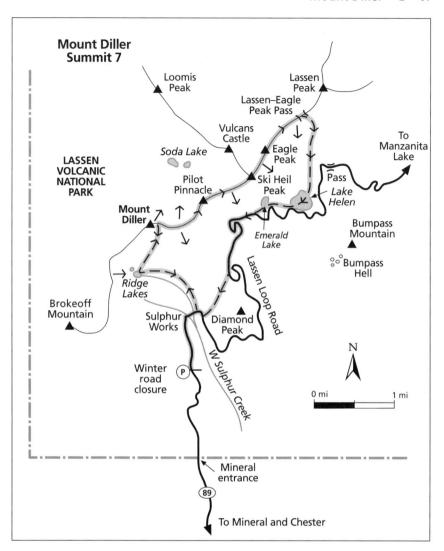

the bridge, leave the road by turning left (north) at the point where the road makes a sharp bend to the right (south). Follow West Sulphur Creek to the Ridge Lakes, staying on the right side and some distance away from the creek where the terrain is less steep and the trees are not as thick.

From the Ridge Lakes ascend open slopes to the saddle between Pilot Pinnacle and Mount Diller. If you have the time and desire, climb to the summit of Pilot Pinnacle by traversing around to the north of the peak. There is great bowl skiing off Pilot Pinnacle's north side. A drop of about 1,000 feet will bring you to Soda Lake. Climb back up to the saddle between Pilot Pinnacle and Mount Diller, and climb to the summit of Mount Diller.

The views along the ridge are splendid. To the southwest is the northeast face of Brokeoff Mountain—an impressive sight. In the opposite direction is Lassen Peak, dwarfing the many surrounding peaks. Along the ridge linking Brokeoff Mountain and Lassen Peak are Mount Diller, Pilot Pinnacle, Ski Heil Peak, and Eagle Peak. Down below on the unplowed Lassen Loop Road an occasional skier may be spotted passing the frozen form of Emerald Lake or Lake Helen. And just below these lakes is Bumpass Hell, a group of boiling mud pots.

You can descend the way you came, or seek out more open terrain to the east. Alternatively, ski along the crest of the ridge from Mount Diller to the base of Lassen Peak, over the tops of Pilot Pinnacle, Ski Heil Peak, Eagle Peak, and finally the pass between Eagle Peak and Lassen Peak. Descend from the pass on open slopes to Lake Helen and the Lassen Loop Road. This is an excellent route, and can be completed in a long day with an early morning start.

Due to the colder temperatures of Lassen Peak, this area has excellent powder snow. This trip is good between December and April, and is also excellent immediately after a storm.

Chapter 4
LAKE TAHOE REGION

Lake Tahoe is the crown jewel of the Sierra Nevada, one of the highest and most beautiful large alpine lakes found anywhere in the world. There is no other lake like it in all of North America. Lake Tahoe is 12 miles wide and 22 miles long with 72 miles of shoreline. Its crystal-clear waters cover 264 square miles to a depth of 1,645 feet. This lake basin was carved out of the alpine granite terrain by ancient glaciers that covered the region. Lake Tahoe is the second-deepest lake in the United States.

The region is a skier's and snowboarder's paradise. Fourteen alpine ski resorts and eleven cross-country ski areas dot the region. Just to the west of Lake Tahoe and the state's most popular resort areas are two magnificent wilderness areas—Desolation Valley Wilderness Area and Granite Chief Wilderness Area. With their glacier-polished granite lake basins and peaks, these two wilderness areas are favorite summertime destinations for hikers, climbers, and backpackers, and contain ideal backcountry skiing terrain.

Although not included in this guide, Anderson Peak, Tinkers Knob, and Silver Peak (located on the Sierra Nevada crest between Highway 80, Donner

Desolation Valley and Lake Aloha in the winter, with Pyramid Peak (Summit 11) in the background. The south ridge of Pyramid is on the left skyline.

Summit, and Squaw Valley); Twin Peaks and Ellis Peak (south of Alpine Meadows); Jacks Peak (Desolation Valley); Freel Peak and Waterhouse Peak (near Highway 89 and Luther Pass); Stevens Peak (near Red Lake Peak); and Round Top (south of Carson Pass) are other excellent ski and snowboard summits in the Tahoe region.

The Snow Laboratory in Norden, California, has snowfall data for the region going back 119 years. Recorded snowfall has been as much as 68 feet in a single season, with accumulations as high as 15.4 feet from a single storm.

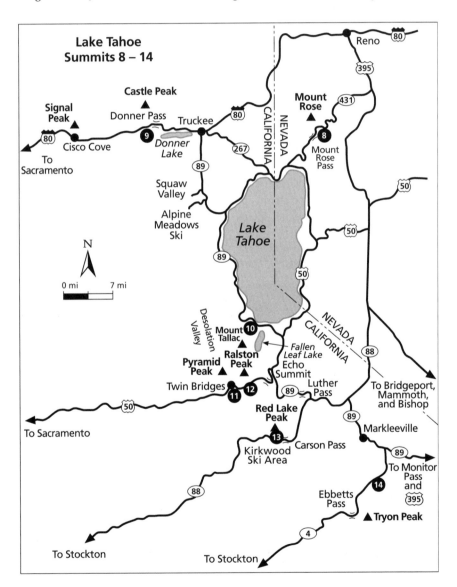

How to get there: For the purposes of this book, the Lake Tahoe region extends from Castle Peak, just north of Donner Pass on Interstate 80, south to Tryon Peak, just south of Ebbetts Pass on Highway 4, a north-to-south distance of about 70 miles. Access to the summits in this region is by way of Interstate 80 (Castle Peak), Highway 50 (Pyramid Peak and Ralston Peak), and Highway 88 (Red Lake Peak). These three trans-Sierra highways remain open through the winter. Highway 4 (a trans-Sierra highway that is closed in the winter) provides access to Tryon Peak from the north and the town of Markleeville. Highway 431 (Mount Rose Highway) provides road access to Mount Rose, and Highway 89 will take you to the start of the climb of Mount Tallac.

The First Winter Crossing of the Sierra Nevada

John C. Fremont, Second Lieutenant in the U.S. Topographical Engineers, is credited with the first sighting of Lake Tahoe, the first crossing of the Sierra Nevada in winter (over Carson Pass—8,574 feet), and the first ascent of Red Lake Peak on February 14, 1844. Fremont's winter crossing was a success, as not a single man was lost in the ordeal. This is in stark contrast to the more famous, ill-fated, well-chronicled expedition of the Donner Party two years later in 1846, when thirty-four of eight-one died attempting to cross the Sierra Nevada near Donner Pass.

Fremont's Second Exploring Expedition set out in the spring of 1843. The party was particularly strong, as it included the famous scouts Kit Carson and Thomas Fitzpatrick. After exploring the Columbia River region and California, Fremont had hoped to return by heading east across the Great Basin to the Rocky Mountains, but his provisions were low and the stock unfit for the eastward journey. He decided instead to cross the Sierra and resupply in the Sacramento Valley. The decision could not have been an easy one, for he was committing his party to an unknown route and to the first Sierra Nevada crossing ever attempted in the winter. As this account begins, they are lost, the snow is deepening, and the winter temperatures are unbearable as they leave Carson Valley, Nevada, and head west toward Carson Pass.

It was the last day of January when Fremont again camped by the waters of the Carson River, supposing himself back on his "Salmon Trout" river (today's Truckee River). By this time the "Pathfinder" was definitely lost. It was beginning to snow again and the men were getting restive. He had to do something. He made a speech, reminding his men "of the beautiful valley of the Sacramento," and assuring them that with one effort they would "place themselves in the midst of plenty."

Fremont was now at his best. No longer hesitant, he boldly led on into the wintry Sierra in frontal attack. Up the East Carson River, past the site of Markleeville, the party began to encounter deep snow. An old Indian warned: "Rock upon rock—rock upon rock—snow upon snow—snow upon snow. Even if you get over the snow you will not be able to get down from the mountain." An Indian who had been engaged as a guide deserted. But Fremont no longer wanted a guide; he would spy out the land himself. On February 6, he set out with a few others on showshoes to reconnoiter. "Crossing the open basin, in a march of about ten miles we reached the top of one of the peaks. Far below us, dimmed by the distance, was a large snowless valley, bounded on the western side, at the distance of about a hundred miles by a low range of mountains which Carson recognized with delight as the mountains bordering the coast. Between us, then, and this low coast range, was the valley of the Sacramento; and no one who had accompanied us through the incidents of our life for the past few months could realize the delight with which at last we looked down upon it."

The following night the thermometer fell to three degrees below zero. "Scenery and weather combined," writes Fremont, "must render these mountains beautiful in summer; the purity and deep-blue color of the sky are singularly beautiful; the days are sunny and bright, and even warm in the noon hours; and if we could be free from the many anxieties that oppress us, even now we would be delighted here; but our provisions are getting fearfully scant." Thus for the moment the spell of the High Sierra was upon him. Almost immediately, however, the perils of the situation were brought back to his attention. The weather changed, the wind rose to a gale, and it began to snow again. For several days the struggle continued through wind and snowfall, followed by bright sun and thaw. Snow blindness, fatigue and hunger were countered by resolution and resourcefulness.

To one member of the party, however, the stark necessities of survival were more important than the scenery. Charles Preuss, the German topographer, was not so inured to hardship as were others of the party. His diary furnishes some realistic commentaries. "We are getting deeper and deeper into the mountains and snow. We can make only a few miles each day. No longer any salt in camp. This is awful. We are now completely snowed in. The snowstorm is on top of us. The wind obliterates all tracks which, with indescribable effort, we make for our horses. It is certain that we shall have to eat horse meat." Soon afterward Preuss's mule was killed, then a little dog. Fremont writes, "We had tonight an extraordinary dinner—pea soup, mule and dog."

On February 14, Fremont mentions almost casually, "With Mr. Preuss, I ascended the highest peak to the right: from which we had a beautiful view of a mountain lake at our feet, about 15 miles in length, and so entirely surrounded by mountains that we could not discover an outlet." Here is the first recorded mention of one of the great scenic features of the Sierra, Lake Tahoe. It is also the first account of an identifiable mountain ascent in the Sierra. They were on Red Lake Peak.

But though the illusion of spring was in the air, it was nevertheless midwinter and the party was in a serious predicament. They had gained the Sierra crest at a point a little south of the present Carson Pass and now considered themselves victorious over the mountain. They soon found out, however, that many difficulties intervened between them and the promised land. The second day after they crossed the pass they "were forced off the ridges by the quantity of snow among the timber, and obliged to take to the mountainsides, where, occasionally, rocks and a southern exposure afforded us a chance to scramble along. But these were steep, and slippery with snow and ice; and the rough evergreens of the mountain impeded our way, tore our skins, and exhausted our patience." That afternoon they reached the South Fork of the American River, a short distance from Strawberry Valley. Carson, who was in advance, leaped across at a narrow spot between two rocks, but when Fremont attempted it his smooth moccasin slipped and he fell into the water; whereupon Kit jumped in and rescued him. They dried off before a large fire—a scene to be recalled when driving along U.S. 50 on a winter's day.

The barrier had been surmounted, and, although hunger and hardship were still with them, from that time on they were definitely on the way to warmth and safety. On the sixth of March the advance party was greeted by Captain Sutter at New Helvetia and two days later the others, emaciated and exhausted, at last found haven. Of the large band who started across the mountain not one had failed to arrive, although one man did come in somewhat deranged in his mind. Of the sixty-seven horses and mules, thirty-three reached Sutter's Fort. Had the winter been as severe as some of those immediately before and after, the story would have been quite different and Lieutenant Fremont's career would have ended abruptly.

—Francis P. Farquhar, *History of the Sierra Nevada*

Mount Rose

Height: 10,776 feet

Route: Galena Creek

Best time to go: January through March

Trip duration: 1 day

Elevation gain: 2,676 feet

Effort factor: 5.2

Level of difficulty: Intermediate in the Galena Creek drainage; advanced (Black Diamond) above 8,600 feet

Mileage: 5 miles to the summit

Snowboards: Recommended, but there is a relatively flat section for the first 2 miles

Map: Mount Rose

Even though Mount Rose is on the California border just within the state of Nevada, this summit is too good to overlook. Mount Rose and the many nearby summits have been a favorite of skiers for many years. This area offers excellent

Mount Rose as seen from the air. Photo by Colin Fuller

snow conditions, a variety of terrain, and a choice of numerous secondary peaks.

From either Reno, Nevada, or Incline Village, California, take the Mount Rose Highway (Highway 431) to the Mount Rose Ski Area. Park at the Mount Rose parking area or just west of the resort on Highway 431.

From the parking area (8,300 feet) ski west, dropping gradually to cross the creek that drains from Tamarack Lake and then Galena Creek near 8,100 feet. Continue west up the right side of Galena Creek to around 8,800 feet. Turn northwest up a side tributary to Galena Creek, and ascend the creek to the saddle between Mount Houghton and Mount Rose at the 9,731-foot level. Follow the southwest ridge to the summit of Mount Rose.

From the top of Mount Rose, descend the southwest ridge or the south face into the Galena Creek valley. Continue down the Galena Creek drainage to the major switchback in Highway 431 or ski out to the Sky Tavern Ski Area. Hitch a ride back up the road to your car. Due to the southerly exposure, you should make sure there is ample snow for this trip. Since Mount Rose is east of the Sierra Nevada Crest, it receives substantially less snow.

An easier, more gentle approach, more suited for the intermediate skier, starts just west of Mount Rose Pass on Highway 431. Ski up the unplowed road that intersects the highway at 8,840 feet; this will take you up a beautiful valley into Third Creek (9,400 feet). From here the route steepens. To your left, due west, you should see an old tramway and radio tower; turn north at this point, then traverse northeast into Galena Creek, joining the first route and continuing to the saddle at 9,731 feet. This alternate route adds about 2 miles to your approach, but it is worth the effort, for its varied terrain provides additional ski options. This approach takes you by Mount Houghton (10,450 feet) and Relay Peak (10,338 feet), both of which have excellent ski descent routes.

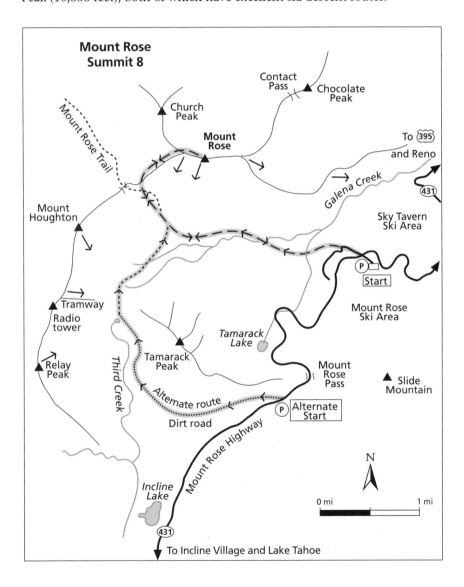

Castle Peak

Height: 9,103 feet	
Route: West Ridge	
Best time to go: December through March	
Trip duration: 1 day	
Mileage: About 3 miles to the summit	
Elevation gain: 2,000 feet	
Effort factor: 3.5	
Level of difficulty: Strong intermediate, with some steeper slopes near the summit	
Snowboards: Recommended, but includes a flat 1-mile approach	
Maps: Norden, Cisco Grove	

This area has been a backcountry ski destination for many decades. The gentle terrain and the ease of access contribute to the area's popularity. The Sierra Club's Peter Grubb Hut is located in Round Valley, due west of Castle Peak. There are several fine but short descent routes off the summit ridge, and for the adventurous there are a number of steep descents on the north side of Castle Peak down Coon Canyon and North Fork Prosser Creek.

Drive to Donner Pass on Interstate 80 (west of Truckee). Take the Boreal Ski Area/Castle Peak turnoff and proceed to the well-signed Sno-Park, located just beyond the motel. Daily or annual Sno-Park permits may be purchased at the motel (they accept cash only).

From the Sno-Park, it is a short walk back under the freeway to the north side and the start of the trip. A well-traveled unplowed road leads toward Castle

The three summits of Castle Peak as seen from Basin Mountain. The far peak is the highest pinnacle. The ascent route is from the right up the ridge that crests near the summit of Castle Peak.

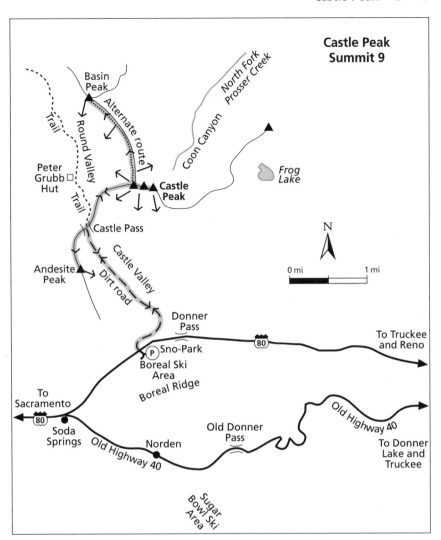

Peak and Peter Grubb Hut. Ski or snowshoe up the road to Castle Pass (7,900 feet). From Castle Pass, ascend the ridge to the summit. You may need crampons, as the upper slopes may be icy.

As you near the summit, there is a particularly fine timbered bowl (off to your left) that offers good skiing and snowboarding with protection from the winds during bad weather. This descent will take you down into Round Valley and Peter Grubb Hut. Continuing to the summit ridge, you'll have a number of options. You can ski the peak's back side, down several steep chutes that drop off to the northeast. These are steep at the top but soon lead to gentler terrain and a nice descent to the 7,600-foot level. These steep gullies may be avalanche prone, so use caution.

There are three other descent options to the north and northeast. Ski the ridge toward Basin Peak and descend into Round Valley; there is good skiing and snowboarding off Basin Peak on all sides. A second option would be to descend the west ridge, following your ascent route. Or a third option would be to traverse the south face of the peak, staying just below the three summit blocks, and descend either the far (easternmost) gully or the center gully (the more difficult route).

There is also intermediate skiing on Andesite Peak, located to the south of Castle Pass. From Castle Pass follow the ridge south to the summit at 8,219 feet. Ski the east slopes down into Castle Valley and the road back out to Interstate 80.

SIGNAL PEAK

An alternative to Castle Peak is a ski ascent of Signal Peak (see Lake Tahoe region map). Signal Peak has everything that Castle Peak has but without the crowds. Drive 10 miles west of the Boreal Ski Area on Interstate 80 and take the Cisco Grove turnoff. Park on the north side of the freeway (5,700 feet), and ski or walk up Fordyce Road. After about 1.5 miles, leave the road and ascend north to the southwest ridge leading to the summit, passing the old Southern Pacific fire lookout at 7,700 feet. Great powder skiing can be found on the northeast side. From the summit (7,841 feet), ski the northeast gully to about 6,600 feet. Return to the summit and ski back down to Fordyce Road. Due to the rather low elevation of the peak and the southerly exposure of the ascent, this route is limited to the winter when there is adequate snow coverage (December through March).

Mount Tallac

Height: 9,735 feet	
Routes: South Ramp, Northeast Bowl	
Best time to go: January through April	
Trip duration: 1 day	
Mileage: 4 miles to the summit via South Ramp, 3 miles via Northeast Bowl	
Elevation gain: 3,335 feet	
Effort factor: 5.3 South Ramp, 4.8 Northeast Bowl	
Level of difficulty: Strong intermediate along South Ramp route; advanced (Black Diamond) along Northeast Bowl	
Snowboards: Northeast Bowl is recommended, as some of the steeper bowls rise directly above the parked car	
Map: Emerald Bay	

This has been a favorite for years, and deservedly so, as the summit of Mount Tallac has a wonderful view of Lake Tahoe, Fallen Leaf Lake, Desolation Wilderness,

The South Ramp of Mount Tallac is along the left skyline, with several excellent chutes descending the east face.

the Crystal Range with Pyramid Peak (Summit 11), Price Peak, Jacks Peak, Freel Peak, and others. Not only does Mount Tallac have superb views, but the ski descent is one of the best in the Lake Tahoe region.

Mount Tallac is perched on the edge of Lake Tahoe, with its northeast face dropping precipitously to lake level. The wilderness setting, surrounded on all sides by glacier-carved lakes, is exceptional. Emerald Bay and Cascade Lake are to the north, Lake Tahoe is to the northeast, and Fallen Leaf Lake bounds Tallac on the east. To the west are Desolation Wilderness Area and Lake Aloha.

Mount Tallac offers many options for both ski ascent and descent. Two ascent routes are described here—the South Ramp and the Northeast Bowl. The South Ramp route is longer and consequently not as steep as the more direct Northeast Bowl. Both routes begin and end at the end of Spring Creek Road.

Once you are on the summit, you have a choice of numerous bowls and chutes to descend. Local skiers call the more popular routes names such as "The Crucifix" and "Corkscrew." Several of the descent routes are described below.

From South Lake Tahoe on Highway 50, proceed northeast on Highway 89 for 4.5 miles. Do not turn off on the road signed "Mount Tallac Trailhead," but continue a short distance to Spring Creek Road. Turn left on Spring Creek Road and follow the road for 1 mile to its end.

SOUTH RAMP

From the end of Spring Creek Road (6,400 feet), ski south following the stream flowing out of Floating Island Lake. After about 2 miles and 1,200 feet elevation gain, you will pass Floating Island Lake and then Cathedral Lake. Here the route steepens and begins to angle to the northwest. In the next 0.5 mile, gain 1,000 feet as the route ascends a wide gully. At the head of this gully (8,600 feet), the route emerges onto the wide, south-facing, upward-sloping summit plateau or South Ramp. Follow this broad ramp to the summit.

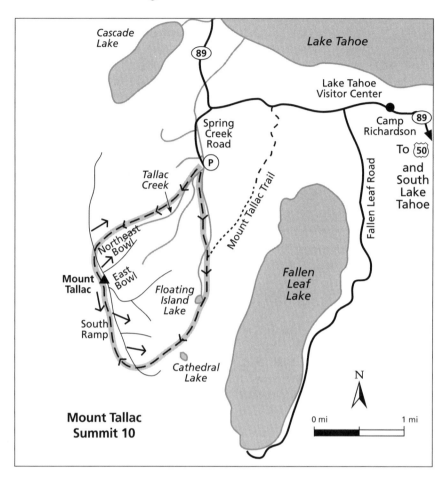

This wide-open ramp offers endless skiing opportunities above the treeline on intermediate terrain. However, due to the southerly exposure, the snow does not last long in the warm spring sun.

Once on the summit, there are several descent options. Follow your ascent route down the South Ramp, or explore the steep chutes that originate from the south ridge and descend the east face of Mount Tallac. One such chute is starts about half a mile south of the summit at 9,200 feet and descends a steep, wide gully to Floating Island Lake, 2,000 feet below. This prominent gully can be seen easily from the highway.

NORTHEAST BOWL
From the end of Spring Creek Road, follow the right fork (north) of Tallac Creek. At the 7,400-foot level, angle away from the creek and climb the ridge to the right of the large and impressive Northeast Bowl. Continue up the ridge and join the main north ridge at 9,200 feet. Follow the north ridge for a short distance and traverse across the top of the Northeast Bowl. Ski through the small pass, just

to the right of the main summit, and ski to the top of Mount Tallac from the west.

The Northeast Bowl provides an excellent advanced (Black Diamond) descent route from the summit. There is good tree skiing in the bowl, but midway down there is a steep cliff band that must be passed on the left. Use caution, as the steep cliffs regularly avalanche into the bowl.

In addition to the Northeast Bowl, there is excellent tree skiing just to the north of the ascent ridge and a large gully that provides excellent ski terrain. This gully is not as steep as the Northeast Bowl and can be viewed at the very beginning of the trip.

The upper bowls and steep chutes avalanche regularly, so use extreme caution. They can also be dangerous in the spring. In the morning before the hard spring snow is softened by the sun, a slip can be fatal. In 1997 a skier slipped at the top of one of these bowls and, unable to arrest his fall, slid to his death.

Pyramid Peak

Height: 9,983 feet	
Route: South ridge	
Best time to go: January through April	
Trip duration: 1 day	
Mileage: 3 miles to the summit	
Elevation gain: 3,983 feet	
Effort factor: 5.5	
Level of difficulty: Strong intermediate	
Snowboards: Recommended, as it is a direct downhill run from the summit	
Map: Pyramid Peak	

Pyramid Peak rises 4,000 feet above the South Fork of the American River Canyon at Twin Bridges. It offers more vertical relief than any other peak in the Tahoe region, along with great open-bowl skiing above timberline. Pyramid Peak is the highest peak in the Desolation Valley Wilderness Area, with fine views of Lake Aloha, Lake Tahoe, Mount Tallac (Summit 10), Fallen Leaf Lake, Ralston Peak (Summit 12), and other lakes and summits in the region. This is a popular summit with skiers in the spring, and provides excellent off-piste skiing and snowboarding in a beautiful setting.

Take Highway 50 to Twin Bridges (6 miles west of Echo Summit) and park on the north side of the road, just west of where Pyramid Creek crosses under Highway 50 (6,000 feet). The route climbs the broad southeast ridge of Pyramid Peak. From the ridge you will be greeted with some impressive views of Horsetail Falls, the sheer rock faces of Lovers Leap, Desolation Valley, and the large cornices that form along the ridge between 8,000 and 8,800 feet.

On Pyramid Peak's corniced south ridge. The route to the summit is up the left skyline.

Due to the southerly aspect of the route, there may be inadequate snow coverage at the start. To avoid the exposed brush on the lower slopes directly above Twin Bridges, skirt around to the right (east) side of the south face. Gain elevation slowly, continuing around southeast of the brush fields, then (in about a quarter mile) angle up steeply toward the main south ridge. Near 7,000 feet you will encounter a small gully that provides an excellent route through the brush, as it holds the snow well. This gully can be seen from Highway 50. Follow the gully until it merges into the main ridge near 7,600 feet. (An alternate approach, preferred by some, is to follow Rocky Canyon from the start. Rocky Canyon crosses Highway 50 about 0.5 mile to the west of Twin Bridges. You'll encounter brush and thick timber on this route.)

Near 8,800 feet, the main south ridge of Pyramid Peak levels off. Ski across this basin, angling to the northwest for the final summit push up the broad, south-facing ridge. The views are outstanding, and the ski descent of Pyramid Peak is one of the best in the region. You can ski from the summit in just about any direction—northwest to Lake Sylvia, down the east face to Pyramid Lake, or back down the south ridge.

This is a strenuous single-day trip but also makes for a great multiday trip. If you plan to spend the night, camp on the ridge near 8,800 feet with its impressive views, or traverse into Desolation Valley to camp. A favorite trip of mine is to cross the ridge near the 8,800-foot level and traverse down to Pyramid Lake to camp. A base camp at Pyramid Lake provides access to great bowl skiing in the large glacial cirques east of Pyramid and Price Peaks.

With a camp in Desolation Valley, the backcountry options are numerous. A ski ascent of Pyramid, Price, and Jacks Peaks are at your tent flap. Pyramid and Price Peaks provide a 1,800-foot descent to Lake Aloha. From Jacks Peak, a little farther away, you can make a 2,000-foot descent down to Susie Lake.

For a description of an alternate approach into Desolation Valley Wilderness Area, see Ralston Peak (Summit 12).

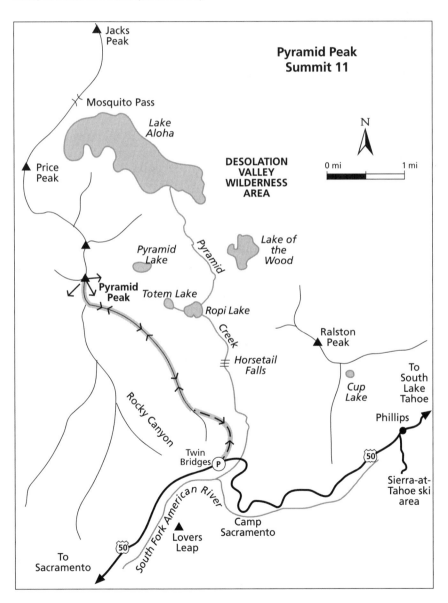

Ralston Peak

Height: 9,235 feet

Route: South slope

Best time to go: December through mid-April

Trip duration: 1 day

Mileage: 2 miles to the summit

Elevation gain: 2,735 feet

Effort factor: 3.7

Level of difficulty: Strong intermediate on south slope; advanced (Black Diamond) in northeast gullies

Snowboards: Recommended; descent finishes at car

Maps: Pyramid Peak, Echo Lake

Ralston Peak rises immediately from the South Fork of the American River canyon. The peak sits on the southern edge of Desolation Valley Wilderness Area with a commanding view of Lake Aloha, Echo Lake, Lake Tahoe, Pyramid Peak (Summit 11), Price Peak, Jacks Peak, Dicks Peak, Mount Tallac (Summit 10), and the numerous lakes and peaks in the wilderness area. This is a great intermediate trip in an outstanding setting.

Take Highway 50 to Sierra Pines Road (about 1.8 miles east of Twin Bridges and 5 miles west of Echo Summit). Park on the side of Highway 50 near 6,500 feet, or along Sierra Pines Road (a private road). Parking along either is limited due to snow-removal restrictions.

Begin your ascent by following the summer trail in a northerly direction along Tamarack Creek. The trail begins at Camp Sacramento, a wide spot in

Mount Ralston's excellent ski and snowboard slopes directly above Highway 50 near the turnoff to the Sierra-at-Tahoe ski area. The main summit is in the far background.

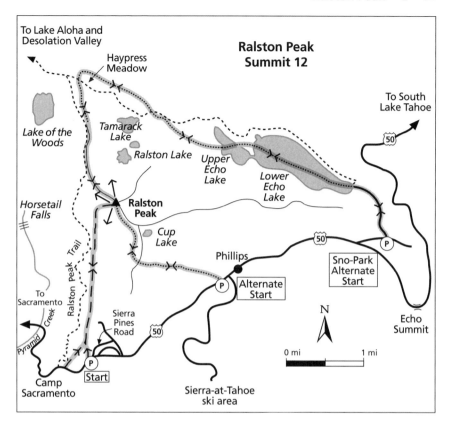

Highway 50 a short distance below Sierra Pines Road, and at Sierra Pines Road (there is no parking at Camp Sacramento). On your left is the steep Pyramid Creek canyon with wonderful views of Horsetail Falls. The falls occasionally freeze over for short periods during an extreme winter cold snap, presenting a spectacular sight indeed. Your route steepens between 7,200 and 8,000 feet above which the slope backs off a bit. Continue to the summit of Ralston Peak. The views to the north and down into Echo Lake are rewarding.

An alternate approach begins a short distance east on Highway 50, just west of Phillips. Check the snow coverage, as this approach is on the south-facing slopes. Park at Milestone 47 (Aspen Creek Tract) or at the turnoff to the Sierra-at-Tahoe ski area. Ski up the steep, open bowl past Cup Lake to the summit of Ralston Peak.

For those not ready to ski back immediately, there are numerous descent routes off the north side of the peak. The northeast face contains a number of Black Diamond and Double Black Diamond gullies and bowls; use caution, as these avalanche regularly. Alternatively, the north ridge provides an intermediate-level descent to Haypress Meadow or Ralston Lake. Whatever route you select, the 1,600-foot ski run to Ralston Lake is a worthy descent with an enjoyable climb back to the summit via the north ridge.

When you are ready to head down to the car, there are several descent routes from which to choose. You can descend the way you came, or ski over to Cup Lake and descend from there. Cup Lake, set in a perfectly symmetrical bowl, is a uniquely beautiful spot.

A third approach to Ralston Peak and Desolation Valley Wilderness Area is farther to the east, across Echo Lake. Take the Echo Lake/Berkley Camp turnoff (Johnson Pass Road), which intersects Highway 50 about 1 mile west of Echo Summit, to the Echo Lake Sno-Park. Ski up the unplowed road to Upper and Lower Echo Lakes and across the frozen lakes. (Caution: Early in the season the ice may not be sufficiently formed to allow safe skiing.) At the upper end of the lake, head toward Tamarack Lake and climb up to Haypress Meadow. (To ski into Desolation Valley Wilderness Area, you can ski through the meadow and onto Lake Aloha, which lies at the base of Pyramid and Price Peaks.) To ascend Ralston Peak, turn up its north ridge near Haypress Meadow and follow it to the summit. This is a bit longer than the previously noted routes but more scenic. It is about 7 miles to the top, with an elevation gain of 2,000 feet. If you leave a car on Highway 50, a quick descent gets you down. Or return the way you came down the north ridge and across Echo Lake.

Red Lake Peak

Height: 10,061 feet

Route: Ascend from the south, descend via the northeast ridge or Northeast Bowl

Best time to go: January through mid-May

Trip duration: 1 day

Mileage: 3 miles to the summit, 2-mile descent

Elevation gain/loss: 1,561-foot ascent, 2,661-foot descent

Effort factor: 3.1

Level of difficulty: Strong intermediate

Snowboards: Recommended; short approach with a long, steep descent

Maps: Carson Pass, Caples Lake

Red Lake Peak is rich in California history, for it was here that John C. Fremont and his party made the first winter crossing of the Sierra Nevada (see sidebar), a journey of 30 days and much hardship. Hopefully your climb and ski descent will not be as traumatic. Modern-day skis and clothing, and convenient access (Highway 88), make for an enjoyable single-day tour with views of Lake Tahoe, Hope Valley, Round Top, and the hundreds of peaks in the region.

Drive to Carson Pass (named for Kit Carson) on Highway 88 and park in the Sno-Park area on the north side of the highway, just west of the pass. Place a shuttle car several miles down the highway on the east side of the pass at around the 7,400-foot level near the unplowed road to Crater Lake.

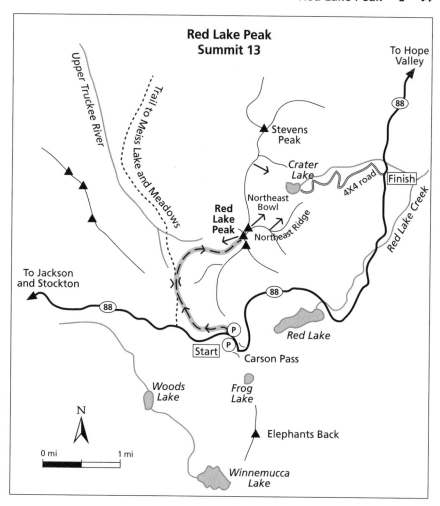

**Red Lake Peak
Summit 13**

From the Sno-Park, begin by skiing west, gaining little elevation. After a half-mile traverse, ski into a small valley. Turn north and climb to an unnamed pass at 8,800 feet. The Upper Truckee River's headwaters originate to the north of this pass. As you reach the pass, Lake Tahoe will come into view. Traverse up to the northeast, passing the unnamed peak to the east of the pass. Gain the summit of Red Lake Peak from either the south or the north.

Various ski descent options are available. If you return to Carson Pass directly, there is excellent skiing in the trees that grow high on the northwest shoulder of the peak. The trees provide protected skiing from the frequent winds. Nearby is a prominent gully that offers great skiing.

If you planned a car shuttle or do not mind hitchhiking, there are at least three options, each with a drop of over 2,600 feet. The northeast ridge leads down past Crater Lake. This route avoids the steep drop into Crater Lake by passing it to the south. Another option is to ski toward Stevens Peak and the low gap

Red Lake Peak and the Crater Lake bowl

north of Red Lake Peak; from the gap, descend to the north and then to the east, passing the steep drop into Crater Lake to the north. A third option is to ski or snowboard down the center of the Northeast Bowl. This prominent bowl can be seen from the highway. This route includes the steep drop down to Crater Lake. Descend with caution. If inadequate snow or avalanche hazard exists, traverse to the right. The slope angle lessens as you near the northeast ridge.

Tryon Peak

Height: 9,920+ feet

Route: Northeast Bowl

Best time to go: January through April

Trip duration: 3 or more days

Mileage: 8 miles to the summit (from the upper winter closure gate) near 7,000 feet

Elevation gain: 3,120 feet

Effort factor: 7.1

Level of difficulty: Strong intermediate

Snowboards: Not recommended due to long approach over varied terrain

Maps: Ebbetts Pass, Wolf Creek

The twin summits of Tryon Peak are located on the Sierra Nevada Crest about 2 miles south of Ebbetts Pass. This beautiful peak is not the tallest in the region but has some wonderful ski descents in its northeast bowl. In January, February, and March the powder skiing can be exceptional. In April expect spring corn.

Before leaving for this trip, check with the Caltrans Road Maintenance Station at Woodfords (see Appendix 5) to determine how far Highway 4 is open. After a major storm, the road may be closed at Wolf Creek; this will add 4 miles of road skiing to your trip. The road is normally kept open to the upper winter closure gate just below Nobel Creek Campground on Highway 4 (near 7,000 feet). This trip is an excellent opportunity to use a snowmobile, as the approach follows an unplowed road (Highway 4).

In the winter when Monitor Pass (Highway 89) is closed, the only road access to the town of Markleeville is from the north and Highway 88 and then south on Highway 89/4. From the small town of Markleeville, Alpine County, continue south on Highway 89/4 toward Ebbetts Pass. At the junction to Monitor Pass (Highway 89) continue along the East Fork Carson River on Highway 4 to the road closure gate near 7,000 feet.

Ski or snowmobile up the road past Nobel Creek Campground, and continue up the three major switchbacks in the highway. At the third switchback, follow the route of the summer trail up Nobel Creek. On your traverse into the valley, stay high; do not prematurely drop down into the creek, as you will encounter rough terrain and large boulders. Follow the creek for the next couple of miles in thick trees and an occasional meadow.

Around 7,800 feet the slopes open up considerably. Leave the creek and the route of the summer trail, slowly gaining elevation to the east of the creek; this is necessary to avoid the narrow, steep portion of Nobel Canyon near the 8,400-foot level and the large rock bluff between 8,400 and 8,700 feet. Once above this barrier, traverse on gentle terrain into the Nobel Lake basin. This is an ideal place to camp, with great views of Tryon Peak. It is also an ideal place to set up a base camp before you explore the upper slopes of Highland Peak and the 10,037-foot peak just to the east of Tryon Peak.

Ascend to 9,700-foot Tryon Pass to the southeast of Tryon Peak, and follow the ridge to the summit. Great skiing awaits in the northeast bowl of Tryon Peak. Ski from either the south summit or the north summit down excellent slopes to Nobel Lake and base camp. The ridge and summits are heavily corniced, so be careful as you ascend the ridge and in selecting your descent route.

The twin summits of Tryon Peak from the Nobel Lake area—great powder skiing, as you can see from our tracks

Just beyond the pass to the southwest is Tryon Meadow, and Hiram and Folger Peaks. These two peaks have excellent ski descents. (See H. J. Burhenne's *Sierra Spring Ski-Touring* for a description of Hiram Peak.)

In the spring, when the road to Ebbetts Pass is open, it may be easier to reach Tryon Peak by driving to Ebbetts Pass (5.8 miles beyond the upper winter closure gate at 7,000 feet), then skiing along the west side of the Sierra Nevada crest. Alternatively, you can drive or ski up a dirt road to Tryon Meadows that leaves Highway 4 about 1.5 miles west of Ebbetts Pass.

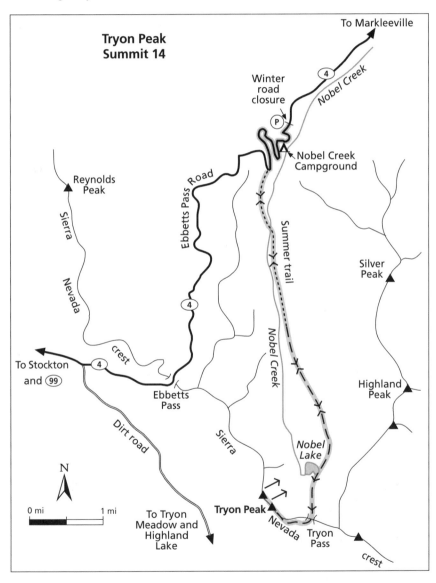

Chapter 5
YOSEMITE NATIONAL PARK

Yosemite's eastern boundary follows the crest of the Sierra Nevada for approximately 50 miles, roughly paralleling Highway 395 between Bridgeport in the north and June Lake in the south. Ranging in elevation from 2,000 feet near its western boundary to 13,114 feet (Mount Lyell) on its eastern boundary, the park has four major features: deep river gorges, including Yosemite Valley (the valley floor is at 4,000 feet); groves of giant sequoias on the western slopes (between 6,000 and 8,000 feet); Tuolumne Meadows (8,000 to 9,000 feet); and the superb glaciated alpine wilderness of the rugged and remote mountains, culminating in the summits of Matterhorn Peak, Mount Dana, Mount Lyell, and Mount Conness.

When the Sierra Nevada region lay beneath an ancient sea 500 million years ago, thick layers of sediment accumulated on the seabed, which eventually was folded, twisted, and thrust above sea level. Simultaneously, molten

Skiing west of Mount Lyell in Yosemite National Park

rock welled up from deep within the Earth and cooled slowly beneath the layers of sediment to form granite. Erosion wore away much of the overlying rock and exposed the granite. As the uplifts continued to form the Sierra Nevada, the glaciers went to work to carve the valley, polish the granite faces, and form the glaciated lakes.

Yosemite Valley, "The Incomparable Valley," is probably the world's best-known example of a glacier-carved canyon. Its spectacular waterfalls, sheer cliffs, glaciated domes, and massive monoliths make it a dramatic natural wonder. Alpine glaciers cut through the weaker sections of granite, leaving the harder, more solid granite structures such as El Capitan, Half Dome, and Cathedral Rocks intact. As the glaciers began to melt, a terminal moraine dammed the melting glacier water to form the ancient Lake Yosemite. Sediment eventually filled the lake, forming the flat valley floor we see today.

Tuolumne Meadows and the high country to the east of Yosemite Valley are surrounded by some of the most rugged scenery in the Sierra Nevada, including alpine meadows, jeweled lakes, and towering peaks. Tuolumne Meadows is the largest subalpine meadow in the Sierra Nevada. At Tioga Pass, Highway 120 crosses the Sierra Nevada crest at 9,945 feet, the highest automobile pass in California.

Located 2 miles east of Tioga Pass, Tioga Pass Winter Resort (see Appendix 5) makes for a luxurious base camp for touring in the area of Saddlebag Lake, Tioga Pass, and Tuolumne Meadows, and for ski mountaineering on Mount Dana, Gaylor Peak, False White, White Mountain, North Peak, and Mount Conness.

How to get there: For purposes of this guide, the Yosemite region stretches from Sonora Pass (Highway 108) in the north to the small town of June Lake (Highway 158) in the south. Highway 395, located to the east of Yosemite National Park and the Sierra Nevada crest, provides north–south access to the area. From Highway 395, five east–west laterals provide access to the trailheads: Highway 108/Sonora Pass Road (for Leavitt Peak); Twin Lakes Road out of Bridgeport (for Mount Walt, Cleaver Peak, and Matterhorn Peak); Virgina Lakes Road (for Dunderberg Peak); Tioga Pass Road/Highway 120 (for Mount Dana); and Highway 158 (for Koip Peak and Mount Lyell). Highways 108, Highway 120 (Tioga Pass Road), and Virgina Lakes Road are closed in the winter and do not open until late April or early May under normal winter snowfall conditions. In heavy snow years the roads can remain closed much longer. On occasion, Sonora Pass and Tioga Pass Roads have remained closed well into June because of a deep snowpack.

Call the Caltrans statewide road information number to determine whether a particular road in the area is open, or call the Caltrans Maintenance Station in Bridgeport, Sonora Junction, or Lee Vining for an estimated opening date for roads that have been closed for the winter (see Appendix 5, "Road Conditions and Sno-Park Information," for phone numbers).

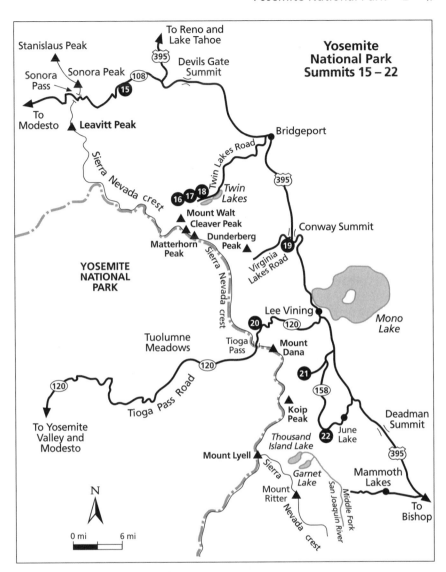

Stanislaus Peak ▲

To Reno and Lake Tahoe ↑

(395) Devils Gate Summit

Yosemite National Park Summits 15 – 22

Sonora Pass

Sonora Peak ▲ (108)

15

To Modesto ▲ **Leavitt Peak**

Bridgeport ●

Sierra Nevada crest

Twin Lakes Road

(395)

16 17 18 *Twin Lakes*

Mount Walt Cleaver Peak ▲

Conway Summit

Matterhorn Peak ▲

Dunderberg Peak ▲

19

YOSEMITE NATIONAL PARK

Sierra Nevada crest

Virginia Lakes Road

Lee Vining ●

Mono Lake

20 (120)

Tuolumne Meadows

Tioga Pass

Mount Dana

(120)

21

(120)

Tioga Pass Road

(158)

Koip Peak ▲

Deadman Summit

To Yosemite Valley and Modesto

Thousand Island Lake

22 June Lake

(395)

Mount Lyell ▲

N

0 mi   6 mi

Garnet Lake

Mount Ritter ▲

Sierra Nevada crest

San Joaquin River Middle Fork

Mammoth Lakes

To Bishop ▲

The Discovery of Living Glaciers

When John Muir arrived in Yosemite Valley in 1869, the conventional thinking among the scientists and explorers of this era was that there were no active glaciers in the Sierra Nevada, the weather being too warm and the mountains too far south. After extensive exploration in the region, John Muir soon reached a different conclusion when he discovered the first active glacier in the autumn of 1871 in what is today known as Yosemite National Park. The glacier is situated in the upper drainage of Illilouette Creek between Red and Black Peaks in the Merced group, about 16 trail miles southwest of Yosemite Valley.

Prior to the autumn of 1871 the glaciers of the Sierra were unknown. In October of that year I discovered the Black Mountain Glacier in a shadowy amphitheater between Black and Red Mountains, two of the peaks of the Merced group. At the time of this interesting discovery I was exploring the névé amphitheaters of the group, and tracing the courses of the ancient glaciers that once poured from its ample fountains through the Illilouette Basin and the Yosemite Valley, not expecting to find any active glaciers so far south in the land of sunshine.

Beginning on the northwestern extremity of the group, I explored the chief tributary basins in succession, their moraines, roches moutonnées, and splendid glacier pavements, taking them in regular succession without any reference to the time consumed in their study. The monuments of the tributary that poured its ice from between Red and Black Mountains I found to be the most interesting of them all; and when I saw its magnificent moraines extending in majestic curves from the spacious amphitheater between the mountains, I was exhilarated with the work that lay before me. . . .

Evening came on just as I got fairly within the portal of the main amphitheater. It is about a mile wide, and a little less than two miles long. The crumbling spurs and battlements of Red Mountain bound it on the north, the somber, rudely sculptured precipices of Black Mountain on the south, and a hacked, splintery col, curving around from mountain to mountain, shuts it in on the east. . . .

Early next morning I set out to trace the grand old glacier that had done so much for the beauty of the Yosemite region back to its farthest fountains, enjoying the charm that every explorer feels in Nature's untrodden wildernesses. The voices of the mountains were still asleep. . . . The scenery became more rigidly arctic, the Dwarf Pines and Hemlocks disappeared, and the stream was bordered with icicles. As the sun rose higher rocks were loosened on shattered portions of the cliffs, and came down in rattling avalanches, echoing wildly from crag to crag.

The main lateral moraines that extend from the jaws of the amphitheater into the Illilouette Basin are continued in straggling masses along the walls of the amphitheater, while separate boulders, hundreds of tons in weight, are left stranded here and there out in the middle of the channel. Tracing the stream back to the last of its chain of lakelets, I noticed a deposit of fine gray mud on the bottom. It looked like the mud worn from a grind stone, and I at once suspected its glacial origin, for the stream that was carrying it came gurgling out of the base of a raw moraine that seemed in process of formation.

Not a plant or weather-stain was visible on its rough, unsettled surface. It is from 60 to over 100 feet high, and plunges forward at an angle of 38 degrees. Cautiously picking my way, I gained the top of the moraine and was delighted to see a small but well characterized glacier swooping down from the gloomy precipices of Black Mountain in a finely graduated curve to the moraine on which I stood. The compact ice appeared on all the lower portions of the glacier, though gray with dirt and stones embedded in it. Farther up the ice disappeared beneath coarse granulated snow. The surface of the glacier was further characterized by dirt bands and the outcropping edges of the blue veins, showing the laminated structure of the ice.

The uppermost crevasse, or "bergschrund," where the névé was attached to the mountain, was from 12 to 14 feet wide, and was bridged in a few places by the remains of snow avalanches. Creeping along the edge of the schrund, holding on with benumbed fingers, I discovered clear sections where the bedded structure was beautifully revealed. The surface snow, though sprinkled with stones shot down from the cliffs, was in some places almost pure, gradually becoming crystalline and changing to whitish porous ice of different shades of color, and this again changing at a depth of 20 or 30 feet to blue ice, some of the ribbon-like bands of which were nearly pure, and blended with the paler bands in the most gradual and delicate manner imaginable.

A series of rugged zigzags enabled me to make my way down into the weird under-world of the crevasse. Its chambered hollows were hung with a multitude of clustered icicles, amid which pale, subdued light pulsed and shimmered with indescribable loveliness. Water dripped and tinkled overhead, and from far below came strange, solemn murmurings from currents that were feeling their way through veins and fissures in the dark. The chambers of a glacier are perfectly enchanting, notwithstanding one feels out of place in their frosty beauty. I was soon cold in my shirt-sleeves, and the leaning wall threatened to engulf me; yet it was hard to leave the delicious music of the water and the lovely light. Coming again to the surface, I noticed boulders of every size on their journeys to the terminal moraine—journeys of more than a hundred years, without a single stop, night or day, winter or summer.

The series of small terminal moraines which I had observed in the morning, along the south wall of the amphitheater, correspond in every way with the moraine of this glacier, and their distribution with reference to shadows was now understood. When the climatic changes came on that caused the melting and retreat of the main glacier that filled the amphitheater, a series of residual glaciers were left in the cliff shadows, under the protection of which they lingered, until they formed the moraines we are studying. Then, as the snow became still less abundant, all of them vanished in succession, except the one just described; and the cause of its longer life is sufficiently apparent in the greater area of snow-basin it drains, and its more perfect protection from wasting sunshine. How much longer this little glacier will last depends, of course, on the amount of snow it receives from year to year, as compared with melting waste.

On August 21, I set a series of stakes in the Maclure Glacier, near Mount Lyell, and found its rate of motion to be little more than an inch a day in the middle, showing a great contrast to the Muir Glacier in Alaska, which, near the front, flows at a rate of from five to ten feet in twenty-four hours.

After this discovery, I made excursions over all the High Sierra, pushing my explorations summer after summer, and discovered that what at first sight in the distance looked like extensive snow fields, were in great part glaciers, busily at work completing the sculpture of the summit-peaks so grandly blocked out by their giant predecessors.

—John Muir, *The Mountains of California*

Leavitt Peak

Height: 11,570 feet

Route: East Ridge

Best time to go: December through early May

Trip duration: 2 or more days (1 day in spring, from Leavitt Road turnoff)

Mileage: 8 miles to the summit (from the second road closure gate at Leavitt Meadows)

Elevation gain: 4,370 feet

Effort factor: 8.4

Level of difficulty: Intermediate

Snowboards: Not recommended due to long approach and rolling terrain

Maps: Sonora Pass, Pickel Meadows

This superb midwinter tour is one of the easier trips in this guide and is an excellent introduction to overnight winter camping.

One of many corniced ridges in the area. The summit ridge of Leavitt Peak is in the background.

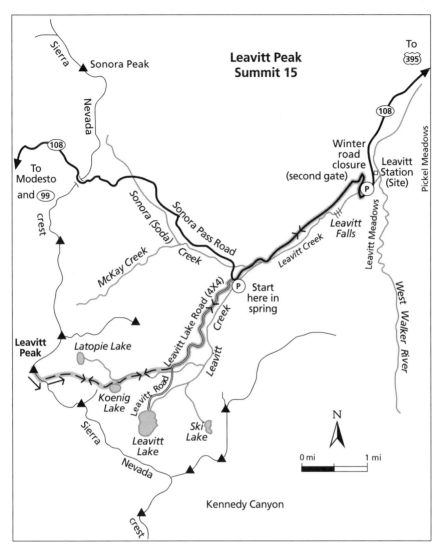

Sierra

Sonora Peak

**Leavitt Peak
Summit 15**

To
(395)

Nevada

(108)

(108)

To
Modesto
and (99)

crest

Sonora (Soda)

Sonora Pass Road

Creek

McKay Creek

Creek

Leavitt Lake Road (4X4)

(P) Start
here in
spring

Creek

Winter
road
closure
(second gate)

Leavitt
Station
(Site)

(P)

Pickel Meadows

Leavitt
Falls

Leavitt Creek

Leavitt Meadows

West Walker River

Leavitt
Peak

Latopie Lake

Leavitt Road

Leavitt

Koenig
Lake

Sierra

Leavitt
Lake

Ski
Lake

Nevada

Kennedy Canyon

crest

N

0 mi   1 mi

Take Highway 395 to the Sonora Pass Road (Highway 108) turnoff, about 13 miles south of Walker and 16.5 miles north of Bridgeport. In the winter, drive west on Highway 108 past the Marine Corps Cold Weather Camp to the first gate across the road at 5 miles from Highway 395 (6,800 feet) or the second gate at Leavitt Meadows (near 7,200 feet), another 2.5 miles. (If there is little or no snow, drive around the first gate and continue to the second gate.) If you have access to a snowmobile, you could shorten the approach by being ferried up Highway 108 to Leavitt Lake Road.

From the road closure point, ski or snowmobile up Sonora Pass Road to the turnoff to Leavitt Lake (8,400 feet), and turn south. Although Leavitt Lake Road goes all the way to the lake, leave the road after about 2 miles and follow the creek that drains Koenig Lake and Latopie Lake. Pass by Koenig Lake and ski west up the broad ridge to the summit of Leavitt Peak, the highest peak in the area.

On the approach many of the lower ridges may be heavily corniced. There may also be an impressive cornice on the summit ridge, as this area is hit by high winds during winter storms. Stay well back from the lip of these cornices. From the summit you will have an unobstructed 360-degree view of the terrain and the many snow-capped peaks in the area. Far below will be the snow-covered Sonora Pass Road.

Retrace your ascent route or choose from several obvious ski descent options. Leavitt Peak offers an excellent intermediate-level descent of nearly 3,000 feet. The ski back to the car will go quickly, helped by the downhill slope of the road.

This is also an excellent spring trip. If you plan your trip after Sonora Pass Road is plowed to the Leavitt Lake Road turnoff (usually by April), the trip can be done in a single day. Check with Caltrans (see Appendix 5 for phone numbers) for an estimated date of opening.

There are several other excellent peaks in this area, as described in H. J. Burhenne's outstanding book *Sierra Spring Ski-Touring*.

Mount Walt

Height: 11,480+ feet	
Route: North Ridge Ramp	
Best time to go: February through May	
Trip duration: 1 day	
Mileage: 4 miles to the summit	
Elevation gain: 4,380+ feet	
Effort factor: 6.4	
Level of difficulty: Advanced (Black Diamond)	
Snowboards: Recommended; approach is direct and short	
Maps: Buckeye Ridge, Twin Lakes, Matterhorn Peak	

The view of Mount Walt from Bridgeport and Twin Lakes is striking. It is the prominent peak on the far northwestern end of the Sawtooth Range, northwest of The Cleaver, Cleaver Peak, and Blacksmith Peak. Much of the North Ridge Ramp route can be seen from the U.S. Forest Service office on Highway 395 at the south end of Bridgeport.

Mount Walt was the name given to this peak by H. J. Burhenne in 1971 in memory of his close friend, Walter W. Herbert. It is not officially named on the USGS maps but is the 11,581-foot peak on the 15-minute topo and the 11,480-plus-foot peak on the newly revised 7.5-minute topo, located 0.6 mile northwest of Glacier Lake and 1 mile due east of Kettle Peak. (Do not confuse Mount Walt with Eocene Peak, about 1 mile southwest of Glacier Lake. Both peaks are the same elevation.)

The rugged terrain, magnificent scenery, and views of neighboring peaks make this trip exceedingly enjoyable. It is a short trip and can be completed in a single day if you get an early, pre-dawn start.

From the town of Bridgeport on Highway 395, drive 13 miles on a paved road to the end of Twin Lakes Road at 7,100 feet. There is a small fee to park in Mono Village. Although the resort opens for the start of fishing season each year (around the last weekend of April), the road to the resort is open all year.

Walk through the Mono Village campground and cross the bridge over Robinson Creek. Continue up the creek a short distance, and turn south up Blacksmith Creek; stay to the left of the creek. The climb through the trees is steep for the first 800 feet, but you soon break out of the trees and into an open valley. Near 8,100 feet, Blacksmith Creek splits; follow the right fork. Near 8,600 feet, leave the creek and angle up the wide gully to your right; the route is easily identified by the large rock outcropping in the center. These slopes avalanche regularly, so be aware and cautious. The slope steepens to about 35 degrees. Climb up the gully, using the rock bluff and the treed slopes as natural protection in case of an unexpected avalanche.

Above, the gully opens up into a fine bowl ringed by rock pinnacles. At the head of the bowl is a distinct pinnacle near the 10,200-foot level. At this point, turn left or south onto the North Ridge Ramp. Near 11,000 feet what seems to be the summit comes into view. The ramp continues toward the summit, with the east face dropping precipitously (2,000 feet) to Blacksmith Creek.

Descending the upper slopes of Mount Walt

Continue upward, following the North Ridge to the summit. Drop your skis or board, and scramble the last 100 feet over exposed Class 3 rock. The 4,000-foot ski or snowboard descent is over varied terrain, making for a rewarding run all the way back to the bridge over Robinson Creek.

The views from the upper reaches of Mount Walt are spectacular. The sheer granite face of Blacksmith Peak is equally imposing and inspiring. Beyond Blacksmith Peak are Glacier Col, Cleaver Peak (Summit 17), The Cleaver, Cleaver Notch, and the impressive Sawtooth Range.

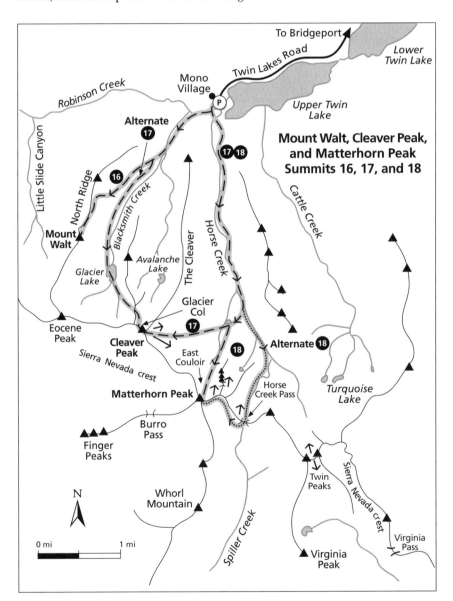

Cleaver Peak

Height: 11,760+ feet
Route: Northeast face
Best time to go: February through May
Trip duration: 1 or 2 days
Mileage: 5 miles to the summit
Elevation gain: 4,660+ feet
Effort factor: 7.2
Level of difficulty: Strong intermediate
Snowboards: Recommended; continuous downhill from the summit
Maps: Buckeye Ridge, Twin Lakes, Matterhorn Peak, Dunderberg Peak

Short approaches coupled with inspiring views and steep terrain make this an excellent and popular area for the backcountry skier and snowboarder. Sawtooth Ridge is well known for its superb alpine mountaineering as well as a wide variety of ski terrain, from intermediate to expert. The relatively short approach to Cleaver Peak makes it a particularly good peak for snowboarding.

You can see the ragged peaks of Sawtooth Ridge from Highway 395 and the town of Bridgeport, jutting above the glaciers and permanent snowfields. From Bridgeport drive 13 miles, on a paved road, to the end of Twin Lakes Road at 7,100 feet. A small fee is charged for parking at Mono Village. Although the resort does not open until the start of fishing season each year (the last weekend in April), the road is open all year.

Follow the trail up Horse Creek as it switchbacks up the steep lower slopes. Around 8,200 feet the slope lessens and a beautiful valley is revealed. This valley is the home of an industrious beaver population; they have dammed Horse Creek and created numerous ponds, killing hundreds of trees. Continue up the valley and ascend a steep slope to 9,300 feet, where the valley levels off again. (There are a couple of good campsites nearby; see the writeup for Matterhorn Peak, Summit 18.) Leave the valley by turning right, and climb a steep slope below a rock cliff. Top out near a small unnamed lake near 9,800 feet, with Matterhorn Peak and the glacial cirque on its north face directly above. Leave this lake and the Matterhorn Peak drainage by angling up and to your right. You will soon be ascending in the wide-open bowls below Cleaver Peak.

Climb/ski the snow-covered upper slopes of Cleaver Peak until you are stopped by exposed rock. Drop your skis or board, and scramble to the summit of Cleaver Peak by following a series of rock ledges and blocks on the northeast face. Gain the arête and follow it to the summit. The climb is Class 3.

Descend following your ascent route. Great open skiing stretches across the face of Cleaver Peak under The Sawblade, The Three Teeth, The Doodad, and The Dragtooth. This is a superb ski and snowboard descent that, in early spring, is skiable all the way back to the car.

The Northwest Face of Blacksmith Peak is on the right. To its left is Cleaver Peak, and between the two is Glacier Col. Cleaver Notch (lower left) is the gap in the rock rib extending from Cleaver Peak.

A longer and more difficult alternate route to Cleaver Peak parallels the approach to Mount Walt (Summit 16). This superb route is for the experienced and highly skilled ski mountaineer. Walk through the camping area of Mono Village and cross the bridge over Robinson Creek. Follow the creek a short distance and head up Blacksmith Creek as it rises steeply above Robinson Creek (see Mount Walt description). Near 8,100 feet the creek splits; follow the right fork to Glacier Lake. With great bowl skiing in the cirque above it, Glacier Lake is an excellent place to camp.

From Glacier Lake, ski up and through a small notch (10,800 feet) southeast of the lake, located just below the steep arête leading to the summit of Blacksmith Peak. Continue a high traverse to Glacier Col (11,560 feet) just northwest of Cleaver Peak. From the col, traverse up and left to a broad depression on the northwest face. Class 3 climbing leads to the summit of Cleaver Peak.

From the summit or from Glacier Col, descend either via Glacier Lake or Avalanche Lake. Alternatively, carry your skis over the summit and ski down via Horse Creek, completing a spectacular traverse of Cleaver Peak.

Matterhorn Peak *

Height: 12,279 feet	
Routes: East Couloir, East Ridge Ramp	
Best time to go: February through May	
Trip duration: 1 long, strenuous day, or 2 to 3 days	
Mileage: 5 miles to the summit	
Elevation gain: 5,179 feet	
Effort factor: 7.7	
Level of difficulty: East Couloir and East Ridge are expert (Double Black Diamond) at the top	
Snowboards: Recommended, as the terrain and scenery are superior	
Map: Buckeye Ridge, Twin Lakes, Matterhorn Peak, Dunderberg Peak	

Matterhorn Peak is the highest and most striking summit along the jagged Sawtooth Ridge, which includes such aptly named peaks as The Three Teeth, The Sawblade, The Cleaver, Cleaver Peak (Summit 17), The Dragtooth, and Blacksmith Peak. These peaks are majestic when viewed from Highway 395 in the vicinity of Bridgeport and are even more imposing to climb. This area contains some of the finest alpine climbs in the Sierra Nevada.

The basins below Matterhorn Peak and Sawtooth Ridge include a number of impressive but small glaciers. Due to abundant snowfall and a northern exposure, this area holds the snow well into the summer, providing some fine skiing late into the season.

The approach is the same as that for Cleaver Peak (see Summit 17). Park in Mono Village at the end of Twin Lakes Road (7,100 feet). Follow the trail up Horse Creek as it switchbacks up the steep lower slopes, or if there is ample snow coverage ski directly up the drainage. At around 8,200 feet the slope lessens and a beautiful valley is revealed. Continue up the valley and ascend a steep slope to 9,300 feet. Here the valley levels off again. If you plan an overnight trip, this is a good place to camp. Ski past a couple of large boulders and camp in the trees to the west of the last large boulder (about 9,400 feet). You will usually find running water at the base of the upper boulder. A camp here provides access to Twin Peaks and the southeast slopes of Matterhorn Peak via Horse Creek Pass.

Leave the valley by turning right (west). Climb a steep slope below a band of cliffs. Top out near a small, unnamed lake located near 9,800 feet (an alternate campsite). Matterhorn Peak and the glacial cirque on its north face are directly above. From this vantage point, the views of Matterhorn Peak are impressive. As you ascend toward your goal, you will see three skiable ramps leading up toward the summit of Matterhorn Peak: On the left (the East Ridge Ramp) is a broad but steep slope that crests about a quarter mile to the east of the peak; this is by far the best of the three slopes for skiing but is quite steep. On the right is the West Couloir, and in the center is the East Couloir, which

The shaded East Couloir lies to the left of the rock face of Matterhorn Peak. The steep snow slopes of the East Ridge Ramp route can be seen to the left of the East Couloir in the bright morning sun.

crests just east of the main summit. The East Couloir approaches 35 degrees near the top, and there may be inadequate snow coverage the last one hundred feet or so. At the top of the couloir, drop your skis or board and traverse an open slope to the far ridge; follow this far ridge to the summit.

Descend the East Ridge Ramp or East Couloir to the large bowl below and retrace your ascent route down to the small unnamed lake. An alternate descent is to ski up and over an 11,100-foot notch between the main Sierra crest and a large rock buttress (11,200 feet) that divides the creek drainage below the East Couloir (first tributary of Horse Creek) from the second tributary of Horse Creek. There is great open-bowl skiing from this notch to your camp at 9,400 feet below.

If you want to climb Matterhorn Peak but do not want to ascend the steep East Couloir, ski up Horse Creek to Horse Creek Pass (10,800 feet). From the pass it is still 1,500 feet to the summit on terrain much less challenging than that of the East Couloir. Above Horse Creek Pass the snow may be too thin for skiing. Drop your skis or snowboard and continue to the summit. You will be rewarded with splendid views of Sawtooth Ridge, Twin Lakes, Virginia Canyon, and Tuolumne Meadows.

Dunderberg Peak

Height: 12,374 feet

Routes: North Couloir, Northeast Ridge, and Southeast Gullies

Best time to go: January through early May

Trip duration: 2–3 days from Highway 395 or 1 day from the Virginia Lakes Pack Station

Mileage: About 7 miles from Highway 395, or about 2 miles from the pack station

Elevation gain: 4,236 feet from Highway 395, or 2,874 feet from the pack station to the summit

Effort factor: 7.7 from Highway 395, or 3.9 from the pack station

Level of difficulty: North Couloir, advanced (Black Diamond); Northeast Ridge, intermediate; Southeast Gully No. 1, advanced (Black Diamond); Southeast Gully No. 2, intermediate

Snowboards: Recommended when the road is plowed into Virginia Lakes or with snowmobile access in the winter

Best time to go: January through early May

Maps: Dunderberg Peak, Lundy

As you approach Conway Summit from Bridgeport, the twin summits of Dunderberg Peak are prominent from Highway 395. The peak offers numerous descent opportunities on all sides; the best are the two to the northeast and two to the southeast, described here.

This is a superb midwinter trip of moderate difficulty—an excellent introduction to overnight winter ski camping, as the ski into base camp follows the easy grade of Virginia Lakes Road. Besides Dunderberg Peak, the area provides fine ski descents from Excelsior Mountain and Black Mountain.

Proceed to Conway Summit (8,138 feet) on Highway 395, about 13 miles south of Bridgeport and 13 miles north of Lee Vining. Turn west on Virginia Lakes Road. In the winter, park 0.4 mile from Highway 395 and ski up the road or take a snowmobile to the turnoff to the Virginia Lakes Pack Station (about 4.5 road miles). Within the first 0.2 mile of your ski or snowmobile ride in, there is an opportunity to reduce the road mileage by taking a natural shortcut bypassing the long, sweeping switchback in Virginia Lakes Road. After crossing Virginia Creek, leave the road by angling to the left, gradually climbing to rejoin the road above the switchback. Continue along Virginia Lakes Road to the pack station turnoff, just beyond the junction of Dunderberg Meadow Road. Look for a good campsite in this area, or continue up Virginia Lakes Road to the creek that drains Trumbull Lake. For better views of the peak and the route up, ski north toward Dunderberg Peak. You will soon ski out of the trees into open terrain.

The route to the main summit of Dunderberg Peak follows the main gully that ascends the slopes between the east summit of Dunderberg Peak and a subpeak (11,700 feet) to the east. If you are concerned about slope stability and the potential for avalanches, climb the ridge that leads to the summit of the subpeak and follow the main ridge over the east summit and onto the main west summit.

From the summit of Dunderberg Peak there are impressive views of Yosemite's Mount Lyell (Summit 22), Lyell Glacier, Mount Maclure, Mount Dana (Summit 20), Dana Glacier, Mount Conness, Conness Glacier, and the steep snow and ice couloir of North Peak (see Summit 20 description). To the east, Mono Lake dominates the view. From the summit there are numerous enjoyable descent routes for the intermediate and advanced skier. Southeast Gully No. 2, originating from the top of the east summit, is an excellent descent route to your base camp. Southeast Gully No. 1 (advanced) is a much steeper and more difficult gully descending from the saddle between the east and west summits. If you plan to ski Gully No. 1, first scout the route by ascending it or visually inspecting it from Trumbull Lake.

From the top of the higher, west summit of Dunderberg Peak there is an excellent descent of the Northeast Ridge down to the unnamed lake at the head of Dunderberg Creek, over intermediate ski terrain. A steeper route also begins at the summit but descends a hidden couloir just beneath the small, northeast-facing summit headwall. This gully is about 35 degrees and drops over 1,000 feet before it merges into the Northeast Ridge route. From here, ski down to the unnamed lake at the head of Dunderberg Creek, then head east toward Dunderberg Meadow Road. Once on Dunderberg Meadow Road it is about 1.5 miles back to Virginia Lakes Road.

The northeast side of Dunderberg as seen from Highway 395 west of Conway Summit. The far summit is the high point. Ski and snowboard routes descend to the left and to the right of the main summit.

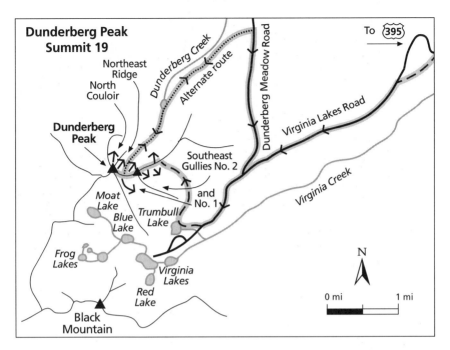

This is an excellent single-day spring tour, as well, once the road in to the summer cabins near Trumbull Lake is opened, usually in April. (Call the Caltrans Maintenance Station at Bridgeport to find out when the road will be opened; see Appendix 5.)

Mount Dana

Height: 13,057 feet

Route: Dana Couloir

Best time to go: April through May (after Tioga Pass Road is opened)

Trip duration: 1 day

Mileage: 4 miles to the summit

Elevation gain: 3,407 feet

Effort factor: 5.4

Level of difficulty: Expert (Double Black Diamond)

Snowboards: Recommended after Tioga Pass Road is opened in the spring

Map: Tioga Pass, Mount Dana

Superb backcountry ski terrain makes the Tioga Pass area a favorite of many skiers in winter and spring. Due to the high elevation and ample snow depths,

Mount Dana, with the Dana Couloir to the left and the Solstice Couloir to the right of the summit. The Dana Plateau is in the foreground, with the top of the Ellery Bowl visible at the lower left.

skiing remains good into early June. Unfortunately for winter skiers, Tioga Pass Road is not plowed until April or May, depending on the amount of snowfall accumulation during the winter.

This trip description assumes that you can drive to Tioga Lake. (The tour can be completed earlier in the season but requires walking or skiing an additional 6 miles up Tioga Pass Road.) Tioga Pass Winter Resort (see Appendix 5) is an excellent base camp for a tour of Mount Dana and the peaks west of Tioga Lake.

From Lee Vining on Highway 395, proceed west on Tioga Pass Road to Tioga Lake (9,650 feet). Start at the upper end of Tioga Lake and ski east up Glacier Canyon to Dana Lake (11,100 feet), situated at the base of Mount Dana and the Dana Glacier. The impressive Dana Couloir crests the ridge to the left of Mount Dana, while the equally steep Solstice Couloir reaches the skyline to the right of the summit. From Dana Lake angle south and climb Dana Couloir, which approaches 40 degrees. At the head of the couloir, turn right and make your way along the ridge to the summit of Mount Dana. You will be rewarded with impressive views of Mono Lake, Tuolumne Meadows, and Mount Conness.

An alternate route is to follow the route of the summer trail up the northwest slopes of Mount Dana, starting at Tioga Pass. The ski or snowboard descent of these slopes is an enjoyable run of moderate difficulty (intermediate terrain). Due to the westerly exposure, the snow melts off this route quickly each spring.

If you are planning to ski the Dana Couloir for the first time, it is recommended that you climb the route. Not only will this allow you to check the route for potential avalanche conditions and the condition of the snow, but you will know you are in the correct couloir: the entire chute is not visible from the top, so approaching from the summit can be intimidating. The couloir's entry slopes are inviting enough but they steepen quickly, preventing the skier from seeing all the way to the bottom.

An additional bonus after skiing the Dana Couloir is to descend the expert

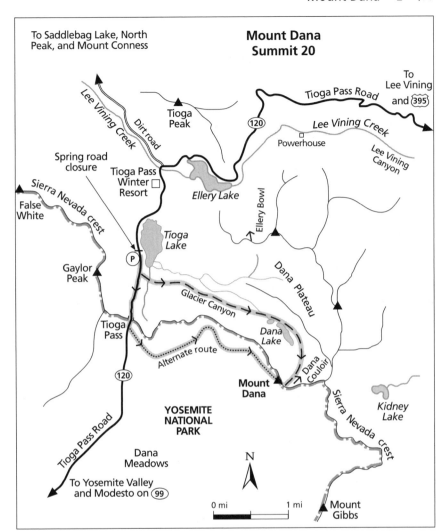

(Double Black Diamond) Ellery Bowl. From Dana Lake, traverse north onto the Dana Plateau and make your way to the north end of the plateau. The bowl (visible from Ellery Lake) is steep, especially at the top, and is often blocked by a large cornice. Use caution, as this wide bowl avalanches often.

In addition to Mount Dana, there is superb skiing on the peaks west of Tioga Lake on Gaylor Peak, White Mountain, False White, and the slopes above Saddlebag Lake, including Mount Conness and North Peak. The north side of North Peak contains three extremely steep chutes that are popular ice-climbing routes in the fall when the snow turns to ice. The upper gully (the chute furthest to the right when viewed from below) makes for an excellent ski descent for the expert skier and is about 40 degrees. For more information on North Peak, see *Sierra Classics: 100 Best Climbs in the High Sierra,* by John Moynier and Claude Fiddler.

Koip Peak

Height: 12,979 feet	
Route: East Ridge	
Best time to go: January through early May	
Trip duration: 1 day	
Mileage: 6 miles to the summit	
Elevation gain: 5,079 feet	
Effort factor: 8.1	
Level of difficulty: Advanced (Black Diamond)	
Snowboards: Recommended	
Map: Koip Peak	

This is a long, single-day summit with over 5,000 feet of elevation gain, so get an early start. Koip Peak is one of the highest peaks in the area and is much higher than it appears. Mount Dana, 6 miles to the north, seems significantly higher but exceeds Koip Peak by only a few feet.

The names of Koip Peak and nearby Kuna Peak are thought to be of Mono Indian origin. In the closely related Northern Paiute dialect, *koipa* means "mountain sheep."

Take Highway 395 to the northern junction of June Lake Loop (Highway 158), about 5 miles south of Lee Vining (see Yosemite National Park map). Drive about a mile and turn right on the well-signed dirt road to the Parker Lake trailhead. Follow this road for about 3 miles to the trailhead (7,900 feet).

Looking up the Parker Lake basin at Koip Peak (center)

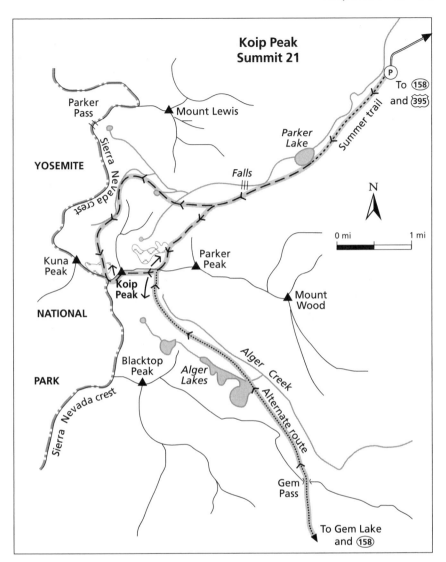

**Koip Peak
Summit 21**

Ski or hike along the summer trail to Parker Lake (just below 8,400 feet). Continue up the prominent valley and the creek that flows into Parker Lake. Above 9,600 feet the valley and cascading creek steepen dramatically; you may encounter difficulties in this area under icy conditions. Take an ice axe and crampons.

Near 10,000 feet a vertical ice bulge forms in the creek at the waterfall. This can be passed either on its left or right. This ice usually remains in good condition through April and provides an excellent area for ice climbing practice. The ice bulge is about two pitches in height.

At the 10,800-foot level, the narrow canyon of Parker Creek opens up into a large bowl and the slope slackens. The summer trail traverses this basin on a natural bench on its way between Parker Pass to the north and the Koip Peak/Parker Peak Pass to the south. Here you have two great routes to the summit of Koip Peak. Ski up to the small lake near 11,700 feet to the northwest of the peak, cross the small glacier, and gain the ridge at the Koip Peak/Parker Peak Pass. Follow the ridge to the summit. Alternatively, from the natural bench at the 10,800-foot level, turn and head northwest for about one-half mile and then southwest up the creek to the glacier east of Koip Peak. Ascend to the pass southwest of Koip Peak and follow the ridge to the summit.

From the summit, you will have great views of Banner Peak, Mount Ritter (Summit 23), Mount Lyell (Summit 22), Mount Dana (Summit 20), and Mono Lake. Ski either route back down to the car. Both are excellent, the east ridge being the steeper of the two descents.

An alternate route is recommended for a winter ascent (January–March) of Koip Peak. When the road to Parker Lake is blocked by snow (usually until the end of March), drive to the community of June Lake and begin at the SCE hydroelectric power plant near Silver Lake on Highway 158. Head toward Agnew and Gem Lakes (for detailed directions, follow the start of the Mount Lyell route, Summit 22). At the upper end of Gem Lake, ascend Gem Pass and continue past Alger Lakes and then up to the Parker Peak/Koip Peak pass to the summit of Koip. This route is not recommended after April 1, because Agnew Lake and Gem Lake become unsafe to cross when they fill with spring runoff. Additionally, the rugged terrain makes skiing around these lakes very time-consuming.

Mount Lyell ⋆

Height: 13,114 feet	
Route: Lyell Glacier	
Best time to go: February through early May	
Trip duration: 4 days	
Mileage: About 12 miles to the summit	
Elevation gain: 6,500 feet	
Effort factor: 12.5	
Level of difficulty: Strong intermediate	
Snowboards: Not recommended due to length of the approach over varied terrain	
Maps: June Lake, Koip Peak, Mount Ritter, Vogelsang Peak, Mount Lyell	

Mount Lyell is the highest peak in Yosemite National Park, and its glacier is the second largest in the Sierra Nevada. This peak is frequently climbed in the summer but seldom visited in the winter. This is an ideal late winter/early spring backcountry tour and summit descent for those willing to spend a little extra effort to ski into this splendid high alpine region. The views from the summit are outstanding.

Take Highway 395 to Highway 158 (June Lake Loop, southern junction). The turnoff is about 12 miles south of Lee Vining and 15 miles north of Mammoth Lakes. Drive through the town of June Lake, past the June Mountain Ski Resort to the Southern California Edison (SCE) Rush Creek Hydroelectric Power Plant at Silver Lake (7,200 feet). This is the end of the plowed road in winter. Park at the end of the road, not on SCE property.

Climb or hike up the steep slopes above the power house, following the route of the tramway to Agnew Lake at 8,500 feet. Your route is up Rush Creek and the chain of lakes (Agnew, Gem, and Waugh Lakes) that have been dammed by SCE as part of their Rush Creek Hydroelectric Project. Pass the dams for Gem and Waugh Lakes on the left. Above Waugh Lake (9,400 feet) pick up the route of the John Muir Trail and ski over Donohue Pass (11,056 feet). Donohue Pass overlooks the Lyell Canyon and the Lyell Fork of the Tuolumne River.

Ski down and traverse southeast to near 10,600 feet. This area makes for an excellent campsite. Mount Lyell is only 2 miles away and a 2,500-foot climb. Ski up the valley to the glacial cirque above and to the north of the buttress that divides the Lyell Glacier into two segments. Ski up the western portion of the glacier toward the Mount Maclure–Mount Lyell notch and onto the summit.

From the summit of Mount Lyell, the ski mountaineer has a commanding view of Banner Peak and Mount Ritter (Summit 23) and the peaks of Yosemite National Park to the west and north. Ten miles to the southwest are Merced Peak, Red Peak, Gray Peak, and Mount Clark, where John Muir discovered the first living glaciers of the Sierra Nevada more than a hundred years ago (see sidebar). In the distance are Half Dome and Yosemite Valley.

The approach via Rush Creek takes one across Agnew, Gem, and Waugh Lakes. These reservoirs are drained in the fall and winter, providing direct winter access to the backcountry and Donohue Pass. Caution: by early April these

Mount Lyell and Mount Lyell Glacier in February. The route skirts the rock buttress (to its right) and ascends the peak along the right skyline.

reservoirs become unsafe to ski as they fill with water from spring runoff. Skiing around these lakes is time-consuming, making this route undesirable.

When these reservoirs begin to fill in the spring, an alternate route is to drive to Mammoth Mountain Ski Resort and start the trip to Mount Lyell by skiing over Minaret Summit, down to Agnew Meadows, onto Thousand Island Lake, over Island Pass picking up the featured route above Waugh Lake (see Summit 23 description).

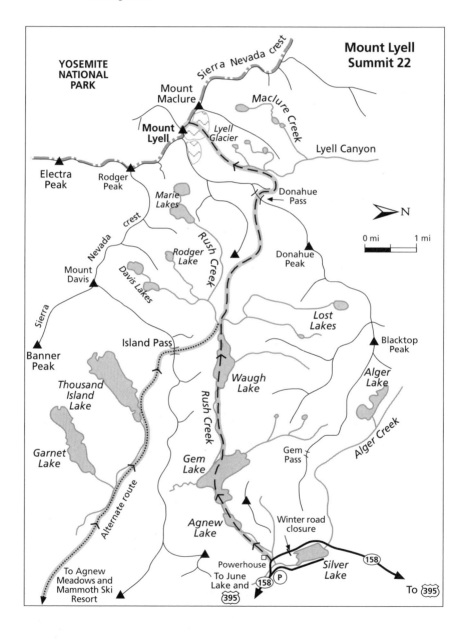

Chapter 6
MAMMOTH LAKES REGION

The Minarets are a striking sight from Highway 395 south of Mammoth Lakes. The highest and most prominent of the twenty Minaret spires is Clyde Minaret, backed by the needlelike spire of Michael Minaret. To the north, the region is dominated by Mount Ritter and Banner Peak. Mount Ritter (Summit 23), first climbed by John Muir in 1872 (see sidebar), is the best of this region's fine ski summits.

The Mammoth Lakes are favorite fishing and sailboarding destinations. The mountains attract climbers, backpackers, mountaineers, snowboarders, and skiers from around the world, and the nearby thermal springs of Hot Creek are enjoyed by all. The resort town of Mammoth Lakes is a popular year-round playground. One of the largest ski areas in the country is Mammoth Mountain Ski Resort, a good place to improve your backcountry skiing and snowboarding skills.

The Mammoth Crest, near Mammoth Lakes, is a backcountry skier's and snowboarder's paradise containing all types of terrain: gentle valleys, frozen lakes, ridge tops with grand views of the Sierra Nevada, and many steep chutes for the expert skier and snowboarder.

Ascending the glacier below the summit plateau of Mount Ritter (Summit 23)

Just 15 miles south of Mammoth Lakes is Rock Creek Winter Lodge, a rustic resort for backcountry skiers and the gateway to excellent backcountry ski terrain in the Little Lakes Valley (see Summits 26 and 27). This high valley, a large glacial basin, is rimmed by magnificent 13,000-foot peaks—Mount Morgan (South), Bear Creek Spire, Mount Dade, Mount Abbot, Mount Mills, and Mount Starr. In the summer the valley is an oasis of streams, meadows, and more than sixty lakes. In the winter the lakes are frozen and covered with snow, making travel up the valley simply a matter of skiing from lake to lake. The valley is an ideal place for winter and spring ski tours in a postcard-perfect setting, and

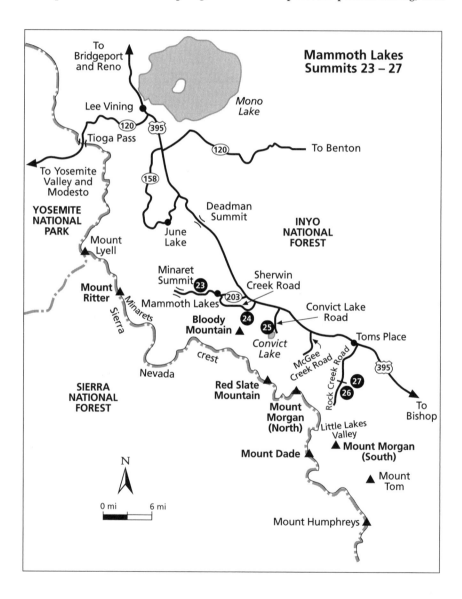

provides an excellent introduction to the joys of snow camping. The terrain in the Little Lakes Valley is gentle (intermediate), and the route past Box Lake and Long Lake to the Treasure Lakes and Dade Lake, with the peaks towering above, makes for a spectacular tour. For advanced and expert skiers, Mount Dade, Mount Morgan (South), Treasure Peak, Mount Mills, and other summits in the area offer numerous challenging descents.

How to get there: For purposes of this book, the Mammoth Lakes region stretches from the turnoff to Mammoth Lakes (Highway 203) south to Toms Place at Sherwin Summit, a relatively short distance of about 15 miles along Highway 395. Approaching from the south, take Highway 395 to Bishop. Toms Place and the turnoff to Mammoth Lakes are about 26 miles and 41 miles, respectively, north of Bishop. If approaching from the north, the Mammoth Lakes turnoff (Highway 203) is about 26 miles south of Lee Vining, and Toms Place is another 15 miles south.

From Highway 395, east–west laterals provide access to the peaks: Highway 203 for Mount Ritter, Sherwin Creek Road for Bloody Mountain, Convict Lake Road for Red Slate Peak, and Rock Creek Road at Toms Place for Mount Dade and Mount Morgan (South).

The Untouched Summit of Ritter

In October 1872, after exploring the glaciers of the Mount Lyell area, John Muir decided to "make an excursion to the untouched summit of Ritter." Starting in Yosemite Valley, he hiked past Vernal and Nevada Falls to Mount Lyell and on to Mount Ritter.

Mount Ritter is king of the mountains of the middle portion of the High Sierra, as Shasta of the north and Whitney of the south sections. Moreover, as far as I know, it had never been climbed. I had explored the adjacent wilderness summer after summer, but my studies thus far had never drawn me to the top of it. Its height above sea-level is about 13,300 feet, and it is fenced round by steeply inclined glaciers, and cañons of tremendous depth and ruggedness, which render it almost inaccessible. But difficulties of this kind only exhilarate the mountaineer. . . .

On the southern shore of a frozen lake, I encountered an extensive field of hard, granular snow, up which I scampered in fine tone, intending to follow it to its head. The surface was pitted with oval hollows, made by stones and drifted pine-needles that had melted themselves into the mass by the radiation of absorbed sun-heat. These afforded good footholds, but the surface curved more and more steeply at the head, and the pits became shallower and less abundant, until I found myself in danger of being shed off like avalanching snow. I persisted, however, creeping on all fours, and shuffling up the smoothest places on my back, as I had often done on burnished granite.

Arriving on the summit of this dividing crest, one of the most exciting pieces of pure wilderness was disclosed that I ever discovered in all my mountaineering. There, immediately in front, loomed the majestic mass of Mount Ritter, with a glacier swooping down its face nearly to my feet, then curving westward and pouring its frozen flood into a dark blue lake, whose shores were bound with precipices of crystalline snow. After gazing spellbound, I began instinctively to scrutinize every notch and gorge and weathered buttress of the mountain, with reference to making the ascent. The entire front above the glacier appeared as one tremendous precipice, slightly receding at the top, and bristling with spires and pinnacles set above one another in formidable array. Massive lichen-stained battlements stood forward here and there, hacked at the top with angular notches, and separated by frosty gullies and recesses that have been veiled in shadow ever since their creation; while to right and left, as far as I could see, were huge, crumbling buttresses, offering no hope to the climber. The head of the glacier sends up a few finger-like branches through narrow couloirs; but these seemed too steep and short to be available, especially as I had no ax with which to cut steps, and the numerous narrow-throated gullies down which stones and snow are avalanched seemed hopelessly steep, besides being interrupted by vertical cliffs; while the whole front was rendered still more terribly forbidding by the chill shadow and the gloomy blackness of the rocks.

I could not distinctly hope to reach the summit from this side, yet I moved on across the glacier as if driven by fate. Contending with myself, the season is too far spent, I said, and even should I be successful, I might be storm-bound on the mountain; and in the cloud-darkness, with the cliffs and crevasses covered with snow, how could I escape? No; I must wait till next summer. I would only approach the mountain now, and inspect it, creep about its flanks, learn what I could of its history, holding myself ready to flee on the approach of the first storm-cloud. But we little know until tried how much of the uncontrollable there is in us, urging across glaciers and torrents, and up dangerous heights, let the judgment forbid as it may.

I succeeded in gaining the foot of the cliff on the eastern extremity of the glacier, and there discovered the mouth of a narrow avalanche gully, through which I began to climb, intending to follow it as far as possible, and at least obtain some fine wild views for my pains. I thus made my way into a wilderness of crumbling spires and battlements, built together in bewildering combinations, and glazed in many places with a thin coating of ice, which I had to hammer off with stones. The situation was becoming gradually more perilous; but, having passed several dangerous spots, I dared not think of descending; for, so steep was the entire ascent, one would inevitably fall to the glacier in case a single misstep were made. Knowing, therefore, the tried danger beneath, I became all the more anxious concerning the developments to be made above, and began to be conscious of a vague foreboding of what actually befell; not that I was given to fear, but rather because my instincts, usually so positive and true, seemed vitiated in some way, and were leading me astray.

At length, after attaining an elevation of about 12,800 feet, I found myself at the foot of a sheer drop in the bed of the avalanche channel I was tracing, which seemed absolutely to bar further progress. It was only about forty-five or fifty feet high, and somewhat roughened by fissures and projections. The tried dangers beneath seemed even greater than that of the cliff in front; therefore, after scanning its face again and again, I began to scale it, picking my holds with intense caution. After gaining a point about halfway to the top, I was suddenly brought to a dead stop, with arms outspread, clinging close to the face of the rock, unable to move hand or foot either up or down. My doom appeared fixed. I must fall. There would be a moment of bewilderment, and then a lifeless rumble down the one general precipice to the glacier below.

When this final danger flashed upon me, I became nerve-shaken for the first time since setting foot on the mountains, and my mind seemed to fill with a stifling smoke. But this terrible eclipse lasted only a moment, when life blazed forth again with preternatural clearness. I seemed suddenly to become possessed of a new sense. The other self, bygone experiences, Instinct, or Guardian Angel,—call it what you will,—came forward and assumed control. Then my trembling muscles became firm again, every rift and flaw in the rock was seen as through a microscope, and my limbs moved with a positiveness and precision with which I seemed to have nothing at all to do. Had I been borne aloft upon wings, my deliverance could not have been more complete.

Above this memorable spot, the face of the mountain is still more savagely hacked and torn. It is a maze of yawning chasms and gullies, in the angles of which rise beetling crags and piles of detached boulders that seem to have been gotten ready to be launched below. But the strange influx of strength I had received seemed inexhaustible. I found a way without effort, and soon stood upon the topmost crag in the blessed light.

How truly glorious the landscape circled around this noble summit!—giant mountains, valleys innumerable, glaciers and meadows, rivers and lakes, with the wide blue sky bent tenderly over them all. Looking southward along the axis of the range, the eye is first caught by a row of exceedingly sharp and slender spires, which rise openly to a height of about a thousand feet, above a series of short, residual glaciers that lean back against their bases; their fantastic sculpture and the unrelieved sharpness with which they spring out of the ice rendering them peculiarly wild and striking. These are "The Minarets."

Beyond them you behold a sublime wilderness of mountains, their snowy summits towering together in crowded abundance, peak beyond peak, swelling higher, higher as they sweep on southward, until the culminating point of the range is reached on Mount Whitney, near the head of the Kern River, at an elevation of nearly 14,700 feet above the level of the sea.

—John Muir, *The Mountains of California*

Mount Ritter ★

Height: 13,157 feet
Route: Southeast Glacier
Best time to go: March through May
Trip duration: 3 days or more
Mileage: 12 miles to the summit
Elevation gain: 5,432 feet
Level of difficulty: Advanced (Black Diamond)
Snowboards: A long approach to Lake Ediza, but the boarding is supreme from the summit
Effort factor: 11.4
Maps: Mammoth Mountain, Mount Ritter

The Banner Peak and Mount Ritter area is one of the most exquisite in the Sierra Nevada. In the summertime the base of these peaks can be reached with a short hike of a couple of hours. The spires of the Minarets, the high glacial cirques, and the sparkling lakes, cascading falls, and lush meadows make this a favorite of many summer backpackers, hikers, and rock climbers. Its beauty is magnified in the winter. The area is a true winter wonderland that you will probably have all to yourself in late winter or early spring.

A ski or snowboard descent of Mount Ritter is the focus of this trip, but the area offers many great touring options. Tours to Iceberg Lake, Nydiver Lakes, Garnet Lake, and Thousand Island Lake can all be made from Ediza Lake. A climb to the Banner-Ritter col and the descent of the glacier to Lake Catherine is a more serious endeavor but a great side trip to the main attraction.

Mount Ritter and Banner Peak (right). The summit snowfield is visible to the left of Mount Ritter, but much of the descent route and the glacier are hidden from view.

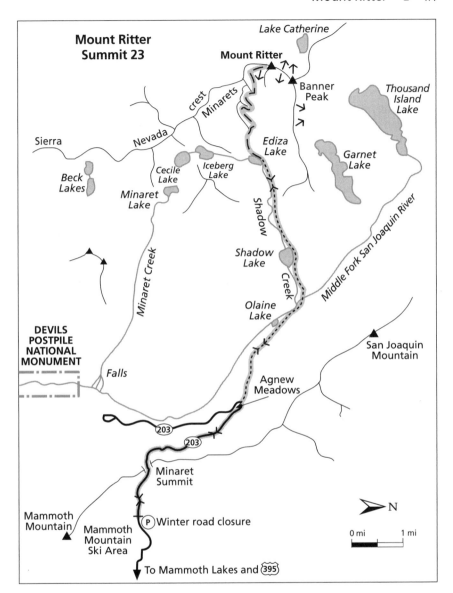

The best time to ski Mount Ritter is in the spring before the road is plowed to Agnew Meadows. The road is closed at the Mammoth Mountain Ski Resort and is not normally opened until mid-May or after the Memorial Day weekend. In most years, the road could be easily opened much earlier but does not receive the attention and priority that it should from the public officials. This inconvenience adds about 4 miles to the approach.

Take Highway 395 to the Mammoth Lakes (Highway 203) turnoff, and drive through the town of Mammoth Lakes. At the far end of town, turn right to Mammoth Mountain Ski Resort and Minaret Summit. Park your car at the resort (8,900 feet); check with the lodge on the north side of the road for the best place to park your car overnight. Ski up the road to Minaret Summit (9,175 feet) and down to Agnew Meadows (8,335 feet). Where the road doubles back to the left, continue on to the campground and trailhead to the right.

Follow the trail to the Middle Fork of the San Joaquin River and past Olaine Lake, then take the trail's left fork to Shadow and Ediza Lakes. You will soon cross the river on a bridge (8,100 feet) and begin a steep but short climb to Shadow Lake (8,800 feet). Continue along Shadow Creek, reaching Ediza Lake (9,300 feet) in a couple of miles.

The upper part of the Ediza Lake basin is an excellent place to camp. The old-growth trees offer protection in a storm, yet are widely spaced to provide wonderful views and great opportunities for photos of this exceptional setting.

For the ascent of Mount Ritter, follow the prominent valley toward the Banner-Ritter col. Near 9,800 feet, take the first gully to your left and follow it to its crest near 10,800 feet. Swing to the right, following a generally upward traverse. Ski below the base of the prominent cliff (around 11,200 feet) and into the high glacial cirque. Ski west up the glacier to the steep headwall. Near the headwall, turn right (north) and up a steep section to the upper glacier and the summit plateau. Follow the plateau to the summit.

Beyond the prominent foreground view of Banner Peak, you will be rewarded with great views of Yosemite, Mount Lyell, and Mono Lake. It is a superb ski back along your ascent route to Ediza Lake, a descent of nearly 4,000 feet, with the Minarets as the backdrop.

24
Bloody Mountain

Height: 12,544 feet
Routes: Bloody Couloir, North Ridge Ramp
Best time to go: Late April through May
Trip duration: 1 day
Mileage: 3 miles to the summit
Elevation gain: 3,544 feet
Effort factor: 5.0
Level of difficulty: Bloody Couloir, expert (Double Black Diamond); North Ridge Ramp, advanced (Black Diamond)
Snowboards: Recommended; steep terrain and short approach
Maps: Bloody Mountain, Old Mammoth

The impressive north face and the distinctive couloirs of Bloody Mountain can be seen from as far away as Conway Summit on Highway 395, more than 40 miles to the north. This popular descent is one of the more difficult in the region.

Ascending Bloody Couloir. The best route is to the left of the large buttress in the center of the couloir.

Nevertheless, Bloody Couloir is a superb descent for the expert skier. There are also other descent routes, allowing one to avoid the steep main couloir.

Turn southwest on Sherwin Creek Road, which leaves Highway 395 about 1.5 miles south of the Mammoth Lakes turnoff. In 1.5 miles turn left on Laurel Lakes Road (high-clearance, four-wheel-drive vehicle required) and drive until the snow blocks your progress; early in the season, this will be well below the end of the road. Hike or ski up the 4.5-mile-long road to Laurel Lakes.

The easiest route to the summit is to ascend the snow ramp (North Ridge Ramp), far to the left of Bloody Couloir. Start your climb from the lower end of the first Laurel Lake. This snow ramp crests the summit ridge about 0.5 mile north of the main summit. This is an excellent descent route and not nearly as steep as the main couloir.

If you plan to ski the main couloir, it is best to ascend it to check for conditions, obstacles, and steepness of the route. Follow Laurel Lakes Road to the upper lake and begin your ascent of Bloody Couloir. Bring crampons and an

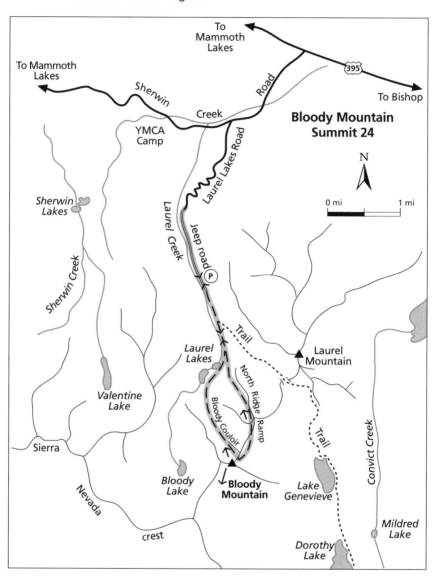

To
Mammoth
Lakes

To Mammoth
Lakes

395

To Bishop

Sherwin

Road

Creek

YMCA
Camp

**Bloody Mountain
Summit 24**

Laurel Lakes Road

N

0 mi   1 mi

Sherwin
Lakes

Laurel Creek

Jeep road

P

Sherwin Creek

Trail

Laurel
Lakes

North Ridge Ramp

Laurel
Mountain

Valentine
Lake

Bloody Couloir

Trail

Convict Creek

Sierra

Nevada

Bloody
Lake

↓Bloody
Mountain

Lake
Genevieve

crest

Mildred
Lake

Dorothy
Lake

ice axe. The main couloir is divided by two large rock towers; as you climb, stay to the left of these rock islands. The Bloody Couloir is steep, and depending on snow conditions you may not be able to arrest a fall.

The view from the summit includes Mount Morrison, Red Slate Mountain (Summit 25), Convict Canyon, Mammoth Mountain Ski Resort, Banner Peak and Mount Ritter (Summit 23), and the spectacular Minarets.

A less steep alternate route up Bloody Mountain is to approach the peak from Convict Lake, via Edith Lake; see the description and map for Red Slate Mountain (Summit 25).

Red Slate Mountain ★

Height: 13,163 feet
Routes: Northwest Couloir, Red Slate Couloir
Best time to go: January through April
Trip duration: 2 to 3 days
Elevation gain: 5,583 feet
Effort factor: 8.6
Level of difficulty: Northwest Couloir, advanced (Black Diamond);
Red Slate Couloir, expert (Double Black Diamond)
Mileage: 6 miles to the summit
Snowboards: A long approach but great boarding up high
Maps: Bloody Mountain, Convict Lake

The climb and ski or snowboard descent of Red Slate Mountain is a great three-day trip in some rugged terrain. The approach to this peak is often easier on skis in the winter and spring than on foot in the heat of the summer.

From the junction to Mammoth Lakes, drive 4 miles southeast on Highway 395 to Convict Lake Road. Proceed south for 2 miles to Convict Lake and park.

Depending on snow conditions, walk or ski around the north (right) side of Convict Lake following the route of the summer hiking trail. Do not ski on the lake, as the ice may be dangerously thin; in recent years a number of people have fallen through the ice and drowned. At the upper end of the lake, the trail swings around a prominent ridge and heads south up the hidden valley of Convict Creek. The route takes you under the impressive face of Sevehah Cliff. Numerous avalanche chutes are obvious as you make your way up the canyon. The contrasting colors of the various rock formations are impressive—at every turn there is a new array of reds, blacks, grays, and whites.

Red Slate Mountain in the early February morning light with the Red Slate Couloir in the center. The main route to the summit is via the saddle on the right, then up the right skyline.

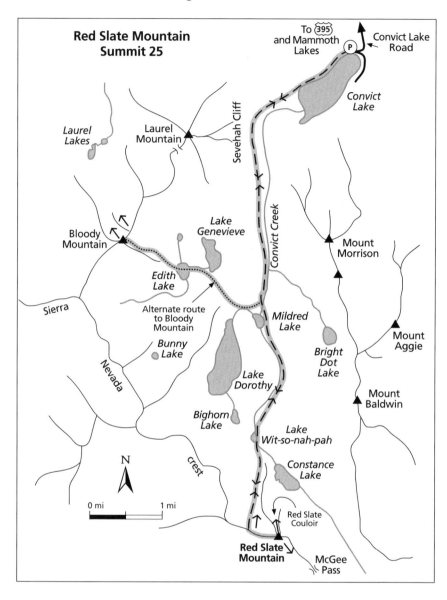

Red Slate Mountain
Summit 25

To ③⑨⑤
and Mammoth
Lakes

Convict Lake
Road

P

Convict
Lake

*Laurel
Lakes*

*Laurel
Mountain*

Sevehah Cliff

*Bloody
Mountain*

*Lake
Genevieve*

Convict Creek

Mount
Morrison

*Edith
Lake*

Sierra

Alternate route
to Bloody
Mountain

*Mildred
Lake*

Mount
Aggie

*Bunny
Lake*

Nevada

*Lake
Dorothy*

*Bright
Dot
Lake*

Mount
Baldwin

*Bighorn
Lake*

*Lake
Wit-so-nah-pah*

N

crest

*Constance
Lake*

0 mi   1 mi

Red Slate
Couloir

**Red Slate
Mountain**

McGee
Pass

Ski past the two summits of Mount Morrison and the stream that flows from Bright Dot Lake. In about 4 miles and 2,300 feet elevation gain you will reach Mildred Lake. Continue on up the narrow, relatively flat valley for another 0.7 mile to the snow survey marker, located in an opening on the right side of the valley floor near where the creek forks to Lake Wit-so-nah-pah. This is a good place to camp, as it is sheltered by the nearby trees and there is usually running water, even in the dead of winter. Alternatively, ski an additional 600 feet in elevation and camp at Lake Wit-so-nah-pah. From here you will have great views of Red Slate Mountain and the large bowl to the west of the summit.

The route from the lake is obvious. Ski up to the broad saddle to the west of Red Slate Mountain and climb the steep snow slopes to the summit. (These upper slopes approach 35 degrees for about 400 feet.) The view from the summit is impressive—Banner and Ritter and Mono Lake to the north, the Rock Creek area (Bear Creek Spire, Mount Dade, and Mount Morgan) to the near south.

From the summit there are three descent routes to choose from, all excellent. You can ski the slopes you climbed, a fast route back to base camp. For the expert (Double Black Diamond) skier, there is the Red Slate Couloir, a steep (1,000-foot), prominent couloir bisecting the north face of the peak. The couloir approaches 40 degrees, and it is wise to climb it if you plan to descend it, as finding the correct entrance from the summit ridge can be tricky. A third alternative is to ski off the southeast ridge toward McGee Pass, then turn north toward Constance Lake, returning to your camp.

Besides the descent of Red Slate Mountain, there are numerous other ski mountaineering opportunities in this compact area. The northeast bowls above Lake Dorothy and the north bowl above Bunny Lake provide excellent skiing. This guide includes a separate descent of Bloody Couloir on Bloody Mountain (Summit 24), but a less difficult ascent and descent of Bloody Mountain can be made from this side of the peak via Edith Lake.

Mount Dade ★

Height: 13,600+ feet
Route: Hourglass Couloir
Best time to go: February through early May
Trip duration: 2 or more days
Elevation gain: 4,700+ feet
Effort factor: 9.7
Level of difficulty: Below the Hourglass Couloir, intermediate; the Hourglass is advanced (Black Diamond)
Mileage: 10 miles to the summit
Snowboards: There is a long approach, but the boarding above Long Lake is excellent
Maps: Toms Place, Mount Morgan, Mount Abbot

The Little Lakes Valley is a popular area for backpackers in the summer. More than sixty small lakes fill the glacial valley, and the trail passes countless meadows, abundant wildflowers, and numerous streams. The summits of Mount Mills, Mount Abbot, Mount Dade, and Bear Creek Spire are popular summertime destinations for peak baggers and mountaineers. The ease of access and the superb ski terrain make this area nearly as popular with skiers and ski mountaineer

A wonderful view of Mount Dade (right) with the Hourglass Couloir (center), taken from the summit of Mount Morgan (to the south). The Treasure Lakes are just out of the photo, at the base of the Hourglass Couloir.

guides. The area provides something for everyone, from gentle terrain in the valley to advanced and expert terrain in the high glacial cirques.

On Highway 395, proceed to Sherwin Summit and the small community of Toms Place. Turn west on the paved Rock Creek Road for 6 miles and park at the Sno-Park (8,900 feet). From here it is a short 2-mile ski up the road to Rock Creek Winter Lodge, and another 3 miles to Mosquito Flat (10,200 feet). Thanks to Rock Creek Winter Lodge, the entire distance to the John Muir Wilderness boundary is groomed, allowing for a quick approach to the backcountry.

For the beginning of this approach, refer to the map for Mount Morgan (Summit 27). From the end of the road at Mosquito Flat, ski up the chain of lakes (Marsh, Heart, Box, and Long Lakes) as you make your way up the Little Lakes Valley toward the Treasure Lakes. The lakes are located near the base of a sheer, triangular rock face and the obvious Hourglass Couloir. This triangular rock face is fractured by bands of light rock running across its black face and is prominent from the chain of lakes below.

There are many excellent tours in this area; two are described here. From a base camp at Long Lake, you can ski up the shallow, well-defined gully to Treasure Lakes, across the westernmost lake, and up the creek that flows into the lakes. Then ski up the steep southeast slopes to the Mount Abbot–Treasure Peak col (12,500 feet). (Treasure Peak is just east of Mount Abbot.) After cresting the col, ski down past Mills Lake and Ruby Lake back to the Little Lakes Valley; or ski down past Mills Lake and near 11,400 feet ski east down a gully that terminates at Long Lake. Another route to the col, which avoids the steep slopes above the Treasure Lakes, is to approach from the east and north, leaving the narrow gully below the Treasure Lakes near the 10,800-foot level and skiing west passing an unnamed lake at 11,600 feet up to the hanging valley north of the col. This route takes you beneath the sheer north face of Treasure Peak.

Another magnificent loop tour ascends to a small glacial cirque above Dade Lake, which provides great skiing beneath the north face of Bear Creek Spire. From the outlet of the Treasure Lakes, turn left (east) and ascend a rounded ridge to the plateau at 11,600 feet, then ski over flat terrain to Dade Lake. Descend via the Gem Lakes to Long Lake.

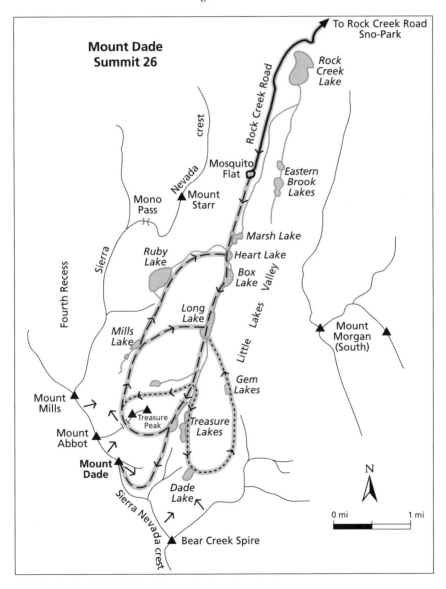

The featured summit is Mount Dade and the descent of the Hourglass Couloir (also called the Dade or East Couloir). Long Lake or the Treasure Lakes make an excellent base camp for a climb and descent of Mount Dade. Following the same route to the Treasure Lakes, ski across the westernmost Treasure Lake and up the Hourglass Couloir. Just as the triangular rock face is so prominent from below, so is the Hourglass Couloir which ascends alongside it. Use judgment in climbing the couloir, as it is avalanche prone. When it is icy or hard packed, a slip on the climb up or a fall on the descent may be difficult to arrest. The couloir is steep and approaches 35 degrees for about 400 vertical feet. Crampons may be necessary.

Above the Hourglass Couloir, continue into the beautiful glacial cirque to the south of Mount Dade and up southeast slopes to the summit. Great views await. Enjoy the 2,400-foot descent to the Treasure Lakes.

27
Mount Morgan (South)

Height: 13,748 feet

Route: North Ridge

Best time to go: February through April

Trip duration: 1 long day or an overnight trip

Mileage: 8 miles to the summit

Elevation gain: 4,848 feet

Effort factor: 8.9

Level of difficulty: North Ridge, intermediate; headwall couloirs, advanced (Black Diamond)

Snowboards: A long approach, but the boarding in the headwall chutes is superior

Maps: Toms Place, Mount Morgan

Mount Morgan (South) is an ideal introduction to backcountry winter camping. Approaching the peak, the terrain is gentle and campsites can be selected in the protected shelter of the trees near Kenneth Lake. In the event of an unexpected storm, you can quickly retreat to Rock Creek Road and your car. For a variety of reasons, the snow does not accumulate to typical depths expected on a peak of this elevation in the Sierra Nevada. Because of the potential for sparse snow coverage, this summit should be skied in mid- to late winter or early spring.

The steep chutes below the summit of Mount Morgan (South). Excellent powder skiing can be found in these protected gullies. Photo by Colin Fuller

On Highway 395, proceed to Sherwin Summit and the small community of Toms Place. Drive southwest on Rock Creek Road for 6 miles and park at the Sno-Park (8,900 feet). Ski up the road for about 3 miles to Rock Creek Lake and follow the road around the left shore to the start of the summer trail (9,600 feet). This route climbs gradually up a secluded valley among widely spaced trees. Continue east around the base of the north end of the north ridge, gradually turning southeast to Kenneth Lake and finally south to Francis Lake. A

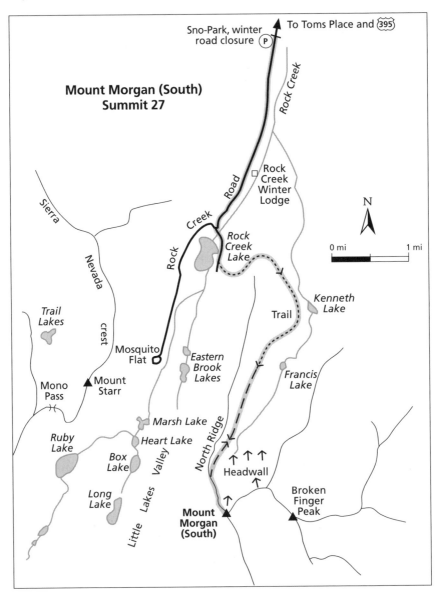

more direct route would be to slowly gain elevation as you ski around the end of the North Ridge, gaining the plateau above and to the west of Kenneth and Francis Lakes; this plateau leads directly to the large cirque above 12,000 feet and the crest of the North Ridge, which gives excellent access to the summit plateau by skirting the 1,000-foot headwall and couloirs that bisect it. Above the headwall you will emerge onto the summit plateau.

Gain the summit of Mount Morgan by continuing up the North Ridge or by traversing to the left across the summit plateau to the far ridge and a prominent notch; follow the ridge from this notch to the summit. Often the snow conditions are superior on this far side of the summit plateau, providing fine powder skiing.

From the summit you will be rewarded with excellent views of the Little Lakes Valley directly below, with Bear Creek Spire, Mount Dade and the Hourglass Couloir (Summit 26), and Mount Abbot in the near distance. A bit farther away, to the southeast, is the impressive massif of Mount Tom (Summit 28). To the north is Red Slate Mountain (Summit 25), along with hundreds of other fine backcountry peaks.

Descend the North Ridge or ski one of the numerous steep couloirs that divide the headwall. The major couloir nearest the North Ridge is about 35 degrees and drops 1,000 feet from the summit plateau to the glacial cirque below. If you plan to ski one of the couloirs, check it out carefully on your ascent. These are steep gullies, so be cautious and aware of avalanche conditions. These gullies provide excellent skiing for the advanced (Black Diamond) and expert (Double Black Diamond) skier.

MOUNT MORGAN (NORTH)

A few miles to the north, at the McGee Creek turnoff from Highway 395, Mount Morgan (North) is also a favorite of many skiers. Take the McGee Creek Road turnoff from Highway 395 (see Mammoth Lakes region map), and ski or drive for 2 miles to the pack station on McGee Creek. Leave the road just beyond the pack station near the pay phone. Cross the creek on a nearby single-plank bridge, and ascend the steep, lower slopes of Esha Canyon. (Use caution, as these slopes avalanche.) Near 11,000 and 11,200 feet you will encounter the second and third lakes below two impressive headwall cirques. At either lake, leave the canyon by skiing east up steep terrain to the summit plateau. Three peaks ring the summit plateau, with Mount Morgan (North) at the center (13,005 feet). The upper slopes of the peak are usually devoid of adequate snow, so bypass the main summit and ski to the top of the peak (12,984 feet), located 0.5 mile to the west.

Chapter 7
BISHOP REGION

This splendid backcountry region includes Evolution Valley and the Evolution Basin, popular summer backpacking areas on the John Muir Trail. This lake-filled, glacier-carved valley is a popular destination in the summer, but back-country skiers will have hundreds of square miles to themselves during the winter and spring. Evolution Basin is absolutely beautiful in the winter. In 1895, Theodore S. Solomons explored the region and named six peaks after famous evolutionists—Lamarck, Darwin, Huxley, Spencer, Wallace, and Haeckel. In 1942, the Sierra Club proposed adding a seventh name, Mendel, to the "Evolution Group."

Muir Pass (12,000 feet elevation) is the high divide between the Evolution Basin to the north (see map for Summit 33) and LeConte Canyon and the Middle Fork Kings River to the south. The John Muir Trail crosses this pass on its route from Yosemite Valley to the summit of Mount Whitney. The Muir Hut, built of natural stone from the area, sits atop Muir Pass. One of the most inaccessible parts of the Sierra Nevada is to the immediate south and west of Muir Pass. The rugged, remote Ionian Basin and the Enchanted Gorge were the last areas of the Sierra Nevada to be accurately mapped (see sidebar).

Although this region includes such intriguing destinations as Enchanted Gorge, Disappearing Creek, Black Giant, Ragged Spur, Devils Crag, Scylla, Charybdis, and the Ionian Basin, the featured attractions in this remote region are Mount Goddard and Mount Darwin, which have elevations of 13,658 and 13,831 feet, respectively. Although earlier attempts had been made, it was not until 1879 that Mount Goddard was climbed by Lil A. Winchell and Louis W. Davis. E. C. Andrews and Willard D. Johnson were the first to climb Mount Darwin in 1908. To the east of Evolution Basin and much closer to civilization are the equally impressive summits of Mount Tom, Basin Mountain, Mount Humphreys, and Mount Lamarck. With the exception of Mount Lamarck, these summits are clearly visible from the town of Bishop and Highway 395.

How to get there: All the peaks in this region can be approached from, or near, the town of Bishop on Highway 395. Pine Creek Road, about 10 miles north of Bishop, provides access to the base of Mount Tom. Road access to all the other peaks is gained from Highway 168, which intersects Highway 395 in Bishop.

The author on the exposed summit block of Mount Darwin Photo by Colin Fuller

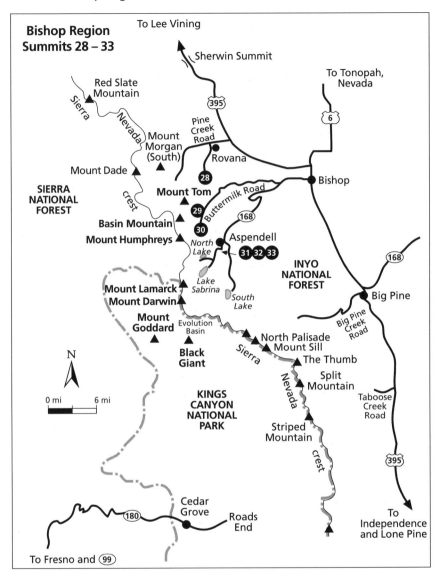

Bishop Region Summits 28 – 33

The Enchanted Gorge

We were caught in a storm while on Mt. Goddard, and were glad to camp at the highest clump of tamarack shrubbery we could find. This happened to be considerably above the big frozen lake, and ice and snow lay all about us. I have never passed a night in a higher altitude than this, nor do I care to, for we must have been nearly 13,500 feet high. We had no sooner built a fire than the snow began to fall, and though for a time it was nip and tuck between the two elements, our pitch-saturated logs conquered at last.

In the morning we climbed round the southern base of the mountain, and made our way along the divide in a blinding storm, which becoming monotonous after six or eight hours, we determined to descend a deep gorge that had captured our admiration and aroused our curiosity when on the summit of Goddard. At half-past one this gorge lay directly south of us, and in an hour we had descended to its head, which we found was guarded by a nearly frozen lake, whose sheer, ice-smoothed walls arose on either side, up and up, seemingly into the very sky, their crowns two sharp black peaks of most majestic form. A Scylla and a Charybdis they seemed to us, as we stood at the margin of the lake and wondered how we might pass the dangerous portal.

By a little careful climbing we got around the lake, and stood at the head of the gorge. Instead of the precipice we had feared to find, the narrow bottom was filled with snow, furnishing us a kind of turnpike, down which we fairly flew. Down, down, by sinuous curves, our road conducted us, as though into the bowels of the earth; for the walls, black, glinting, weird, rose a thousand and two thousand feet almost perpendicularly over our heads, and were lost in the storm-clouds that were discharging upon us a copious rain. For at least three miles we sped over the snow, when of a sudden the gorge widened into a kind of rotunda, the snow disappeared, and the stream which I expected to emerge from under it was conspicuous by its absence, nor could the roar of its subterranean flow be even faintly heard. Imagine a well a thousand feet wide and nearly twice as deep, its somewhat narrow bottom piled with fragments of rock, from the size of pebbles to that of buildings, the walls and floor of every hue that lends itself readily to a general effect of blackness, and the rotunda is pictured. Several torrents fell over the perpendicular western wall into a lake that had no visible outlet.

After an hour's struggle over the gorge floor, the roughness of which defies description, we reached the lower end of the rotunda and the beginning of another shorter stretch of snow. The walls had now taken on the metallic luster of many shades of bronze, the brilliancy of which was heightened by the polish imparted by the glacier which had formerly filled this deep gorge. The snow floor again giving place to monster rock fragments again we struggled over the uneven surface; when, without warning, below a little moraine-like embankment, out gushed a great torrent of water, which on reaching a part of the gorge so narrow that the snow yet filled it, burrowed underneath, darted out a hundred yards beyond, soon met another drift of snow under which it burrowed, as before, and in the middle of which it formed a lake with perpendicular banks of snow fully thirty feet in height, only to plunge again under the snow, this time leaving a roof so thin that my companion's feet pierced the crust, and he fell in up to his waist. With great coolness and dexterity, however, he extricated himself before I had more than grasped the situation. And so, till the fast-gathering gloom warned us to seek a camping-spot, we worked our way among the manifold wonders of that marvelous gorge. When finally we found trees on a kind of shelf, high above the stream, and wearied with our day's toil, prepared to camp, the barometer registered a drop of nearly six thousand feet from the Goddard divide.

Next day we continued the descent of the gorge to its confluence with Goddard Creek, which from Mt. Goddard we had identified as heading in a number of lakes on the southeastern base of the mountain. Five miles below the confluence of the stream draining the Enchanted Gorge, Goddard Creek empties into the main Middle Fork of the King's River, twenty miles above Tehipitee Valley, the deepest "Yosemite" in the range. We explored and photographed this Middle Fork country and the Tehipitee, securing a number of excellent negatives, and then took the Granite Basin trail to our destination, the King's River Cañon, which we reached on July 28, 1895, hungry and tattered, but in superb physical condition.

So accustomed had we become to our packs during the latter week of our trip, that it is no exaggeration to say that we had not felt the weight of the knapsacks, though when we reached our journey's end they weighed not less than twenty pounds apiece. The little expedition had been an entire success. In sixteen days we had covered fully three times as much territory as we could have hoped to explore had we traveled with a mule or burro. Yet my eyes had constantly been on the alert for passages practicable for animals; and to such good purpose had the quest been pursued that the Sierra Club will shortly place on file in its Club Rooms maps and descriptions which will enable the enterprising mountaineer to leave the Yosemite Valley with loaded animals, and to thread his way to the King's River Cañon through the very heart of the High Sierra.

—Theodore S. Solomons, from "Mount Goddard and its Vicinity" (reprinted in *Treasury of the Sierra Nevada,* edited by Robert Leonard Reid)

 Mount Tom ⋆

Height: 13,652 feet
Route: Elderberry Canyon
Best time to go: March through early May
Trip duration: 1 long, strenuous day
Mileage: About 5 miles to the summit
Elevation gain: 7,352 feet
Effort factor: 9.9
Level of difficulty: The gullies in the headwall, expert (Double Black Diamond); from the North Ridge to the amphitheater, advanced (Black Diamond)
Snowboards: Recommended; the descent is long and continuous
Maps: Mount Tom, Mount Morgan, Rovana

Mount Tom is one of the premier ski and snowboard descents in the Sierra Nevada. It also happens to be one of the longest descents in the state, nearly 6,000 feet from the North Ridge (12,240 feet) to the road at the bottom of Elderberry Canyon (6,300 feet).

Mount Tom and Elderberry Canyon at sunrise. The 6,000-foot descent of Elderberry Canyon is hard to beat on skis or snowboard. Photo by John Moynier

From Bishop, proceed north 10 miles on Highway 395. Turn left onto Pine Creek Road and drive to the town of Rovana. From Rovana, head southwest on first a paved road, then a dirt road to the base of Elderberry Canyon. The road is passable in a car, although you may have an occasional clearance problem and may have to park about 0.5 mile short of the end of the road.

From the entrance of Elderberry Canyon, climb up snow or follow an old mining trail as it switchbacks up the canyon to Lambert Mine (10,800+ feet). An alternate approach is to cross the bottom of Elderberry Canyon and follow an abandoned jeep road as it switchbacks up the face of the mountain to the far left (south) of the canyon. Follow this road to where it seems to fade and disappear, then traverse right over a slight ridge, near 8,200 feet, into Elderberry Canyon.

The ascent up Elderberry Canyon follows a series of steps until you arrive at the large amphitheater near 10,900 feet, which lies in the large cirque at the base of the north headwall of Mount Tom. As you approach the Mount Tom headwall, continue your ascent by turning to the right (west) up a steep ramp to the North Ridge. From here, it is about a mile to the summit on moderate terrain. There may be inadequate snow on the ridge to ski. As you continue up the ridge, numerous gullies descend the face of the headwall.

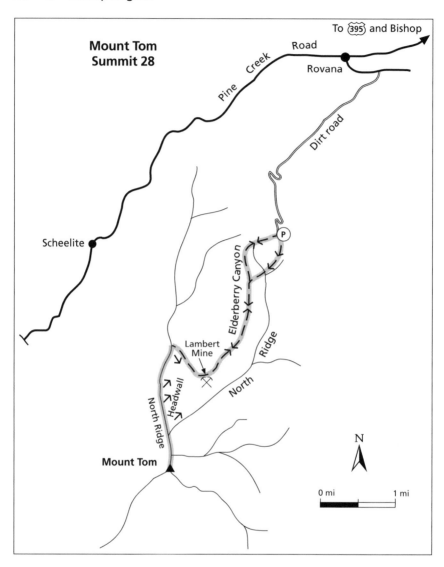

The skiing on the face of the headwall is expert (Double Black Diamond). The descent down the steep ramp to the amphitheater is advanced (Black Diamond), and the terrain in and below the amphitheater is a challenging intermediate.

It is critical to get an early start, as the spring snow is at its best normally in late morning; after 1:00 P.M., you'll find soft snow and less-than-ideal conditions. Since the elevation gain is so great, a partial ascent the night before with a light sleeping bag and a few bites for breakfast and lunch may be necessary for a timely descent.

Basin Mountain

Height: 13,181 feet
Route: Basin Couloir
Best time to go: March through early May
Trip duration: 1 day
Mileage: About 2 miles to the summit
Elevation gain: 4,800+ feet
Effort factor: 5.8
Level of difficulty: Advanced (Black Diamond)
Snowboards: Recommended
Maps: Mount Tom, Tungsten Hills

Like Mount Tom only 3 air miles to the north, Basin Mountain is one of the premier ski descents in the area. The peaks are similar in a number of ways: both have striking couloirs plainly visible from Highway 395; both couloirs face northeast, ensuring superior snow conditions late into the ski season; and both are popular, being two of the longer descents in the Sierra Nevada with excellent skiing.

From Bishop, proceed west on Highway 168 (West Line Street). In about 7.5 miles and just past the 7,000-foot marker, turn right onto Buttermilk Road. There are many side roads off Buttermilk Road, but keep to the most heavily used road. In about 6.1 miles, around 7,500 feet, turn right toward the trailhead for the Horton Lakes (road not signed) and proceed 0.6 mile and park; or, if you have a four-wheel-drive vehicle, continue another 0.3 mile to the gate and the Horton Lakes trailhead (8,000 feet).

Basin Couloir lies in the shadow of the morning sun. Skiers ascend to the top of the couloir (left of the summit) and drop their boards or skis to climb to the top of Basin Mountain. Photo by John Moynier

The ascent route is obvious. From the summer hiking trail/mining road, climb the gully that heads to the small notch to the left of the summit, or continue up the trail/road a short distance until you can turn up an old mining road as it switches back and forth up the slope to an abandoned mine near 10,800 feet. Continue up the Basin Couloir (northeast couloir) to the notch (about 12,800+ feet) between the main summit and the subpeak to the south. Drop your skis or snowboard and make the short scramble to the summit. Great views of Mount Tom, Mount Humphreys, the White Mountains, and the surrounding terrain are well worth the slight additional effort of climbing to the summit.

Again, as with Mount Tom, the timing of your descent is critical. If you are skiing in the spring, plan to descend no later than 1:00 P.M., as later in the afternoon the snow normally becomes too soft for ideal skiing.

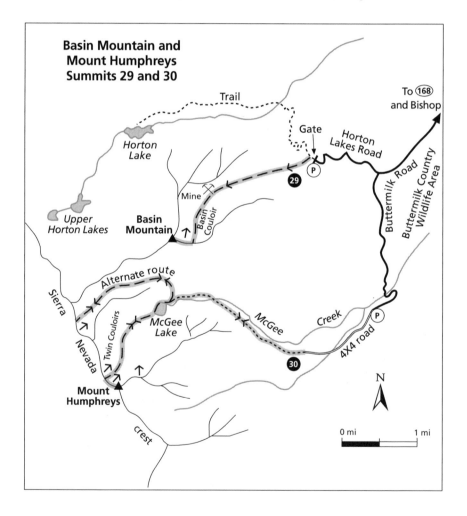

Mount Humphreys ★

Height: 13,986 feet

Route: Humphreys Couloirs

Best time to go: March through May

Trip duration: 1 or 2 days

Mileage: 5 miles to the summit

Elevation gain: 5,586 feet from the 8,400-foot level

Effort factor: 8.1

Level of difficulty: Expert (Double Black Diamond) above the bergschrund, intermediate below

Snowboards: Recommended; the short approach and a steep couloir make for good snowboarding

Maps: Mount Tom, Tungsten Hills

Like the nearby summits of Mount Tom and Basin Mountain, Mount Humphreys is easily visible from Bishop, and the view of Humphreys' twin couloirs on the peak's north face is indeed impressive. From afar, these couloirs appear much too steep to ski but, surprisingly, do not exceed 40 degrees. The couloirs are snow/ice climbing routes in the summer and fall, and provide excellent expert ski and snowboard terrain in the winter and spring.

From Bishop, proceed west on Highway 168 (West Line Street). In about 7.5 miles and just past the 7,000-foot marker, turn right onto Buttermilk Road. There are many side roads, but keep to the most heavily used road. In about 6.4 miles cross a cattle guard and the boundary of the Buttermilk Country Wildlife Area. From here the road deteriorates but continues to be passable by car. Cross McGee Creek in another 1.5 miles and pass Dutch Jones Meadow Road (7S01) in another 0.6 mile (8,200 feet). In 0.2 mile there are several good places to park near the 8,400-foot level; if you have a four-wheel-drive vehicle, continue another mile to the end of the road.

Mount Humphreys with its two couloirs ascending to the right. The prominent Humphreys Couloirs can be seen from Bishop.

From the 8,400-foot level, hike or ski up the road to its end, then follow the route of the summer trail up gentle slopes along the south side of McGee Creek. Initially, the trail and the best winter route stay a good distance south of the creek. Near 9,600 feet the trail crosses to the north side of the stream. Continue to McGee Lake (10,700 feet). The flat area just below the small dam of McGee Lake makes for a sheltered place to camp, with excellent views of Mount Humphreys' twin couloirs.

From your base camp below McGee Lake, consider taking a side tour up the couloir immediately to the north. This exploratory tour will take you to the crest of the Sierra Nevada near 12,800 feet, with great views of the Humphreys Basin and Desolation Lake to the west. This hidden valley contains some exceptional intermediate and advanced skiing in large, open bowls.

For the ascent of the Humphreys Couloirs, ski across McGee Lake and climb to the glacier on the north face of Mount Humphreys. The glacier steepens around 12,400 feet as you approach the couloir. A bergschrund (a giant crevasse formed at the glacier's upper limit) blocks the entrance to the couloir but can be passed on either the left or right. Partway up, the main couloir forks; the left couloir is a bit steeper and narrower than the right fork, but both lead to the summit ridge. The climb is long and continuous, with the slope approaching 40 degrees. You may need a short rope for the rock scramble to the summit, as an exposed Class 4 move is required; with plastic ski boots, this might feel a bit cumbersome.

Enjoy the superb 3,000-foot ski or snowboard descent back to McGee Lake. There is an additional 2,400 feet of elevation loss over easy terrain back to the car. If you get an early start in the morning, you can complete the trip in one long, strenuous day.

31
Mount Lamarck

Height: 13,417 feet

Route: Lamarck Col

Best time to go: January through early May

Trip duration: 1 day

Mileage: 7 miles to the summit (from Aspendell)

Elevation gain: 4,917 feet (from Aspendell)

Effort factor: 8.4 (from Aspendell)

Level of difficulty: Intermediate

Snowboards: Recommended

Maps: Mount Thompson, Mount Darwin

This has been a popular summit for many years. The intermediate terrain is ideal for a large number of skiers, and under spring conditions the skiing can

The view, from near North Lake, of the route to Lamarck Col (center) and Mount Lamarck (right). This ski/snowboard descent has been a favorite for many years.

be incredible as you blast down the mountain at full speed and, hopefully, in complete control.

From Bishop on Highway 395, drive southwest on Highway 168 (Lake Sabrina Road) to Aspendell (8,500 feet); or, when the road is plowed in late spring, continue to the North Lake Road turnoff (9,000 feet). Ski or hike up the road to North Lake and to the campground at the end of the road. From here cross the creek and follow the route of the summer trail past Grass Lake. Do not follow the route of the trail to Lower or Upper Lamarck Lakes, but rather follow the stream that drains into the south end of Grass Lake, well to the east of Lower Lamarck Lake, as it ascends toward Lamarck Col and Mount Lamarck. From Grass Lake, at an elevation just under 10,000 feet, it is a 3,500-foot climb over about 4 miles to the top of the peak. The climb is continuous but gradual.

There seems to be some dispute over the location of the actual summit of Mount Lamarck and the placement of the summit register. The map clearly indicates that the summit is the first major high point about a quarter mile northwest of Lamarck Col. However, once you gain this summit it is obvious that there is a slightly higher peak another quarter mile to the northwest. Over the years the summit register has been moved back and forth between these two summits.

From the summit, the near views of Mendel Couloir, the Darwin Glacier, and Mount Darwin are impressive, and there are farther views of Black Giant, Mount Goddard (Summit 33), and the hundreds of peaks and valleys in the Evolution Basin and the Enchanted Gorge area.

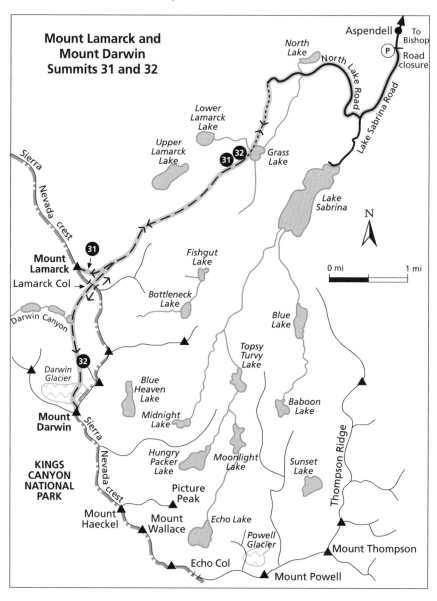

Mount Lamarck and
Mount Darwin
Summits 31 and 32

Lamarck Col is due south of Lamarck's summit and provides access to Mount Darwin (see Summit 32 for route description). From Lamarck Col it is a 1,200-foot descent to the Darwin Lakes and 2 miles to Mount Darwin.

The descent from Mount Lamarck back to the car is one of the better intermediate runs in the Sierra Nevada. Open, gentle bowls allow the skier to descend quickly to Grass Lake and on to North Lake Road.

Mount Darwin  ⋆

Height: 13,831 feet
Route: Darwin Glacier
Best time to go: March through May
Trip duration: 2 to 3 days
Mileage: 9 miles (from Aspendell)
Elevation gain: 6,917 feet (from Aspendell)
Effort factor: 11.4 (from Aspendell)
Level of difficulty: Expert (Double Black Diamond)
Snowboards: A long approach with a 1,200-foot drop over Lamarck Col to the base of Mount Darwin; once there, the climb and descent of Darwin Glacier are superb
Maps: Mount Thompson, Mount Darwin

This trip description assumes that you have reached Lamarck Col by following the route detailed in the writeup for Mount Lamarck (Summit 31). From North Lake, ascend to the top of Lamarck Col and ski down the west side, dropping about 1,200 feet to the upper Darwin Canyon Lake. This makes an excellent base camp for your ascent and descent of Darwin Glacier.

Mount Darwin from Lamarck Col. The skis frame the Darwin Glacier and the route to the summit. Just below the corniced summit plateau, the route ascends the small snow finger angling left to the summit skyline.

There is no more inspiring sight in the Sierra Nevada than the view of Mendel Couloir and the Darwin Glacier as you crest Lamarck Col. From this vantage point, the upper slopes of the Darwin Glacier appear much too steep to ski. Don't be intimidated; due to foreshortening, the route appears to be much steeper than it really is.

As you view the north face of Mount Darwin, two prominent rock ribs divide Darwin Glacier; your route is to the left (east) of the left rib. The main part of the glacier extends to about 13,600 feet, with a small snow finger that passes under a large cornice, reaching the summit plateau. Follow this snow finger as it ascends the upper 200 feet to the summit plateau (13,800 feet). To climb the actual summit block, hike across the plateau, descend about 100 feet, and climb up a steep gully, approaching the summit from the east.

The views from the summit of Mount Darwin are striking, especially those of the ski descent routes of Mount Goddard and Black Giant (Summit 33), a short distance to the south. There are also great views of the Evolution Basin, the Ionian Basin, the Palisades, and hundreds of peaks in all directions.

The skiing on Darwin Glacier is simply superb. Even late in the spring, I have enjoyed excellent skiing on 12 to 16 inches of light, dry powder. Be cautious of avalanches, as avalanche debris has been observed on this route. At the top, in the narrow snow finger, the descent approaches 45 degrees for about 200 feet; it widens as you descend to the main glacier, and the slopes become more forgiving, lessening to 30–35 degrees.

The descent of Mount Darwin is one of my favorites, providing two great runs in one trip. The descent of the Darwin Glacier is rewarding enough, but this trip comes with the added bonus of a wonderful ski descent from Lamarck Col (Summit 31) back to North Lake Road.

33
Mount Goddard ⋆

Height: 13,568 feet
Route: North Ridge
Best Time to go: March through mid-May
Trip duration: 5 days or more
Mileage: About 16 miles to the summit (from Aspendell)
Elevation gain: About 7,000 feet (from Aspendell)
Effort factor: 15.0 (from Aspendell)
Level of difficulty: From the summit, advanced (Black Diamond)
Snowboards: Not recommended due the extremely long approach
Maps: Mount Goddard, Mount Darwin, Mount Thompson

This trip is truly a wilderness classic, traversing some of the finest, most rugged backcountry ski terrain found anywhere. The approach to Mount Goddard

Skiing across the upper lake to begin the climb of Mount Goddard

takes the adventuresome backcountry skier over Echo Col, Muir Pass, and through the unique wilderness of the Ionian Basin, territory seldom visited even in the summer. This trip has so many possibilities that weeks could be spent exploring the many summits, lake basins, and glacial cirques in the area. A descent of Black Giant is a highlight of this trip.

It wasn't until the 1890s that Theodore S. Solomons explored the Ionian Basin and the Enchanted Gorge and climbed Mount Goddard (see sidebar). Even today, the Enchanted Gorge is considered by many to be the most inaccessible section of the Sierra Nevada.

To reach the trailhead, drive to the town of Bishop on Highway 395. Proceed west on Highway 168 toward Lake Sabrina for about 16.5 miles to Aspendell. The road is not plowed beyond this point in the winter and early spring. Park at the gate (8,500 feet).

You can complete Mount Goddard as a simple up-and-back tour, returning via your approach route from Lake Sabrina. However, by adding a day or two to the overall length of the trip, you can make a wonderful loop through the Evolution Basin, over Alpine Col, and out Piute Pass, returning to Aspendell via North Lake Road.

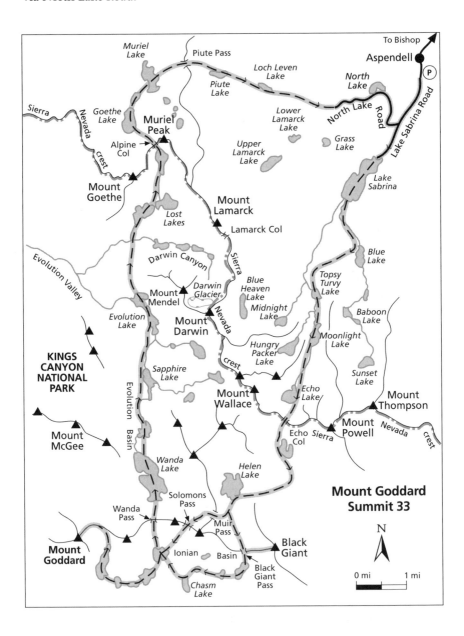

Mount Goddard
Summit 33

Begin by skiing 2 miles up the road from Aspendell (8,500 feet) to Lake Sabrina (9,128 feet). In the winter it is possible to ski across the lake, but if conditions are unsafe, ski around the left shore of the lake to the upper end. Follow the creek to Blue Lake (10,398), a steep but short climb. From Blue Lake, do not ascend the creek that flows into the lake but rather traverse to your right (west) and into the Middle Fork of Bishop Creek, past the Emerald Lakes, above Dingleberry Lake, and on to Topsy Turvy Lake and Moonlight Lake. The prominent face of Picture Peak dominates the view as you ski up this beautiful valley.

Moonlight Lake is an excellent place to camp and provides a marvelous base camp for explorations of Powell Glacier and the large cirque to the northwest of Echo Lake, rimmed by Mount Wallace, Mount Haeckel, and Picture Peak. The cirque and the slopes of Mount Wallace and Mount Haeckel contain many skiing possibilities.

The route steepens as you approach Echo Col. Use caution, as the steep slopes below the col are prone to avalanche after a fresh snowfall.

From the col, descend to the lake directly to the south. Ascend a small pass and descend to the John Muir Trail near 11,200 feet. Ski up to Helen Lake (11,617 feet) and the lake basin west and south of Muir Pass to the base of Black Giant. If you plan to ski Black Giant, camp below the peak in this lake basin, or ski over Black Giant Pass to the unnamed lake at 11,828 feet and camp. Alternatively, ski to Muir Pass and Muir Pass Hut and cross into the Ionian Basin via Solomons Pass (the notch at 12,400+ feet), west of Mount Solomons, and down to the lake at 11,592 feet.

The ascent to the summit of Black Giant is not difficult and provides an exhilarating descent. Ski from the top, either by descending the south ridge and slopes back to the lake at 11,828 feet or the north ridge and slopes to Black Giant Pass.

The ski through the Ionian Basin, as you snake your way through this chain of splendid lakes, is bound to be a rewarding and memorable experience. Chasm Lake (11,000 feet), at the head of the Enchanted Gorge, is appropriately named, as it is sandwiched between the rock faces of Scylla and Charybdis. Ski north and up to the lake at 11,592 feet and gradually up past two unnamed lakes at 11,824 feet and 11,951 feet, respectively, at the base of Mount Goddard.

Mount Goddard's slopes are clearly visible from this third lake. For an ascent of the peak, ski to the upper end of the lake and ski north and west to the summit at 13,568 feet. The slope steepens considerably near the top; there is normally a small cornice on the summit. Enjoy the wonderful descent.

Return by retracing your tracks through the string of lakes in the Ionian Basin. From the large, unnamed lake (11,592 feet) southwest of Solomons Pass, ascend over that pass or Wanda Pass (12,400 feet) and down into the Evolution Basin, past Wanda Lake, Sapphire Lake, and Evolution Lake. This route takes you through the heart of the Evolution region and past peaks, lakes, and glacial basins too numerous to mention. From Evolution Lake (10,852 feet), traverse around the Mount Mendel massif to Darwin Bench, past Darwin Canyon, and up to the three large lakes below Muriel Peak and Alpine Col. Ski over the col and down to Goethe Lake, Muriel Lake, and over Piute Pass to North Lake and the car at Aspendell.

Chapter 8
PALISADES REGION

Rugged peaks, high meadows, and numerous glaciers combine to make the Palisades the most alpine region of the Sierra Nevada. Five summits—Thunderbolt Peak, North Palisade, Mount Sill, Middle Palisade, and Split Mountain (formerly South Palisade)—exceed 14,000 feet, and many others approach that height. Most of the peaks in this region are exceptionally steep on all sides, with no "easy" ski ascent or descent routes. The summits in this region are some of the finest in the Sierra Nevada.

Thunderbolt Peak, North Palisade, and Mount Sill are highly coveted by mountaineers. Thunderbolt's summit pinnacle requires Class 5.9 climbing, with room for only one climber on the top at any one time. Mount Sill is the most massive peak in the area; its Swiss Arête is a classic rock climb. At 14,242 feet, North Palisade is the fourth highest peak in California and the primary goal of climbers in this region. It is striking from a distance, and all routes to the summit require considerable mountaineering skills on rock, snow, and ice. From the east, the U-Notch and V-Notch couloirs become challenging ice climbs in the fall, as the winter snow goes through many melt and freeze cycles before hardening to ice.

The V-Notch (left) and U-Notch (right) Couloirs as seen from the Palisades Glacier

The Palisades region contains the largest concentration of glaciers in the Sierra Nevada. The Palisade Glacier, in the glacial cirque formed by vertical abutments of Thunderbolt Peak, North Palisade, Mount Sill, and Mount Gayley, is the largest glacier in the Sierra Nevada. The twenty-plus glaciers in this region are fed by steep ice-and-snow couloirs originating near the summits of the high peaks. Summer and winter climbing in this region require advanced climbing skills.

In the winter and spring, some of these steep couloirs make for excellent ski and snowboard descent routes. Due to the ruggedness of the region, it is

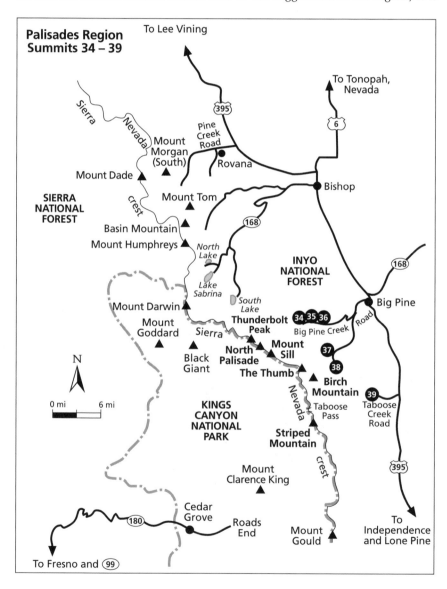

not feasible to ski from the summits of North Palisade, Thunderbolt Peak, or Mount Sill when approaching from the east (Summit 35). Although the ski and snowboard descents start several hundred feet below their summits, these peaks are included in the guide as they provide exceptional skiing and snowboarding opportunities in an outstanding setting.

How to get there: This region stretches to the west of Highway 395 from the town of Big Pine in the north to Independence in the south, a distance of about 30 miles. Big Pine is located 15 miles south of Bishop. Trailheads are accessed from the east. From Highway 395, Glacier Lodge Road (Big Pine Creek Road) out of Big Pine provides access to Mount Sill, North Palisade, and Thunderbolt Peak. Follow this same road and take the fork to McMurry Meadows for the approach to The Thumb and Birch Mountain. Access to the trailhead for Striped Mountain and Cardinal Mountain is up Taboose Creek Road, which intersects Highway 395 about 12 miles south of Big Pine.

A Windstorm in the Forests

High winds are always a concern of backcountry skiers, as they can dampen an otherwise wonderful tour. John Muir describes his now-famous adventure of climbing a 100-foot-tall Douglas Fir to experience first-hand the force and beauty of a fierce Sierra windstorm. This article is particularly pertinent for the backcountry skier, as the wind is no friend of ours. John Muir's thoughts provide a whole new perspective on the subject of the often-cursed and always despised wind.

The mountain winds, like the dew and rain, sunshine and snow, are measured and bestowed with love on the forests to develop their strength and beauty. However restricted the scope of other forest influences, that of the winds is universal. The snow bends and trims the upper forests every winter, the lightning strikes a single tree here and there, while avalanches mow down thousands at a swoop as a gardener trims out a bed of flowers. But the winds go to every tree, fingering every leaf and branch and furrowed bole; not one is forgotten; the winds blessing the forests, the forests the winds, with ineffable beauty and harmony as the sure result.

One of the most beautiful and exhilarating storms I ever enjoyed in the Sierra occurred in December, 1874. The sky and the ground and the trees had been thoroughly rain-washed and were dry again. The day was intensely pure, one of those incomparable bits of California winter, warm and balmy and full of white sparkling sunshine, redolent of all the purest influences of the spring, and at the same time enlivened with one of the most bracing wind-storms conceivable. Instead of camping out, as I usually do, I then chanced to be stopping at the house of a friend. But when the storm began to sound, I lost no time in pushing out into the woods to enjoy it. For on such occasions Nature has always something rare to show us, and the danger to life and limb is hardly greater than one would experience crouching deprecatingly beneath a roof.

It was still early morning when I found myself fairly adrift. Delicious sunshine came pouring over the hills, lighting the tops of the pines, and setting free a steam of summery fragrance that contrasted strangely with the wild tones of the storm. The air was mottled with pine-tassels and bright green plumes, that went flashing past in the sunlight like birds pursued. I heard trees falling for hours at the rate of one every two or three minutes; some uprooted, partly on account of the loose, water-soaked condition of the ground; others broken straight across, where some weakness caused by fire had determined the spot. The Silver Pines were now the most impressively beautiful of all. Colossal spires 200 feet in height waved like supple goldenrods chanting and bowing low as if in worship, while the whole mass of their long, tremulous foliage was kindled into one continuous blaze of white sun-fire. The force of the gale was such that the most steadfast monarch of them all rocked down to its roots with a motion plainly perceptible when one leaned against it. Nature was holding high festival, and every fiber of the most rigid giants thrilled with glad excitement. . . .

Toward midday, after a long, tingling scramble through copses of hazel and ceanothus, I gained the summit of the highest ridge in the neighborhood; and then it occurred to me that it would be a fine thing to climb one of the trees to obtain a wider outlook and get my ear close to the Æolian music of its topmost needles. But under the circumstances the choice of a tree was a serious matter. One whose instep was not very strong seemed in danger of being blown down, or of being struck by others in case they should fall; another was branchless to a considerable height above the ground, and at the same time too large to be grasped with arms and legs in climbing; while others were not favorably situated for clear views. After cautiously casting about, I made choice of the tallest of a group of Douglas Spruces that were growing close together like a tuft of grass, no one of which seemed likely to fall unless all the rest fell with it. Though comparatively young, they were about 100 feet high, and their lithe, brushy tops were rocking and swirling in wild ecstasy. Being accustomed to climb trees in making botanical studies, I experienced no difficulty in reaching the top of this one, and never before did I enjoy so noble an exhilaration of motion. The slender tops fairly flapped and swished in the passionate torrent, bending and swirling backward and forward, round and round, tracing indescribable combinations of vertical and horizontal curves, while I clung with muscles firm braced, like a bobo-link on a reed.

In its widest sweeps my tree-top described an arc of from twenty to thirty degrees, but I felt sure of its elastic temper, having seen others of the same species still more severely tried—bent almost to the ground indeed, in heavy snows—without breaking a fiber. I was therefore safe, and free to take the wind into my pulses and enjoy the excited forest from my superb outlook. The view from here must be extremely beautiful in any weather. Now my eye roved over the piny hills and dales as over fields of waving grain, and felt the light running in ripples and broad swelling undulations across the valleys from ridge to ridge, as the shining foliage was stirred by corresponding waves of air. Oftentimes these waves of reflected light would break up suddenly into a kind of beaten foam, and again, after chasing one another in regular order, they would seem to bend forward in concentric curves, and disappear on some hillside, like sea-waves on a shelving shore. The quantity of light reflected from the bent needles was so great as to make whole groves appear as if covered with snow, while the black shadows beneath the trees greatly enhanced the effect of the silvery splendor. . . .

I kept my lofty perch for hours, frequently closing my eyes to enjoy the music by itself, or to feast quietly on the delicious fragrance that was streaming past. . . . Most people like to look at mountain rivers, and bear them in mind; but few care to look at the winds, though far more beautiful and sublime, and though they become at times about as visible as flowing water. When the north winds in winter are making upward sweeps over the curving summits of the High Sierra, the fact is sometimes published with flying snow-banners a mile long. Those portions of the winds thus embodied can scarce be wholly invisible, even to the darkest imagination. And when we look around over an agitated forest, we may see something of the wind that stirs it, by its effects upon the trees. Yonder it descends in a rush of water-like ripples, and sweeps over the bending pines from hill to hill. Nearer, we see detached plumes and leaves, now speeding by on level currents, now whirling in eddies, or, escaping over the edges of the whirls, soaring aloft on grand, upswelling domes of air, or tossing on flame-like crests. Smooth, deep currents, cascades, falls, and swirling eddies, sing around every tree and leaf, and over all the varied topography of the region with telling changes of form, like mountain rivers conforming to the features of their channels.

After tracing the Sierra streams from their fountains to the plains, marking where they bloom white in falls, glide in crystal plumes, surge gray and foam-filled in boulder-choked gorges, and slip through the woods in long, tranquil reaches—after thus learning their language and forms in detail, we may at length hear them chanting all together in one grand anthem, and comprehend them all in clear inner vision, covering the range like lace. But even this spectacle is far less sublime and not a whit more substantial than what we may behold of these storm-streams of air in the mountain woods. . . .

When the storm began to abate, I dismounted and sauntered down through the calming woods. The storm-tones died away, and, turning toward the east, I beheld the countless hosts of the forests hushed and tranquil, towering above one another on the slopes of the hills like a devout audience. The setting sun filled them with amber light, and seemed to say, while they listened, "My peace I give unto you." As I gazed on the impressive scene, all the so called ruin of the storm was forgotten, and never before did these noble woods appear so fresh, so joyous, so immortal.

—John Muir, *The Mountains of California*

North Palisade ★

Height: 14,242 feet

Route: U-Notch

Best time to go: March through May

Trip duration: 3 or more days

Mileage: About 7 miles to the summit

Elevation gain: 6,200 feet

Effort factor: 9.7

Level of difficulty: U-Notch, expert (Double Black Diamond); below the bergschrund, strong intermediate; V-Notch, extreme; North Couloir Thunderbolt Peak, expert (Double Black Diamond)

Snowboards: Recommended, as the terrain and boarding are superior; however, there is a long approach

Maps: Coyote Flat, Mount Thompson, North Palisade

North Palisade is one of the classic peaks of the Sierra Nevada, and the fourth highest peak in California. All routes to the summit require advanced mountaineering skills on rock, snow, and ice. The U-Notch and V-Notch couloirs become serious, roped ice climbs in the autumn.

From Highway 395 proceed to the town of Big Pine (15 miles south of Bishop). Turn west on Big Pine Creek Road and continue to Glacier Lodge at the end of the road (7,800 feet). In the winter and early spring before Glacier Lodge is open, park your car near the lodge. If you can find a caretaker, ask

The impressive Palisade Glacier amphitheater, as seen from the air. On the left is Mount Sill, and to the right of center is North Palisade. The U-Notch Couloir is in the center, and the V-Notch Couloir is to its left. Thunderbolt Peak can be seen on the right. Photo by Colin Fuller.

permission. Or, park in the trailhead parking lot a short distance down the road from the lodge.

Follow the North Fork Big Pine Creek Trail past First, Second, and Third Lakes. Near 10,400 feet leave the main trail and cross the creek that flows out of Fifth Lake. Depending on the time of year and the amount of snow accumulation during the winter, you may end up carrying your skis to around 10,400 feet before there is adequate snow to start skiing.

After crossing the creek, follow the drainage south to Sam Mack Meadow, near 11,000 feet. Continue up the gully past the small lake south of Sam Mack Lake, near the 11,700-foot level. Stay to the left of the lake and up the left gully that emerges onto the moraine dividing the Palisade and Thunderbolt Glaciers. A base camp here provides excellent views of the surrounding summits. Equally important, it provides convenient access to the Palisade Glacier (Mount Sill and North Palisade), the Thunderbolt Glacier (Thunderbolt Peak and Mount Winchell), and the glaciers north of Mount Winchell and Mount Agassiz. It would be easy to spend a week or more at this base camp exploring the various glaciers and snow-filled couloirs.

As you approach the Palisade Glacier cirque from Sam Mack Meadow, two prominent snow-filled couloirs are unmistakable. The imposing headwall of the Palisade Glacier cirque is bisected by the V-Notch (on the left) and the U-Notch (to the right) and their corresponding snow-and-ice-filled couloirs. Although both have been skied, the V-Notch (extreme) is considerably more difficult than the U-Notch (expert).

For the ascent of the U-Notch, ski up the Palisade Glacier to the bergschrund (a large crevasse at the upper limit of the glacier, between the glacier and the surrounding snowfield or rock face). Just below the 'schrund, the slope steepens. Take off the skis and replace them with your crampons and ice axe. Cross the 'schrund and climb to the top of the U-Notch; the 'schrund is usually passable to the far right side. The ski descent is a serious endeavor (up to 40 degrees), as a single fall could send you down the slope to the bergschrund below.

The twin couloir to the east of the U-Notch is the V-Notch. This, too, has a 'schrund at its base, and the couloir approaches 50 degrees. During the fall season the snow turns to ice, and this becomes an exceptional ice climb, although occasional rockfall detracts from the climb. The ski descent is difficult and is rated extreme. Due to the steepness, it may be impossible to arrest a fall. The bergschrund below adds additional danger to the descent.

The North Couloir of Thunderbolt Peak, another exceptional descent, is easily reached from your base camp. From base camp, ski up the Thunderbolt Glacier toward the Thunderbolt-Winchell Col. Three steep couloirs bisect the steep north wall of Thunderbolt Peak. The first narrow couloir, west of the prow of the northeast buttress, is the Northeast Couloir. The second and widest couloir of the three is the North Couloir. As was the case for both the V-Notch and the U-Notch, the North Couloir is guarded by a bergschrund. Cross the 'schrund and climb the large, Y-shaped, 35-plus-degree, 1,000-foot snow-and-ice couloir. Use caution and check the conditions carefully. This couloir avalanches regularly and may contain avalanche debris. The North Couloir is rated expert (Double Black Diamond).

To ski out, retrace your ascent route. Alternatively, consider skiing the gully in the northwest shadow of Temple Crag; it may provide a longer ski descent, as the snow remains longer in this sheltered gully. (Inspect this potential descent route on your way in to base camp.)

Whether or not you climb and ski/board the U-Notch or any of the other steep chutes in the Palisade Amphitheater, skiing the Palisade, Winchell, and Agassiz Glaciers is an exquisite adventure that will be long remembered.

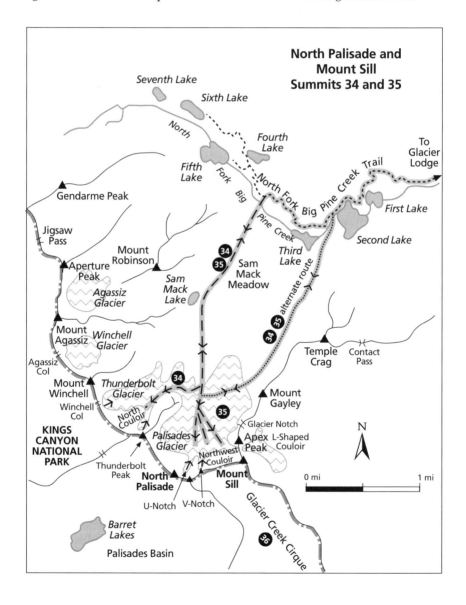

Mount Sill, Northwest Couloir and L-Shaped Couloir

Height: 14,153 feet

Route: Northwest Couloir, L-Shaped Couloir

Best time to go: March through May

Trip duration: 3 or more days

Mileage: About 7 miles to the summit

Elevation gain: 6,200 feet

Effort factor: 9.7

Level of difficulty: From the top of Northwest Couloir, advanced (Black Diamond); below bergschrund, intermediate; L-Shaped Couloir, advanced (Black Diamond)

Snowboards: Recommended, as the boarding and scenery are superb; however, the approach is long

Maps: Coyote Flat, Mount Thompson, North Palisade

Mount Sill is the most massive peak in the area, with one of the best views in the entire Sierra Nevada. Its profile is striking and dominates the skyline. The two ski/snowboard descents described here are also popular climbing routes in the summer and fall.

Follow the same ascent route as described in the North Palisade trip (Summit 34). A base camp on the moraine between the Thunderbolt and Palisade Glaciers is an ideal location from which to explore the entire area; from here it is a short tour to the glacier-filled cirques below Mount Agassiz, Mount Winchell, Thunderbolt Peak, North Palisade, and Mount Sill.

To climb Mount Sill's Northwest Couloir, ski across the Palisade Glacier to the bergschrund at the base of the couloir. The Northwest Couloir approaches 35 degrees and is the snow-filled couloir leading to the notch between Mount Sill and the subpeak to the north known as Apex Peak (13,800 feet). Ascend the couloir either on skis or with crampons.

From here, there is an excellent descent to the east down the L-Shaped Couloir to Elinore Lake, nearly 3,000 feet below. Ski down the broad couloir as far as you desire. At any point in your descent, turn around and ascend to the notch for a return ski down the Northwest Couloir. An alternate route, which avoids the climb back up to the notch between Apex Peak and Mount Sill, is to ski to Glacier Notch (between Mount Gayley and Mount Sill, near 13,100 feet) and descend to the Palisade Glacier. The notch is not the obvious low point in the ridge but rather is located near the base of the north ridge of Apex Peak.

The Northwest Couloir is an excellent ski descent. Be careful of underlying ice in the gully. Ski down the couloir and across the Palisade Glacier back to camp.

The Thunderbolt/North Palisade/Mount Sill Amphitheater contains some of the best mountaineering and ski/snowboard terrain in California. The area is worth visiting any time of the year.

The Northwest Couloir of Mount Sill from near the top of the U-Notch on North Palisade. Apex Peak is on the left. The 'shrunds are starting to open even in early May.

Mount Sill, Glacier Creek Cirque ⋆

Height: 14,153 feet
Route: Glacier Creek Cirque
Best time to go: March through early May
Trip duration: 5 days or more
Mileage: About 16 miles to the summit
Elevation gain: About 9,300 feet
Level of difficulty: Strong intermediate
Snowboards: Not recommended, as there are too many miles on the circumnavigation of the Palisades
Effort factor: 17.3
Maps: Coyote Flat, Mount Thompson, North Palisade

The circumnavigation of the Palisades is a arduous ski mountaineering mini-expedition through some of the most rugged alpine terrain in the Sierra Nevada. From the east, the Palisades form an impregnable wall with few routes to the west. The cols in this area are challenging rock and snow climbs. There is no easy way to get to Glacier Creek Cirque, which is located to the west of the Sierra Nevada crest.

From Highway 395 proceed to the town of Big Pine (15 miles south of Bishop). Turn west onto Big Pine Creek Road and continue to Glacier Lodge at the end of the road (7,800 feet). This trip starts and ends at Glacier Lodge, so a car shuttle is not necessary. Park at the lodge or at the trailhead parking lot near the end of Big Pine Creek Road (see the North Palisade trip, Summit 34). An alternate starting point would be South Lake Road out of Bishop, off Highway 168, with a ski approach by way of South Lake and Bishop Pass. This would require a car shuttle and would not reduce the mileage, unless you made the trip late in the season after the road had been plowed to South Lake.

Follow the North Fork Big Pine Creek Trail past First, Second, and Third Lakes, and continue on to Fifth Lake. From here turn west up the glacial valley toward Jigsaw Pass; this valley makes for a great ski descent. Continue up to Jigsaw Pass, around 12,720 feet. The pass is not the obvious low point in the ridge (which ends in a steep couloir and difficult climbing below), but rather is a short distance to the south and about 100 feet higher in elevation. Locate the pass and climb down easy terrain to skiable slopes below. Continue your descent to Bishop Pass (12,000 feet). You have just completed the crux of the trip.

From Bishop Pass ski past the large, unnamed lake to the east of the pass, traversing under Mount Agassiz and Mount Winchell toward 12,400-foot Thunderbolt Pass. The high wilderness ski traverse from Bishop Pass over Thunderbolt Pass, Potluck Pass, Cirque Pass, and Southfork Pass is through some of the finest alpine terrain in the Sierra Nevada. You will be skiing in the shadows of

Mount Winchell, Thunderbolt Peak, North Palisade, Mount Sill, Norman Clyde Peak, Middle Palisade Peak, and Disappointment Peak—four of which have summits over 14,000 feet. It's considerably easier to ski this route in the spring than it is to hike over, around, and under the car-sized boulders that cover much of this terrain in the summer.

Ski over Potluck Pass and down to the large, unnamed lake (11,600 feet) at the head of Glacier Creek. This makes for an ideal camp, in stable weather, for the ski up Mount Sill via Glacier Creek Cirque. (A note of caution—this is an exposed location and can be hard hit during a storm.) From this camp, ski north and then northwest into the large cirque located below and southwest of Mount Sill. Continue up the glacier past Mount Sill to the top of the crest,

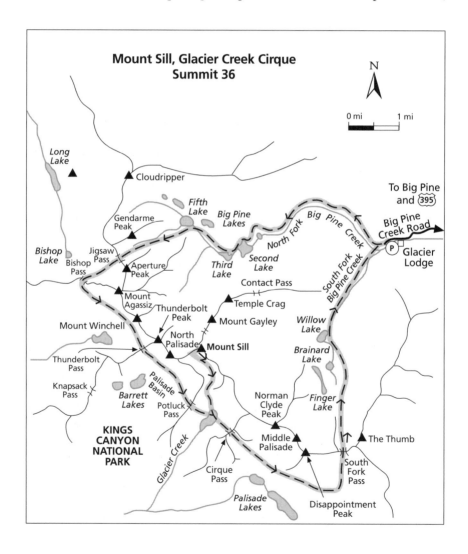

The impressive Glacier Creek Cirque leads to the summit of Mount Sill from the west. Mount Sill is on the right, with North Palisade and Thunderbolt in the background (center). Photo by Colin Fuller

near 14,000 feet. From here, you can look down the other side onto the Palisade Glacier, several thousand feet below.

If you brought your climbing rope, it is a short scramble among rock towers to the top of Polemonium Peak, a minor 14,000-foot peaklet at the head of the U-Notch. From your high point at the top of the glacier, it is a short, easterly traverse to the top of Mount Sill.

The climb and all of the work of the past couple of days are quickly forgotten as you turn your skis downward on this most enjoyable ski descent to camp. This is only half the story, as there is excellent skiing all the way down Glacier Creek to Palisade Creek, for a total run of well over 5,000 feet.

To complete the loop, ski over Cirque Pass (12,400 feet) and traverse above Palisade Lakes near the 11,500-foot level and up into the basin below South Fork Pass. If you have some extra days, a camp at Palisade Lakes provides excellent access to the fine peaks south of the lakes. Additionally, the basin under South Fork Pass provides access to ski descents of Mount Bolton Brown and The Thumb (Summit 37). Ski up and over either of the two passes that comprise South Fork Pass (12,560 feet). Both are passable, although the west pass is not quite as steep and the better of the two. After an enjoyable 3,000-foot descent down to Willow Lake (9,600 feet), you quickly arrive back at Glacier Lodge.

The Thumb ⋆

Height: 13,388 feet
Route: Southeast Ramp
Best time to go: January through early May
Trip duration: 2 days
Mileage: 7 miles to summit
Elevation gain: 6,888 feet
Effort factor: 10.4
Level of difficulty: Advanced (Black Diamond)
Snowboards: Recommended
Maps: Split Mountain, Fish Springs

There is no better ski summit in the Sierra. The scenery, alpine setting, rugged terrain, glaciers, cirques, and skiing are all superb.

The distinct profile of The Thumb, the glacier at the base of the peak, and the prominent ramp through the headwall to the summit are clearly visible from Highway 395, near the town of Big Pine. There is a striking resemblance between The Thumb and Split Mountain, 4 miles to the south: The Thumb's distinct south-facing ramp and vertical east and north faces are mirrored by Split Mountain's prominent north-facing ramp and vertical east and south faces.

From the town of Big Pine, turn west on Big Pine Creek Road toward Glacier

Ascending the narrow-throated snow couloir (left) to the summit ramp. For excellent skiing, follow the ramp to the summit of The Thumb.

Lodge and drive 2.4 miles. Turn left on the lower McMurry Meadows Road, passable in a car (upper McMurry Meadows Road requires a high-clearance vehicle). After 5.7 miles, turn right at the signed turnoff to Birch Lake Trail. This road is not steep but requires a high-clearance vehicle. Follow this road for about 0.7 mile to a barbed-wire cattle gate. Leave the gate the way you found it, up or down. Park here, at about the 6,500-foot level, on the north side of Birch Creek, or if you can clear the large boulder obstruction just beyond the cattle gate, continue up the four-wheel-drive road another 1.5 miles over easy terrain to about 7,100 feet. The route to the trail is not always intuitive, as the road makes a couple of turns away from (to the north of) Birch Creek. Over the 1.5 miles beyond the barbed-wire gate, the road forks twice. At the first fork, where the right fork heads north over a large flat area, turn left. At the next fork, take the right fork, which initially turns away from the creek but soon curves to the west. Follow this fork to its end and the start of Birch Lake Trail. The trail begins by climbing up a narrow valley. A small ridge between the trail and the creek obstructs a view of the creek at the start. Follow the trail to the snow line.

Early in the season when the snow level is still low, you may prefer an alternate approach: Instead of taking the right fork at the second junction, take the left fork and follow the road to where it disappears into the desert sage alongside Birch Creek, around 7,100 feet. At this point, there is a rough, faint, unmaintained trail along the north side of the creek. This trail soon disappears. Follow this trail and continue along the right side of the creek until there is adequate snow on the left side to put on your skis. Cross the creek and ski up the south side of the creek and valley to Birch Lake.

The creek gains elevation rapidly beneath the impressive north-face couloirs of Birch Mountain. The route is pleasant, passing through open terrain scattered with clumps of poplar, aspen, and birch trees. Near 9,000 feet you will be greeted with a spectacular view of The Thumb and your eventual route to the summit. Here, the narrow gully of Birch Creek becomes a beautiful, open valley with great bowl skiing from the top of the unnamed 12,554-foot peak to the west. This is a great place to camp, as is the small bowl at 10,200 feet. Or continue on to camp at Birch Lake, an excellent base from which to climb and ski Birch Mountain and The Thumb.

To ascend Birch Mountain, ski up into the glacial cirque south of Birch Lake and to the col southwest of Birch Mountain. Follow the southwest ridge to the summit. Along the southwest ridge, a number of steep couloirs drop down the northwest face of the peak toward Birch Lake. If there is adequate snow, some of these steep gullies may be skiable. For more information, see the Birch Mountain description (Summit 38).

For an ascent of The Thumb, ski or crampon up "styrofoam" snow to the glacier below the headwall. At the headwall, the glacier narrows. A distinctive couloir (12,000–12,400 feet) leads through the headwall to the upper ramp and the summit 1,000 feet above. The slope of the headwall couloir is 30–35 degrees at the steepest point. The skiing and views are superb at this elevation. Continue to the top. All but the top hundred feet should have adequate snow coverage for your ski descent.

As you climb you will have wonderful views to the south of Split Mountain, Mount Bolton Brown and its impressive north-face couloir, and to the north Disappointment Peak, Middle Palisade, Mount Sill, and North Palisade. The ski descent back to your camp or car is one of the most rewarding in the region.

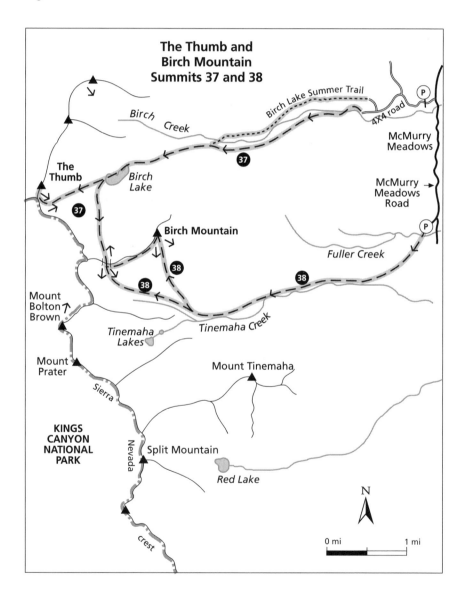

Birch Mountain ★

Height: 13,665 feet
Route: Southeast Face
Best time to go: January through early May
Trip duration: 1 long day or 2 days
Mileage: 6 miles to the summit
Elevation gain: 7,165 feet
Effort factor: 10.2
Level of difficulty: Advanced (Black Diamond)
Snowboards: Recommended; short approach with a continuous descent
Maps: Split Mountain, Fish Springs

Birch Mountain is one of seven east-side summits included in this guide. (Its northwest descents are covered in the previous description, Summit 37.) The other east-side summits included in this guide are Dunderberg Peak, Bloody Mountain, Mount Morgan (North), Mount Morgan (South), Mount Tom, and Basin Mountain. These huge mountains are located to the east of the Sierra Nevada crest and provide the skier and snowboarder with impressively long descents. Mount Tom (Summit 28) and Birch Mountain are arguably the best of the eastside summits, with descents exceeding 6,000 feet.

From the town of Big Pine on Highway 395, turn west onto Big Pine Creek Road toward Glacier Lodge and drive 2.4 miles. Turn left on the lower McMurry Meadows Road, passable in a car (upper McMurry Meadows Road requires a high-clearance vehicle). Continue on McMurry Meadows Road for 7 miles, passing the turnoff to Birch Lake Summer Trail (at 5.7 miles), and then cross both forks of Birch Creek before turning right onto a faint road that soon disappears into the meadow near Fuller Creek (6,500 feet). Park here in the meadow.

Heading west–southwest, hike or ski for about 1.5 miles to Tinemaha Creek (7,800 feet), then follow the creek for about 2 miles to where it forks (near 10,500 feet). Take the right fork. From here you can follow the stream for a

Birch Mountain as seen from the Taboose Creek Trail

short distance, climb to the low saddle southwest of Birch Mountain's main summit, and follow the ridge to the summit. Or you can climb directly up the steep southeast slopes to the summit.

A climb of over 7,000 feet may be more than you want to tackle in a single day. If you choose to spend a night on the mountain, a good place to camp is along Tinemaha Creek between 10,400 and 10,800 feet. To locate the general area in which to camp, draw an imaginary line on your map between the summits of Birch and Tinemaha Mountains.

Once on the summit you will have some grand views of the Palisades and great skiing/boarding back to the car. The Birch Mountain descent is one of the longest in the Sierra Nevada, over 6,000 feet of continuous skiing or boarding. Since the slopes face southeast, they soften early in the day. Start your descent by noon for optimum spring snow conditions. Due to the southerly exposure of this route, Birch Mountain will be one of the earliest peaks to corn up each spring. It is a long and arduous climb to the top but well worth the effort. Birch Mountain is a superb snowboard summit, as the approach to the base of the mountain is short with steep, continuous boarding from the summit.

An alternate route to the summit of Birch Mountain is described in the writeup for The Thumb (Summit 37): Ski up along Birch Creek to Birch Lake on the north side of Birch Mountain. From there, climb to the pass southwest of the summit, and follow the ridge to the summit. A descent of Birch Mountain's great southeast slopes, down to Tinemaha Creek and back to Fuller Creek and McMurry Meadows Road, would make a wonderful summit traverse. A short car shuttle would be required.

Striped Mountain

Height: 13,179 feet
Route: Northeast Bowl
Best time to go: January through early May
Trip duration: 2 to 3 days
Mileage: 8 miles to the summit
Elevation gain: 7,779 feet
Effort factor: 11.8
Level of difficulty: Strong intermediate
Snowboards: Not recommended, due to long approach, but the descents of Cardinal and Striped Mountains are exceptional
Maps: Mount Pinchot, Split Mountain, Fish Springs

This trip's 7,700-foot climb is an arduous endeavor, but it offers numerous options in addition to the excellent ski/snowboard descent of Striped Mountain. The Taboose Pass area offers plenty of slopes for the intermediate skier, and

The steep couloirs of Cardinal Mountain as seen from high on Striped Mountain. Excellent skiing can be found on both Striped Mountain and Cardinal Mountain.

nearby peaks such as Cardinal Mountain provide terrain for the advanced and expert skier/snowboarder.

About 12 miles south of Big Pine and about 15 miles north of Independence on Highway 395, turn west on Taboose Creek Road. Proceed straight on the paved road past the campground. The pavement ends in 1.2 miles. At the first two Ys (1.6 and 1.7 miles from Highway 395), bear right both times. Continue for about 2.1 miles. Along this road segment, you will pass a barbed-wire cattle gate. Leave the gate as you found it, either up or down. At the next Y take the right fork (the left fork is signed to Goodale Creek) and continue for 2 miles to the end of the road (5,400 feet). The dirt road is rough but is passable by car.

The trail begins in the high desert, which is usually in full bloom in the early spring. The red, blue, yellow, and lavender colors of the thistle, cactus, and other desert flowers are striking. The low-elevation start to this trip can be discouraging, but via the steep trail you'll quickly reach the snow line, usually where the trail crosses from the north to the south side of Taboose Creek. Cross the creek and continue on snow up the south side of the stream. The Taboose Creek canyon rises in steep steps, each viewpoint more rewarding than the previous one.

For the climb and descent of Striped Mountain, camp near the 10,200-foot level where a side canyon from the south joins Taboose Creek. There are many excellent campsites here, although you are above the treeline and exposed to storm and wind.

You can also continue on to Taboose Pass (11,400 feet), where there is wonderful skiing in the bowls to the west and north of the pass. Cardinal Mountain (13,396 feet) also offers an impressive descent from near its summit. A steep and spectacular couloir starts just to the east of Taboose Pass and crests

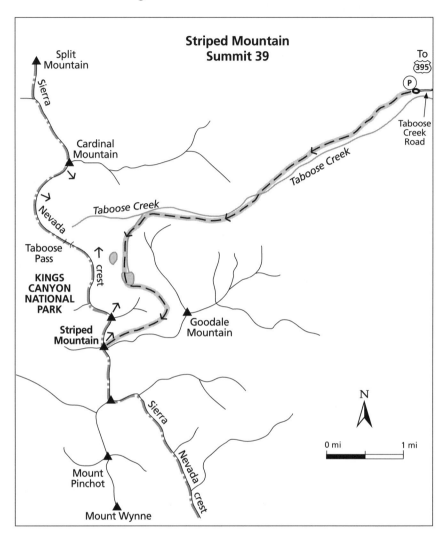

near the summit of Cardinal Mountain. Beware of avalanche potential due to the steepness. These slopes are south facing, so the snow will melt fast.

To climb Striped Mountain from your camp at Taboose Creek, ascend the side canyon (to the left) to a large unnamed lake at 11,400 feet. As you top the couloir just below the lake, an impressive snow-covered summit (12,900 feet) comes into view; this is not Striped Mountain. Striped Mountain is directly behind this peak and several hundred feet higher. Ski up the lake basin to the left of this peak and up steep slopes to the summit plateau of Striped Mountain. From the top, Split Mountain, Cardinal Mountain, Middle Palisade, Mount Sill, Mount Goddard, Black Giant, and hundreds of other snow-capped peaks blanket the landscape for as far as you can see. The ski descent is excellent and quickly takes you back to base camp nearly 3,000 feet below the summit.

Chapter 9
MOUNT WHITNEY REGION

The Mount Whitney region stretches from near Kearsarge Pass in the north to Cottonwood Pass in the south, a distance of about 23 miles. California's two highest peaks, Mount Whitney (14,491 feet) and Mount Williamson (14,375 feet), are found here along with four other peaks over 14,000 feet—Mount Tyndall, Mount Russell, Mount Muir, and Mount Langley—and many other summits nearing that height. Deep gorges, glacial cirques, hanging valleys, serrated ridges, and lofty summits provide all levels of ski terrain and challenge for the ski mountaineer.

Mount Langley was first climbed in 1871 by Clarence King, who mistakenly thought he was making the first ascent of Mount Whitney. (Ironically, he had made a similar mistake in an earlier attempt in 1864, when he climbed Mount Tyndall; see the sidebar "Across the Great Divide" in Chapter 10.) King returned to Mount Whitney in September 1873 to successfully scale the summit, but by then three fishermen from Lone Pine and others had preceded him. In October of that same year, John Muir climbed what is today called the Mountaineer's Route and, two years later, made his ascent of the North Face of Mount Whitney (see sidebar for this chapter); these two ski and snowboard descents are covered in the description for Mount Whitney (Summit 43). The

Ascending the steep snow ramp to Mount Williamson's upper summit plateau

other major peaks in the region were soon climbed, with the exception of Mount Russell, which due to difficult rock faces and exposed ridges was not climbed until 1926 by Norman Clyde.

In 1904 a horse trail to the top of Mount Whitney was completed, and in 1909 a stone shelter was built by the Smithsonian Institution for their astronomers; it is still in use today as an emergency shelter. The summit of Mount Whitney became the site of many scientific experiments in the late 1800s and early 1900s, during which time the U.S. Weather Service used the summit to conduct experiments and observations.

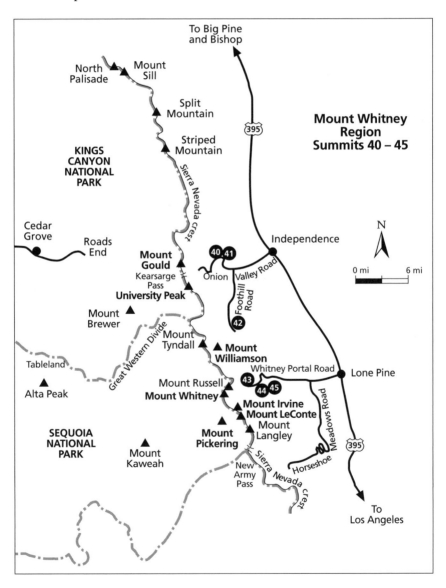

Mount Whitney has become a popular destination for those desiring to climb the highest peak in the lower forty-eight states. It is by far the most climbed peak in California, if not the United States, with as many as 150 day-use permits and 50 overnight permits issued daily between May and October.

How to get there: Access to the peaks is from the east and Highway 395. For Mount Gould, Kearsarge Peak, University Peak, and Mount Williamson, drive to the town of Independence on Highway 395 (about 45 miles south of Bishop) and proceed west on Onion Valley Road. For Mount Whitney, Mount Irvine, Mount LeConte, and Mount Pickering, proceed to Lone Pine, about 60 miles south of Bishop, and drive up Whitney Portal Road.

Mount Whitney—The Early Climbs

When Clarence King received [the disconcerting news that he had ascended Mount Langley, not Mount Whitney] he was naturally greatly surprised and disappointed. He hastened to California, engaged two men at Visalia to accompany him, and he was soon riding over the familiar Hockett Trail to the Kern. At eleven o'clock in the morning of September 19, 1873, he stood at last on the summit of the true Mount Whitney. But, alas for him, he was too late for the first ascent.

At the end of September 1873 the record of ascents of Mount Whitney stood: (1) August 18—Charles D. Begole, Albert H. Johnson, John Lucas; (2) late August—William Crapo, Abe Leyda; (3) September 6—William Crapo, William L. Hunter, Tom McDonough, Carl Rabe; (4) September 19—Clarence King, Frank Knowles. These ascents were made from the southwest, coming north from the Hockett Trail; King and Knowles from Visalia, the others from Lone Pine by way of Cottonwood Pass.

A new epoch begins with the coming of John Muir in October of that year. When Muir left his companions at the foot of Kearsarge Pass, he rode alone southward along the foot of the range and took the usual route from Lone Pine over Cottonwood Pass. Leaving his horse in a meadow, he climbed the false Mount Whitney (Mount Langley) and from there saw, as others had done, the higher peak a few miles away (Mount Whitney). Without delay he ran down, moved his horse to another meadow, and by a very rough way up and down ridges and canyons reached the base of the true Mount Whitney at sunset the same day. As there was not wood for a fire, he made up his mind to spend the night climbing. "I was among summit needles by midnight," he writes in his diary. "Had to dance all night to keep from freezing. Was feeble and starving next morning and had to turn back without gaining the top. Was exhausted ere I reached horse and camp and food." He returned to Independence, ate, and slept all the next day; then, not to be defeated, "set out afoot for the summit by direct course up the east side."

He camped in the sagebrush the first night and next morning made his way up the north fork of Lone Pine Creek and camped at timberline. On the morning of October 21, at eight o'clock, he was on the summit of Mount Whitney. There he found Clarence King's record and a memento left by Rabe with a note, "Notice Gentleman however is the looky finder of this half a Dollar is wellkom to it. Carl Rabe, Sep 6th 1873". Muir sketched, gained glorious views, left the half a dollar where he found it, and descended to the foot of the mountain by the way he came. Many years later Muir wrote, "For climbers there is a canyon which comes down from the north shoulder of the Whitney peak. Well-seasoned limbs will enjoy the climb of 9000 feet required for this direct route, but soft, succulent people should go the mule way." Should someone of the present generation of mountain climbers feel inclined to make light of John Muir's exploit, let him endeavor to duplicate it, starting from Independence (not Lone Pine) on foot, with or without sleeping bag and modern concentrated foods—Muir had neither.

Muir's second visit to Mount Whitney came two years later. This time he took two companions with him. He knew the way and could proceed unerringly. He followed his former route up the North Fork of Lone Pine Creek until he came to the final climb. There he made a variation [see Summit 43], crossing the main crest a little to the north (the Whitney/Russell Col), and descended to a lake (Arctic Lake) on the western side. They passed along the rocky shores, "gradually climbed higher, mounting in a spiral around the northwest shoulder of the mountain, then directly to the summit." The descent is described by Muir in one sentence: "We left the summit about noon and swooped to the torrid plains before sundown, as if dropping out of the sky."

—Francis P. Farquhar, *History of the Sierra Nevada*

Mount Gould

Height: 13,005 feet

Route: East Bowl

Best time to go: February through early May

Trip duration: 1 to 3 days

Mileage: 8 miles to the summit from 7,200-foot level; 3 miles from Onion Valley (9,200 feet)

Elevation gain: 5,805 feet from 7,200-foot level; 3,805 from Onion Valley

Effort factor: 9.8 from 7,200-foot level; 4.3 from Onion Valley

Level of difficulty: Advanced (Black Diamond)

Snowboards: Recommended when the road is open to Onion Valley

Maps: Kearsarge Peak, Mount Clarence King

As is the case with University Peak (Summit 41), Mount Gould's neighbor to the south, the best time to ski Mount Gould is in the spring before or immediately after Onion Valley Road is opened to Onion Valley. The road usually opens in

April or early May. Although Mount Gould can be completed in a long day from Onion Valley, a two- or three-day trip will provide more time to explore the lake basin to the north of Golden Trout Lake, the steep gullies of Dragon Peak, and Kearsarge Peak. This is also an excellent winter overnight trip with a base camp at Golden Trout Lake.

From the town of Independence on Highway 395, drive west on the paved Onion Valley Road. There is no gate closing the road, so you can drive to the snow line; in winter this normally is as far as the northernmost switchback near the 7,200-foot level, about 5 miles and 2,000 feet below the Onion Valley summer trailhead (9,200 feet). In early spring, the road may be passable to 8,000 feet or higher, provided there has not been a large snow or rock slide blocking the road.

From Onion Valley Road, turn north up the Golden Trout Lake watershed. The route climbs rapidly, following a small stream into a hanging valley. Near the 10,800-foot level the valley forks, with the left fork going to Golden Trout Lake. Follow this fork to Golden Trout Lake, located in the large amphitheater formed by the north and east faces of Mount Gould.

Golden Trout Lake has commanding views of Mount Gould and Kearsarge Peak. It also provides access to the unnamed lake basin and Dragon Peak to the north and Kearsarge Peak to the east.

From the upper end of Golden Trout Lake, follow the steep slopes that lead to the upper East Bowl, a large, open bowl cresting the summit ridge near 12,900 feet, just north of the summit. The summit views of Mount Clarence King, Mount Cotter, University Peak, Dragon Peak, and Kearsarge Peak are rewarding, as is the magnificent ski descent of the East Bowl down Golden Trout Lake and all the way back to Onion Valley.

Another descent route is down Mount Gould's southeast slopes and shoulder. These slopes provide excellent spring skiing and can be skied to Flower Lake, near University Peak, or back to Onion Valley. For more information, see the trip description for University Peak (Summit 41).

Mount Gould and the Golden Trout Lake basin as seen from the approach to University Peak via Robinson Lake. The sunlit slopes of Mount Gould provide a great descent to Flower Lake.

KEARSARGE PEAK

Kearsarge Peak and Sardine Canyon offer excellent ski opportunities as well. Follow the route from Onion Valley as described above. At the junction of the two forks in the Golden Trout Lake outlet stream (10,800 feet), climb a steep gully to Kearsarge Peak's summit ridge (12,100 feet). Follow the ridge to the summit (12,600 feet), or ski down Sardine Canyon to an old mining road (7,200 feet). Follow this road back to Onion Valley Road; the two roads join at the northernmost switchback described above.

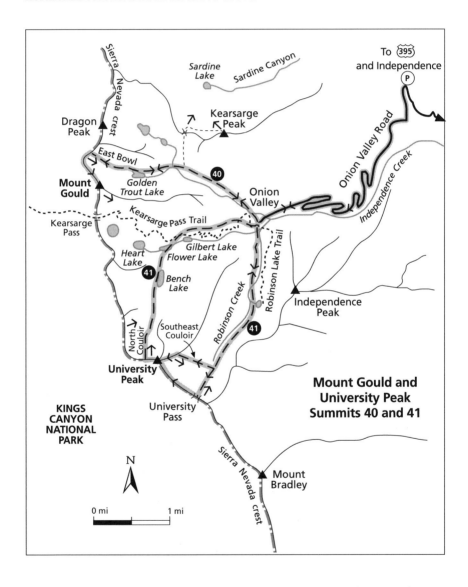

Mount Gould and University Peak Summits 40 and 41

University Peak  ★

Height: 13,589 feet

Routes: University Pass, North Couloir

Best time to go: February through early May

Trip duration: 1 to 3 days

Mileage: 9 miles from 7,200-foot level; 4 miles from Onion Valley (9,200 feet) to the summit

Elevation gain: 6,389 feet from 7,200-foot level; 4,389 feet from Onion Valley

Effort factor: 10.9 from 7,200-foot level; 6.4 from Onion Valley

Level of difficulty: University Pass and Southeast Couloir, advanced (Black Diamond); North Couloir, expert (Double Black Diamond)

Snowboards: Recommended when the road is open to Onion Valley

Maps: Kearsarge Peak, Mount Williamson, Mount Brewer

University Peak offers excellent ski descents from two different approaches. University Pass and the Southeast Couloir, via Robinson Lake, provide fine descents from near the summit. The North Couloir provides a long and steep descent to Bench and Flower Lakes. The powder is often excellent in the North Couloir.

The best time to ski University Peak is in the late winter or early spring, before or immediately after Onion Valley Road is opened to Onion Valley. The road usually opens in April or early May, but this depends upon the amount of snow accumulation during the winter. This trip can also be completed in the winter, but all the routes contain steep gullies above 12,000 feet; be sure to wait until the snow has stabilized and avalanche danger has been eliminated.

To reach the trailhead, follow the directions given in the description for Mount Gould (Summit 40).

ROBINSON LAKE

For the Robinson Lake approach to University Pass and the Southeast Couloir, turn south from Onion Valley and ski up the Robinson Creek valley. The route parallels the creek and the summer trail to Robinson Lake, located about a mile and 1,300 feet above Onion Valley. The lake is nestled against the steep cliffs of Independence Peak, and the large red fir trees in the lake basin make for an excellent and protected campsite.

The terrain above Robinson Lake bears many similarities to that of the North Fork Bairs Creek route on Mount Williamson (Summit 42). Both approaches are up large glacial cirques to the south and east of their respective summits. Both peaks have impressive headwalls divided by one or more steep

University Pass (col) is on the left, and University Peak is just out of the photo to the right.

chutes. And both have a long, steep couloir to the right (north) of the headwall that bypasses the headwall, terminating on an east–west ridge east of the summit. Although there are many similarities, there are considerable differences— Mount Williamson is almost 1,000 feet higher than University Peak, and its approach begins in the desert sagebrush at only 6,200 feet without benefit of an access road or trail above this point. The approach to University Peak is much easier, with a road to 9,200 feet.

From Robinson Lake, ski up the creek into the large glacial cirque located south and east of University Peak. As you approach 12,000 feet, either continue your southwesterly direction by skiing up and over University Pass (the steep couloir in the middle of the headwall that ends in the low point on the ridge), or turn right (northwest) up the prominent Southeast Couloir that continues to the top of the ridge. Both routes lead to the summit; however, the Southeast Couloir leaves you about a quarter mile east of the summit and requires Class 3 climbing along the summit ridge, which is made more difficult with snow on the rocks and ledges. This route does, however, provide for a longer ski descent. The chute begins around 12,200 feet and continues to above 13,300 feet, approaching 35 degrees near the top.

The University Pass Couloir provides an easier route to the top. From the pass, it is an easy 800-foot climb to the summit. However, this south-facing upper plateau may lack adequate snow coverage to permit skiing above the pass.

NORTH COULOIR

For an approach by way of Flower and Bench Lakes and the North Couloir, follow the Onion Valley drainage along the route of the summer trail heading west toward Kearsarge Pass. The route climbs steeply for 1,200 feet and levels off at Gilbert and Flower Lakes. From Flower Lake, turn south and climb about 400 feet to Bench Lake. Bench Lake makes an excellent campsite from which to ski the North Couloir and the bowls to the north. The North Couloir rises nearly 2,500 feet above Bench Lake to the ridge just west of University Peak. From the ridge it is a short scramble to the summit.

The powder in the North Couloir can be superb. The high altitude and the north-facing aspect of the couloir combine to provide expert (Double Black Diamond) terrain and wonderful snow conditions. This is an excellent ski and snowboard descent. Due to the steepness of the couloir, be aware of avalanche conditions.

A camp at Bench Lake also provides a great opportunity to ski the various gullies and bowls in the area. The bowl to the north of the North Couloir is especially good. Also, the southeast slopes and shoulder of Mount Gould (Summit 40) are nearby and can be skied early in the spring season.

Mount Williamson ⋆

Height: 14,375 feet	
Route: North Fork Bairs Creek Glacial Cirque	
Best time to go: February through early May	
Trip duration: 3 days	
Mileage: 7 miles to the summit	
Elevation gain: 8,175 feet	
Effort factor: 11.7	
Level of difficulty: Advanced (Black Diamond)	
Snowboards: A long and strenuous approach, but the snowboarding from the summit can be superb	
Maps: Mount Williamson, Manzanar	

In the Sierra Nevada, Mount Williamson is second in height only to Mount Whitney (Summit 43), 6 miles to the south, and the size of its massif is exceeded only by that of Mount Shasta (Summits 1, 2, and 3), one of the largest stratovolcanoes in the world. Mount Williamson dominates the region, and its immense North Fork Bairs Creek Glacial Cirque and headwall couloir are impressive sights even when viewed from Highway 395.

The combination of rugged terrain, the lack of an approach trail, and the low elevation of the start make this trip one of the more difficult summits in this guide. However, once you have conquered the most challenging part of the trip—the approach below the snow line—the skiing and snowboarding in the grand cirque and summit plateau are rewarding. In heavy snow years it is possible to ski or snowboard from the very summit to 7,200 feet, a descent of over 7,000 feet! In the spring, the lower-elevation snow melts fast, so go early in the season to maximize your turns. This trip is within the California Bighorn Sheep Zoological Area; observe the closure dates that are printed on USGS topo maps for this area.

None of the other approaches to the Mount Williamson summit are very good. Given the low starting point, the brush, and the rugged terrain, there appears to be no easy way to reach the snow other than by helicopter—and helicopters are not allowed within the zoological area or national forests. You can follow the stream and fight the brush and willows. Another option is to gain the south side of the stream and select a route above the stream and the willows; however, the south side of the stream is bluffy and treed, making travel with a snowboard or skis strapped to a pack a trying experience. The third option may be no better, but is described below.

From Independence on Highway 395, proceed 4.3 miles west on Onion Valley Road. Turn left (south) on Foothill Road and drive 6.5 miles to North Fork Bairs Creek and park on the north side of the stream (about 6,200 feet).

Keeping to the north side, wander upstream through the sagebrush, staying away from the willows growing along the creek. Soon you will come to a large, decomposing, white granite cliff blocking your progress. Avoid the cliff by climbing up and onto a rounded ridge above the creek. Follow the ridge to about 7,200 feet. At this point leave the gentle ridge and traverse left across steep terrain and gullies to an obvious notch at 7,200 feet, 400 feet above where the creek turns and flows north to south at an elevation of 6,800 feet. From this notch continue across steep terrain and gullies with scrub oak to North Fork Bairs Creek.

Cross the creek below where it splits at 7,400 feet, and climb up the south side of the creek for about 1,000 feet. Traverse right into the left-hand fork of the creek and follow the stream into the large glacial cirque above. Alternatively, cross the creek where it splits (7,400 feet), hike up the stream for a short distance, and climb the rib to the right of the left fork. In a heavy snow year, early in the season, it may be possible to start skiing where you cross the creek near 7,200 feet. In a normal snow year, skiing may not be possible until 8,600 feet or higher.

The impressive North Bairs Creek Glacial Cirque. Ascending the snow ramp at the head of the cirque (in the shade) takes you to the summit plateau of Mount Williamson.

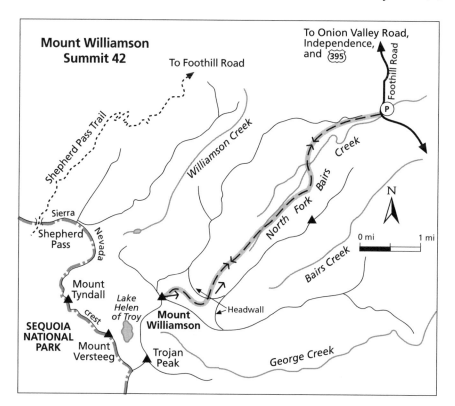

As you continue to climb, the narrow creek canyon begins to open up into the grand cirque that is visible from Highway 395. On your left are the near-vertical walls of the cirque which form an impregnable barrier. Up ahead is the impressive headwall with a U-shaped couloir providing access to the summit plateau. On your right are stands of large red firs. Between 9,600 and 11,200 feet are several excellent places to camp.

Continue up the cirque to the headwall, and ascend the U-shaped couloir in the center of the headwall. The couloir rises from about 12,200 feet and emerges onto an upper cirque near 13,000 feet. This 800-foot ramp approaches 35 degrees. To the far right of the base of the U-shaped couloir is another gully. Avoid this route, as this long, steep gully avalanches regularly and leads to difficult climbing above.

From the top of the U-shaped couloir it is about one mile and an elevation gain of 1,400 feet across the upper cirque and summit plateau to the top. The views are superb: You will see Mount Langley, Mount Whitney (Summit 43), Mount Barnard, Trojan Peak, Versteeg Peak, the Kaweahs (Summit 48), Milestone, Table Mountain, Junction Peak, and Mount Brewer (Summit 46). The view of George Creek Cirque to the south is impressive, and it appears the skiing there would equal the superb skiing in the North Fork Bairs Creek Cirque.

Mount Whitney ★

Height: 14,491 feet

Routes: Mountaineers Route, North Face

Best time to go: February through early May

Trip duration: 2 to 3 days

Mileage: Mountaineers Route, 6 miles; North Face, 8 miles to the summit

Elevation gain: 6,191 feet

Effort factor: Mountaineers Route, 9.2; North Face, 10.2

Level of difficulty: Mountaineers Route, expert (Double Black Diamond) from 14,200 feet; North Face, expert (Double Black Diamond); intermediate below Iceberg Lake

Snowboards: Recommended; excellent trip for snowboards

Maps: Mount Whitney, Mount Langley

The Mountaineers Route is the distinctive couloir on the northeast face and shoulder of Mount Whitney. It is readily seen from Highway 395 and the town of Lone Pine. In the winter and spring it is a challenging 30- to 35-degree snow couloir. In the summer and fall it is scaled by hundreds of rock climbers each year. This challenging route was first skied by Galen Rowell in 1974.

From the town of Lone Pine on Highway 395, turn west on Whitney Portal Road and drive to Whitney Portal (8,300 feet). From the Whitney Portal trailhead, hike up the main Mount Whitney Trail for about 0.7 mile. At the

Day Needle, Keeler Needle, and Mount Whitney. The Mountaineers Route (Couloir) is to the right of the east face of Whitney. Only the upper third of the couloir is visible in this photo.

second creek crossing, leave the main trail and hike up the right side of North Fork Lone Pine Creek, following the well-used, but unmaintained, climber's trail for about a quarter mile to where the trail crosses the creek to the south. If there is adequate snow to cover the brush and talus, continue up the drainage on skis or snowshoes; otherwise, cross the creek and hike up the trail for another quarter mile to where it crosses the stream again and climbs the rock ledges on the north side of the creek known as the Ebersbacher Ledges. Climb up a rock ledge angling east (downstream) until it is possible to climb up to the next level of ledges, turning back upstream. The route stays on the right (north) side of the creek to Lower Boy Scout Lake.

Ski or hike up the main drainage to Clyde Meadow. At the meadow, follow the stream to Upper Boy Scout Lake. From here, ski up toward the impressive east faces of Day and Keeler Needles. Just below Iceberg Lake, climb the steep slope (in the summer this is a rock cliff) to the magnificent lake basin at the base of Mount Whitney's sheer east face and the Mountaineers Route (couloir). Iceberg Lake (12,600 feet) is exposed but a great place for a base camp, as is Upper Boy Scout Lake (11,300 feet). If it's windy, build a 4-foot-high wall of snow blocks around your tent.

From Iceberg Lake, the Mountaineers Route is the obvious snow couloir ascending the right shoulder of the east face of Mount Whitney. Climb to the top of the couloir, which ends in a notch near 14,200 feet. The east ridge and east face of Mount Russell are impressive from the top of the couloir. Angle west, descending ever so slightly, and then turn left toward the summit, climbing a gully that is extremely steep near the top. This gully can be icy, with a cornice at the top. To avoid this gully continue to traverse across the North Face to the next gully and up, or continue west across the upper portion of the North Face to the summit ridge. Follow this north ridge for 5–10 minutes to the summit and rock hut.

Skiing and snowboarding in the chute above 14,200 feet is dangerous (extreme), as it is exposed and usually icy: a fall may be impossible to arrest, resulting in a drop of several thousand feet. However, on my last trip up the Mountaineers Route, I met five snowboarders from Lake Tahoe who had boarded this upper chute—an impressive feat indeed. The skiing from the 14,200-foot notch to Iceberg Lake is advanced (Black Diamond). The skiing below Iceberg Lake down to the snow line is a blast over intermediate terrain.

An alternate ascent and descent route is to climb the Whitney-Russell Col, which is not the lowest point in the ridge between Mount Russell and Mount Whitney, but rather the notch directly above Iceberg Lake. From this pass ski westward, angling up the North Face. Avoid the lower rock bands by traversing to the right (west), and climb steeply to the summit ridge. Above the rock bands the North Face opens up into a large, steep upper bowl. Crest the north ridge near 14,400 feet and walk to the summit on easy terrain.

The summit plateau usually lacks adequate snow coverage to ski from the top. However, you can ski your ascent route starting at near 14,400 feet all the way down to Arctic Lakes—a descent of about 2,000 feet. This route is steep,

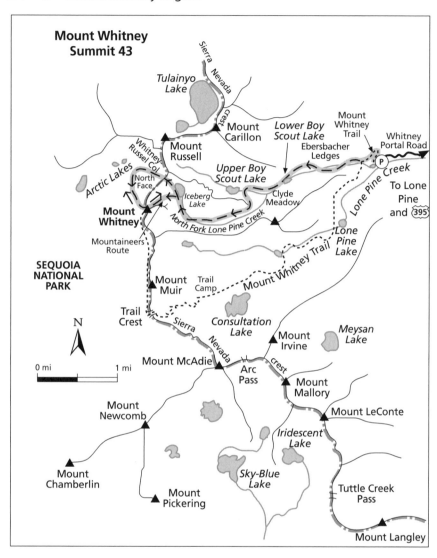

requiring expert (Double Black Diamond) skiing/snowboarding skills. Exploring the isolated Arctic Valley down to Guitar Lake is a rewarding tour seldom done in the summer, let alone in the winter and spring on skis. The route passes the imposing Fish Hook Arête of Mount Russell, a classic rock climb.

Mount Whitney can also be skied by following the summer hiking trail (Mount Whitney Trail) to the top. The route above Trail Crest (13,480 feet) usually lacks adequate snow coverage for good skiing and snowboarding due to the sunny westerly exposure and the high winds that tend to scour the area. From a base camp at Trail Camp, numerous good skiing and snowboarding opportunities are found in the large bowls below Mount Muir, as well as a challenging descent from Arc Pass.

Mount Irvine and Mount LeConte

Height: 13,779+ and 13,845 feet

Route: Meysan Lake Cirque

Best time to go: February through early May

Trip duration: 2 to 3 days

Mileage: 6 miles to the summit of either peak

Elevation gain: Mount Irvine, 5,779+ feet; Mount LeConte, 5,845 feet

Effort factor: 8.8

Level of difficulty: Advanced (Black Diamond)

Snowboards: Recommended; long descents from both summits

Maps: Mount Whitney, Mount Langley

The large Meysan Lake basin is ringed, from right to left, by the four impressive summits of Mount Irvine, Mount Mallory, Mount LeConte, and Lone Pine Peak. A base camp at Meysan Lake is a good location from which to ski Mount LeConte, Mount Irvine, and the numerous high-elevation bowls in the area.

Mount Mallory as seen from Meysan Lake. Skiers ascend the steep snow chute, then follow the summit plateau to the top of Mount Irvine, which is just out of the photo to the right.

From the town of Lone Pine on Highway 395, drive up the Whitney Portal Road to the lower Whitney Portal campground (8,000 feet). Park along the road. Start by walking through the campground and past the summer cabins perched on the mountainside, following the signs to the start of Meysan Lake Trail.

The trail gains elevation rapidly as it ascends the canyon below Meysan Lake. The trail is on the sunny side of Meysan Creek, so it may be free of snow for several miles. The impressive northwest face of Lone Pine Peak towers over the canyon on your left. After a couple of miles you will pass a number of small lakes (the Grass Lakes). From these small lakes, follow the creek to Meysan Lake (11,500 feet) and base camp.

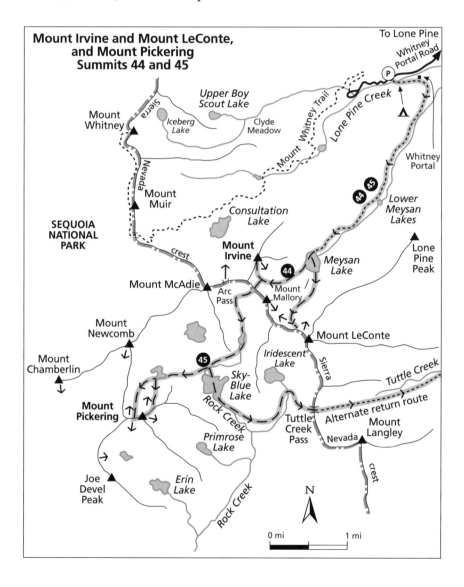

Mount Irvine and Mount LeConte, and Mount Pickering Summits 44 and 45

The large glacial basin above Meysan Lake is split by the rugged east ridge of Mount Mallory. On the left are numerous steep couloirs that descend from the high summit plateau of Mount LeConte. And on the right, the base of the vertical granite face of Mount Irvine rises from near the shore of Meysan Lake.

To climb Mount Irvine, ascend the steep gully to the right of the east ridge of Mount Mallory. This gully is not as steep as it appears, approaching 35 degrees. The gully leads to a large bowl and open slopes to the summit of Mount Irvine, from which you will have a panoramic view of the Mount Whitney region including Mount Muir, Mount Whitney, Mount Russell, and Arc Pass and Trail Camp on the Mount Whitney Trail far below.

To climb Mount LeConte, ascend the chutes to the left of the east ridge of Mount Mallory. Follow these chutes to the high plateau and ridge between Mount Mallory and Mount LeConte. The climb of Mount LeConte is Class 3 but may be made more difficult by snow in the cracks and on the ledges. From the base of the north face, traverse east along an easy but exposed ledge for about 400 feet. When you come to some vertical cracks and ledges, climb approximately 200 feet of exposed Class 3 to the summit.

Both Mount Irvine and Mount LeConte offer excellent skiing from near their summits. The snow holds longer and the snow conditions may be better on Mount LeConte due to its superior northeasterly exposure.

45
Mount Pickering

Height: 13,474 feet	
Route: North Couloir	
Best time to go: February through early May	
Trip duration: 3 or more days	
Mileage: 9 miles to the summit	
Elevation gain: 7,600 feet	
Effort factor: 12.1	
Level of difficulty: Advanced (Black Diamond)	
Snowboards: Not recommended due to the long approach	
Maps: Mount Whitney, Mount Langley	

The Rock Creek and Sky-Blue Lake area is a skier's paradise. A week here would not be sufficient to ski the major summits and couloirs in the area. Joe Devel Peak has an impressive couloir (30–35 degrees) that drops from just north of the peak into the upper end of the Erin Lake Cirque; for the extreme skier, a 50-degree couloir rises from the shore of Erin Lake to near the summit. The slopes of Mount Newcomb and Mount Chamberlin provide a 3.5-mile-long ski descent of Perrin Creek. And up by Arc Pass, the east couloir of Mount McAdie provides challenging skiing. But the best of the group is possibly Mount

Mount Pickering from above Sky-Blue Lake. The ski route ascends the main snow couloir to the skyline (right of the summit) and follows the ridge to the summit.

Pickering, which has numerous descent routes in spectacular and varied terrain.

Follow the route up to Meysan Lake as described in the Mount Irvine trip (Summit 44). Ascend the steep couloir to the right of the east ridge of Mount Mallory and continue to the pass at 13,600 feet. This pass is located between Mount Irvine and Mount Mallory and about 0.5 mile south of the summit of Mount Irvine, the left-most notch. Descend to Arc Pass and the gentle valley leading to Sky-Blue Lake and Rock Creek. Excellent skiing over moderate terrain will bring you to Sky-Blue Lake.

(An alternate approach is to ski up the Mount Whitney Trail to Consultation Lake and up and over Arc Pass and down to Sky-Blue Lake. This is a slightly longer approach in miles but eliminates about 1,000 feet of elevation gain. Arc Pass is quite steep near the top. Pass the steep cliffs near the top by staying to the left.)

From a base camp near Sky-Blue Lake, ski to the uppermost lake (12,000 feet) at the base of Mount Pickering's North Couloir. Climb the main couloir to the ridge just west of the peak or climb the other, less obvious couloir that crests the ridge just east of the peak. Follow either ridge to the summit. Mount Pickering is blessed with excellent views of Mount Whitney, Mount Langley, Discovery Pinnacle, Mount Muir, Mount McAdie, the Kaweahs, and hundreds of other snow-covered peaks.

There are three major summit descent routes from Mount Pickering that will take you back to Sky-Blue Lake and your base camp on Rock Creek. The most direct route is to ski either of the two couloirs on the north side of the peak, the same ascent routes described above. Many times excellent powder can be found in these north-facing couloirs.

There are two other alternatives as well. From the summit of Mount Pickering, ski east down the Primrose Lake headwall and cirque. Or ski in a southerly direction and then east into the Erin Lake cirque, returning to base camp at Sky-Blue Lake via Rock Creek. Both are excellent ski descent routes. If time and energy permit, ski down the Erin Lake cirque to the small unnamed lake (12,200 feet) above Erin Lake and climb the north couloir of Joe Devel Peak.

To ski out, return over Arc Pass or the Mallory-Irvine Pass and back to Whitney Portal Road. Or, for a rewarding loop trip through some spectacularly wild terrain, ski out over Tuttle Creek Pass and down Tuttle Creek. From base camp at Sky-Blue Lake, ski down Rock Creek and climb up to the hidden Iridescent Lake. Just before reaching Iridescent Lake, turn east and climb to the low pass between Mount Langley and the last summit spire of Mount Corcoran. It is a steep climb that may require crampons. The skiing down Tuttle Creek passes through some rugged terrain, but there is always good skiing on moderate slopes. For this descent route, place a car at the bottom of Tuttle Creek. From Lone Pine, drive 3.2 miles up Whitney Portal Road to Horseshoe Meadows Road, turn left on this road and travel 2 miles south, turn right on Granite View Drive for 2.3 miles, and then turn right and follow the road to the end (the last 0.7 mile requires a four-wheel-drive vehicle).

Chapter 10
SEQUOIA AND KINGS CANYON NATIONAL PARKS

Sequoia National Park, known for its majestic giant sequoias and rugged mountain terrain, became the second of our nation's national parks shortly after Yosemite National Park in 1890. Sequoia National Park also has some deep canyons, including the Kern River Canyon (6,000 feet in depth) and the Middle Fork of the Kaweah River Canyon (over 4,000 feet). But it is Kings Canyon National Park that has the really deep canyons. The Kings River Canyon, reaching a depth of 8,200 feet near the confluence of the Middle and South Forks of the Kings River, is deeper than Hells Canyon in Idaho, the Grand Canyon in Arizona, or any other canyon in North America. At Roads End, the start of the Mount Brewer trip (Summit 46), the canyon walls rise nearly a mile above the flat glacial valley.

To the east of the deep canyons and giant sequoias in both parks are magnificent mountains, meadows, glaciated bowls, and alpine lakes. This area is excellent for exploring, hiking, fishing, mountain climbing, and of course ski and snowboard mountaineering. Officially, the Sequoia and Kings Canyon park boundaries extend to the Sierra Nevada crest and include Mount Whitney and many of the other 14,000-foot peaks of California. However, for purposes of this book, the Sequoia and Kings Canyon National Parks region includes those summits west of the Sierra Nevada crest (the Kaweahs, the Great Western Divide, and the Kings-Kern Divide), with road and trail access from the west—Roads End in Kings Canyon National Park, and Wolverton and Mineral King Valley in Sequoia National Park.

Mineral King Valley is a unique and isolated part of Sequoia National Park. In the summer, the wildlife is plentiful—mule deer, mountain lion, coyote, pine martens, fishers, wolverine, black bear, marmot, gray fox, bobcat, and trout. High alpine lakes, meadows, wildflowers, streams, and waterfalls abound. Numerous peaks and high passes ring the valley, providing countless hiking, camping, and fishing opportunities.

In the winter and spring, Mineral King is a backcountry skier's and snowboarder's utopia. It is no wonder that Walt Disney wanted to build a large alpine ski resort in the upper valley. Its steep sides, high passes, and lofty summits provide an ideal setting for the backcountry skier. There are dozens of

The author enjoying the light powder Photo by Gene Leach

tours and descent routes to choose from in this relatively compact area. Three peaks in the Mineral King area are featured here—Sawtooth Peak (Summit 49), Florence Peak (Summit 50), and Vandever Mountain (Summit 51). Ski or snowboard descents of Empire Mountain, Tulare Peak, and White Chief Peak are also briefly described. All are worthy summits with numerous ski and snowboard descent possibilities.

During a normal snow year, the National Park Service does not open the road to Mineral King until Memorial Day weekend, and in heavy snowfall years it can be much later. In 1998, for example, the road was not open to the public until the Fourth of July, even though the road had been plowed weeks earlier. The failure of the park service to provide public access to Mineral King Valley during the spring ski season is regrettable public policy, as the best spring

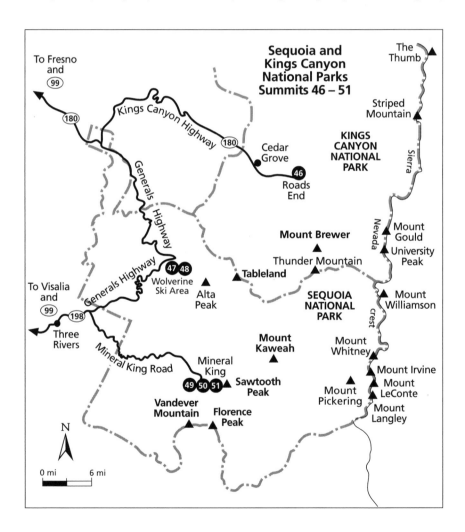

skiing exists from March through May, well before the road is opened. To take advantage of the best skiing conditions, you must ski the road from the snow line, a considerable distance.

I challenge the National Park Service to open the road to Mineral King by April 1 each year so that backcountry skiers and snowboarders can take advantage of the wonderful skiing in the valley. And I would encourage you to write or call the Sequoia National Park Chief Ranger, your U.S. Senator, and your congressional representative requesting that the dirt portions of the road (about 3 of the last 7 miles) be paved so that the road can be plowed and opened to the public by April 1 of each year.

How to get there: The approach and access to this region are from the west. For Mount Brewer, drive to Fresno (Highway 99) and take Highway 180 (Kings Canyon Highway) to Kings Canyon National Park and Roads End. The road is closed in the winter but is usually open by mid-April. For Mount Kaweah and the Tableland, drive east from Visalia on Highway 198 to Sequoia National Park and to the Pear Lake Trailhead/Wolverton Ski Area (7,300 feet). This road is kept open throughout the winter.

For Sawtooth Peak, Florence Peak, and Vandever Mountain in the Mineral King area of the park, drive to Visalia and then east on Highway 198 past the town of Three Rivers. Beyond Three Rivers and about 2 miles before the entrance to Sequoia National Park on Highway 198, turn right onto Mineral King Road, a long, narrow, winding road with 698 curves, to Silver City and Mineral King Valley. This road is closed in the winter, but under normal snowfall conditions the National Park Service attempts to open the road by Memorial Day weekend.

For the appropriate phone numbers to call regarding road conditions and opening dates, see Appendix 4 and Appendix 5.

Across the Great Divide

From 1864 to 1873, Clarence King made four attempts to be the first to climb Mount Whitney. This is his account of his first attempt, in July 1864. From Mount Brewer, King and Dick Cotter spotted what they correctly guessed to be the highest peak in the continental United States, 15 miles away. With six days' provisions, they set out to cross the formidable Kings-Kern Divide, somewhere between Thunder Mountain and Mount Jordan, and to climb Mount Whitney.

There seemed but one possible way to reach our goal; that was to make our way along the summit of the cross ridge which projected between the two ranges. This divide sprang out from our Mount Brewer wall, about four miles to the south of us. To reach it we must climb up and down over the indented edge of Mount Brewer. In attempting to do this we had a rather lively time scaling a sharp granite needle, where we found our course completely stopped by precipices four and five hundred feet in height. Ahead of us the summit continued to be broken into fantastic pinnacles, leaving us no hope of making our way along it; so we sought the most broken part of the eastern descent, and began to climb down.

The heavy knapsacks, besides wearing our shoulders gradually into a black-and-blue state, over-balanced us terribly, and kept us in constant danger of pitching headlong. At last, taking them off, Cotter climbed down until he had found a resting-place upon a cleft of rock, then I lowered them to him with our lasso, afterwards descending cautiously to his side, taking my turn in pioneering downward, receiving the freight of knapsacks by lasso as before. In this manner we consumed more than half the afternoon in descending a thousand feet of broken, precipitous slope. The gorge below us seemed utterly impassable. At our backs the Mount Brewer wall either rose in sheer cliffs or in broken, rugged stairways, such as had offered us our descent. From this cruel dilemma, the sole chance of scaling the divide was at its junction with the Mount Brewer wall. A high granite wall surrounded us upon three sides, recurring to the southward in long elliptical curves; no part of the summit being less than two thousand feet above us. A single field of snow swept around the base of the rock, and covered the whole amphitheatre, except where a few spikes and rounded masses of granite rose through it, and where two frozen lakes, with their blue ice-disks, broke the monotonous surface. Through the white snow-gate of our amphitheatre, as through a frame, we looked eastward upon the summit group; not a tree, not a vestige of vegetation in sight,—sky, snow, and granite the only elements in this wild picture.

There was no foot hold above us. Looking down over the course we had come, it seemed an impossible descent. To turn back was to give up in defeat; and we sat at least half an hour, suggesting all possible routes to the summit, accepting none, and feeling disheartened. About thirty feet directly over our heads was another shelf, which, if we could reach, seemed to offer at least a temporary way upward. On its edge were two or three spikes of granite; whether firmly connected with the cliff, or merely blocks of debris, we could not tell from below.

I said to Cotter, I thought of but one possible plan: it was to lasso one of these blocks, and to climb, sailor-fashion, hand over hand, up the rope. In the lasso I had perfect confidence, for I had seen more than one Spanish bull throw his whole weight against it without parting a strand. The shelf was so narrow that throwing the coil of rope was a very difficult undertaking. I tried three times. At last I made a lucky throw, and it tightened upon one of the smaller protuberances. I drew the noose close, and very gradually threw my hundred and fifty pounds upon the rope; then Cotter joined me, and, for a moment, we both hung our united weight upon it. Whether the rock moved slightly or whether the lasso stretched a little we were unable to decide; but the trial must be made, and I began to climb slowly. The smooth precipice-face against which my body swung offered no foothold, and the whole climb had therefore to be done by the arms, an effort requiring all one's determination. When about half-way up I was obliged to rest, and, curling my feet in the rope, managed to relieve my arms for a moment. In this position I could not resist the fascinating temptation of a survey downward.

Straight down, nearly a thousand feet below, at the foot of the rocks, began the snow, whose steep, roof-like slope, exaggerated into an almost vertical angle, curved down in a long white field, broken far away by rocks and polished, round lakes of ice. Cotter looked up cheerfully and asked how I was making it; to which I answered that I had plenty of wind left. At that moment, when hanging between heaven and earth, it was a deep satisfaction to look down at the wild gulf of desolation beneath, and up to unknown dangers ahead, and feel my nerves cool and unshaken.

A few pulls hand over hand brought me to the edge of the shelf, when, throwing an arm around the granite spike, I swung my body upon the shelf and lay down to rest, shouting to Cotter that I was all right. After a few moments breathing I looked over the brink and directed my comrade to tie the barometer to the low end of the lasso, which he did, and that precious instrument was hoisted to my station, and the lasso sent down twice for knapsacks, after which Cotter came up the rope in his very muscular way without once stopping to rest. We took our loads in our hands, swinging the barometer over my shoulder, and climbed up a shelf which led in zigzag direction upward and to the south, bringing us out at last upon the thin blade of a ridge. It was formed of huge blocks, shattered, and ready, at a touch, to fall. So narrow and sharp was the upper slope, that we dared not walk, but got astride, and worked slowly along with our hands, pushing the knapsacks in advance, now and then holding our breath when loose masses rocked under our weight.

[King and Cotter had reached the crest of the Kings-Kern Divide. To their dismay, a glance ahead revealed that the slope they now had to descend was even steeper than the one they had just come up. As for the ridge itself, it was terrifyingly narrow and unstable. Uncertain of how to proceed, the two men exercised the time-honored choice of mountaineers in difficult situations, which is to sit down and eat lunch.]

I suggested that by lowering ourselves on the rope we might climb from crevice to crevice; but we saw no shelf large enough for ourselves and the knapsacks too. However, we were not going to give it up without a trial; and I made the rope fast round my breast, and, looping the noose over a firm point of rock, let myself slide gradually down to a notch forty feet below. There was only room beside me for Cotter, so I made him send down the knapsacks first. I then tied these together by the straps with my silk handkerchiefs, and hung them off as far to the left as I could reach without losing my balance, looping the handkerchiefs over a point of rock. Cotter then slid down the rope, and, with considerable difficulty, we shipped the noose off its resting-place above, and cut off our connection with the upper world.

The shelf was hardly more than two feet wide, and the granite so smooth that we could find no place to fasten the lasso for the next descent; so I determined to try the climb with only as little aid as possible. Tying it round my breast again, I gave the other end into Cotter's hands, and he, bracing his back against the cliff, found for himself as firm a foothold as he could, and promised to give me all the help in his power. I made up my mind to bear no weight unless it was absolutely necessary; and for the first ten feet I found cracks and protuberances enough to support me, making every square inch of surface do friction duty, and hugging myself against the rocks as tightly as I could. When within about eight feet of the next shelf, I twisted myself round upon the face, hanging by two rough blocks of protruding feldspar, and looked vainly for some further hand-hold; but the rock, beside being perfectly smooth, overhung slightly, and my legs dangled in the air. I saw that the next cleft was over three feet broad, and I thought, possibly, I might, by a quick slide, reach it in safety without endangering Cotter. I shouted to him to be very careful and let go in case I fell, loosened my hold upon the rope, and slid quickly down. My shoulder struck against the rock and threw me out of balance; for an instant I reeled over upon the verge, in danger of falling but, in the excitement, I thrust out my hand and seized a small alpine gooseberry-bush. Its roots were so firmly fixed in the crevice that it held my weight and saved me.

I could no longer see Cotter, but I talked to him, and heard the two knapsacks come bumping along till they slid over the eaves above me, and swung down to my station, when I seized the lasso's end and braced myself as well as possible, intending, if he slipped, to haul in slack and help him as best I might. As he came slowly down from crack to crack, I heard his hobnailed shoes grating on the granite; presently they appeared dangling from the eaves above my head. I had gathered in the rope until it was taut, and then hurriedly told him to drop. He hesitated a moment, and let go. Before he struck the rock I had him by the shoulder, and whirled him down upon his side, thus preventing his rolling overboard, which friendly action he took quite coolly. . . .

—Clarence King, *Mountaineering in the Sierra Nevada*

In this manner they painstakingly descended the cliff, successfully crossing the Kings-Kern Divide, then hiked across easier terrain to their final ascent. After climbing up smooth granite faces and fearfully steep slopes of ice to the summit, they made a startling discovery: "To our surprise, upon sweeping the horizon with my level, there appeared two peaks equal in height with us, and two rising even higher." They were not atop Mount Whitney, but Mount Tyndall, 6 miles north of their goal. Reaching Mount Whitney was now out of the question. With supplies running short, the men were forced to return to their camp near Mount Brewer.

Mount Brewer ★

Height: 13,570 feet

Route: South Face

Best time to go: April through early May (after the road to Roads End is opened)

Trip duration: 4 days, longer if the traverse or crest tour is completed

Mileage: About 14 miles to the summit

Elevation gain: About 9,035 feet to the summit

Effort factor: 16.0

Level of difficulty: Advanced (Black Diamond)

Snowboards: Not recommended; a long approach

Maps: The Sphinx, Sphinx Lakes, Mount Brewer

Mount Brewer is the dominant peak in a region of dominant peaks. Within a 4-mile radius of Mount Brewer there is a cluster of superb peaks, each exceeding 13,000 feet, that are highly prized among climbers—Thunder Mountain, Table Mountain, North Guard, South Guard, and Midway Mountain. From the summit are unobstructed views of the Great Western Divide to the south and the Kings-Kern Divide to the east, and, farther to the east, great views of Mount Tyndall, Mount Williamson (Summit 42), Mount Russell, Mount Whitney (Summit 43), and Mount Muir, all over 14,000 feet.

Two ski descent routes on Mount Brewer—the South Face and the Northwest Face—are described here. Both are approached from Sphinx Lakes.

Drive to Fresno (Highway 99) and proceed east on Highway 180 to Kings Canyon National Park and Roads End (5,035 feet); the road to Roads End is usually plowed by the middle of April. Park here, and hike the South Fork Kings River Trail for 2 miles. At the junction, take the right fork, Bubbs Creek Trail.

The trail gradually climbs out of the main valley floor as it ascends the cascading Bubbs Creek. In 2 miles take another right fork and follow the steep Sphinx Creek Trail as it switchbacks up the granite face for about 2.5 miles. About a quarter mile before the trail crosses Sphinx Creek, leave the trail and follow the main creek past the first four Sphinx Lakes (9,610 to 10,520 feet in elevation). This area makes for a good sheltered camp at the treeline. The Sphinx Lakes basin is ideal ski touring terrain with many opportunities to explore.

The route to Mount Brewer continues up the main branch of Sphinx Creek, past the fifth lake (10,900 feet) and two small tarns (11,300 feet), and through the pass at 12,000 feet. The North Guard–Brewer cirque and the steep Northwest Face of Mount Brewer come into view for the first time at the crest of the pass. Lose a little elevation and make a high traverse near the 11,500-foot level around the sub-ridge of North Guard. Ascend the North Guard–Brewer cirque and the Northwest Face of Mount Brewer, or ski up Brewer Creek through the small notch and the two lakes (near 12,000 feet) nestled in the granite notch just below the grand South Face of Mount Brewer. Camp here or ski down to South Guard Lake (11,600 feet). Both are ideal sites for a base camp for your climb and descent of the South Face.

The center of the South Face is divided by a granite rock rib forming two distinct wide snow gullies. Climb the face by ascending the rib, or climb to one side or the other of the rib. The face is steep and avalanche prone, so be cautious. The prominent rib in the center of the face should afford some protection from snow slides if they do occur. Pick your descent line; the skiing is superb.

OTHER OPTIONS FROM MOUNT BREWER
In addition to Mount Brewer's Northwest and South Faces, this area has many options for the wilderness skier. You could, of course, return following your approach route. Or you could make a west-to-east Sierra traverse, or a north-to-south Sierra-crest tour.

Sierra Traverse to Onion Valley: To traverse the Sierra Nevada west to east, ski over the saddle between Mount Brewer and South Guard, down Ouzel Creek to

From the air, the east ridge of Mount Brewer, with the South Face ski descent route on the left. Photo by Colin Fuller

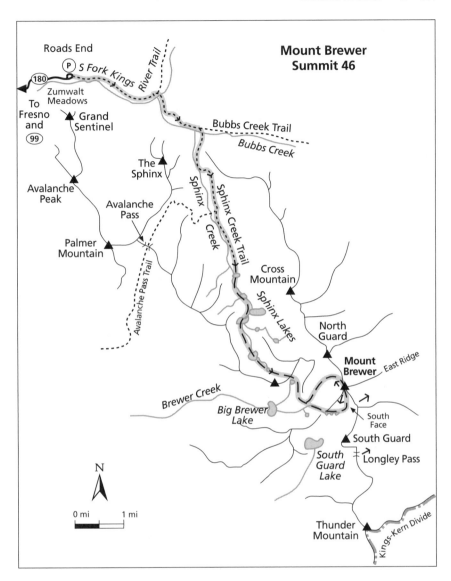

Mount Brewer
Summit 46

East Lake, Junction Meadow, up to Vidette Meadow, and over Kearsarge Pass to Onion Valley Road (see the Mount Whitney region map in Chapter 9 and the trip map for Summits 40 and 41). Or instead of skiing over the saddle between Mount Brewer and South Guard, ski down to South Guard Lake and up over Longley Pass and down to Lake Reflection and East Lake. From South Guard Lake, the traverse east over Kearsarge Pass is about 21 miles. This is 7 miles longer than a direct return to your starting point.

Sierra-Crest Tour (High Sierra Route): A Sierra-crest trip would entail a bit more effort but is one of the grand tours in California. The maps for Summits 47 and 48 show the section from Colby Pass to Wolverton. From the outlet of South Guard Lake, climb up to Longley Pass (12,400 feet) and descend the steep east side of the pass. You are now on the north side of the great Kings-Kern Divide, the great wall that Clarence King and Dick Cotter found so imposing in 1864 (see sidebar). Thunder Pass (12,700+ feet), 0.2 mile east of Thunder Mountain, is the most direct route over the Kings-Kern Divide. However, this route is quite steep. Alternatively, a ski descent to Lake Reflection provides three options for crossing the Kings-Kern Divide—Milly's Foot Pass, Lucy's Foot Pass, and Harrison Pass. Harrison Pass is the farthest but the least steep of the routes.

From any of these four passes, drop down into the upper Kern River basin and turn up Milestone Creek, being careful not to angle too far to the south (left) into the impressive U-shaped cirque. This cirque, rimmed by magnificent vertical granite walls, leads to a dead end. Follow Milestone Creek up to the right, angling toward the prominent summit of Milestone Mountain. Do not cross the obvious gap between Milestone and Midway Mountain, but rather take the less obvious route over the left (southeast) shoulder of Milestone Mountain. Ski down Milestone Bowl to 11,200 feet, south and east of Colby Pass. Again, don't do the obvious: Don't climb up to Colby Pass but rather climb the steep shoulder cresting at 12,000 feet about 0.5 mile south of Colby Pass.

Traverse into a small lake basin, dropping to near 11,300 feet before climbing up to Triple Divide Pass (12,200 feet) and down into upper Cloud Canyon to Glacier Lake (see the map for Summit 48). Ski around and below the steep bluff to the west of Glacier Lake and traverse across the top of Cloud Canyon and Deadman Canyon, returning to the Tableland, Pear Lake Hut, and the ending point at Wolverton Ski Area (see the map for Summit 47). The high traverse across Cloud Canyon and Deadman Canyon is impressive—you have the sense of being on top of the world, with mist and clouds sweeping up from the valleys far below. The descent from the crest of the Tableland down to Pear Lake Hut is one of the best intermediate descents in the Sierra, a remarkable and enjoyable three- to four-mile cruise. For more details on the route from Glacier Lake down to Wolverton, see the trip descriptions for Summits 47 and 48.

You may want to consider reversing the direction of the trip by starting at Wolverton in Sequoia National Park at 7,300 feet rather than the lower Roads End in Kings Canyon National Park at 5,035 feet. In planning your trip, make sure the road to Roads End is open. It is not plowed in the winter but is usually open to the public by the middle of April, while the road to Wolverton is open year round.

From South Guard Lake, the Sierra-crest tour is 23–27 miles, depending on the exact route you choose. This is about 9 miles longer than the direct ski out to your starting point.

47
Tableland

Height: 11,485 feet
Route: Pear Lake Hut
Best time to go: December through early May
Trip duration: 3 days
Mileage: 10 miles to the crest
Elevation gain: 4,425 feet
Effort factor: 9.5
Level of difficulty: Intermediate
Snowboards: Not recommended; a long approach
Maps: Lodgepole, Triple Divide Peak, Mount Silliman

Pear Lake Hut is, by far, the nicest backcountry hut in California and makes an excellent base camp for day tours into the Tableland and some of the finest intermediate ski cruising terrain in California.

Pear Lake Hut, located just below Pear Lake, serves as a great base camp to ski the Tableland, Winter Alta, Mount Alta, and the High Sierra Route. Photo by Steve Leach

Drive to Visalia (Highway 99) and proceed east on Highway 198 to Sequoia National Park. The road is open throughout the winter. Starting at the Pear Lake trailhead, located near the Wolverton Ski Area (7,300 feet), follow the route of the summer hiking trail up and over The Hump (9,440+ feet) and down to Heather Lake (9,200 feet). The trail begins in heavy timber, but the terrain changes markedly as you break out of the trees into the alpine setting near Emerald Lake. Pear Lake Hut, located at 9,200 feet, about 0.5 mile below

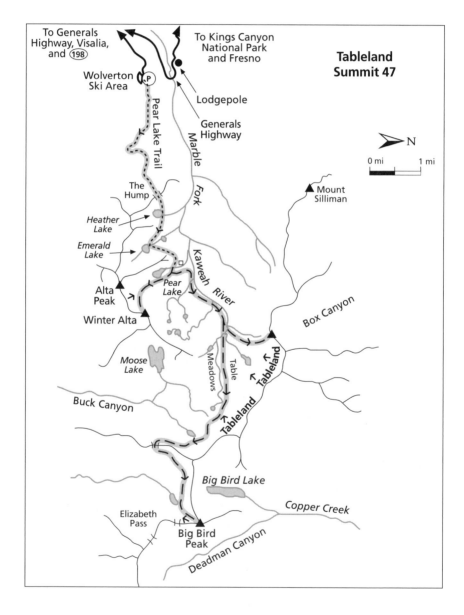

Pear Lake (9,510 feet) and about 6 trail miles from Wolverton, is a popular destination, and reservations are required; contact Sequoia National Park Natural History Association (see Appendix 5, "Cross-Country Ski Lodges and Back-country Huts").

From the hut, continue up the Marble Fork Kaweah River to Table Meadows. At the 10,000-foot level, either turn north and ski up to the crest of the Tableland at 11,485 feet, or continue east along the Tableland to point 11,598 feet. It's worth the extra effort to traverse to Big Bird Peak (11,602), passing through the 10,800-foot saddle south of the 11,598-foot crest and into the lake basin southwest of the peak. From this unnamed lake, ski up the southwest slopes of Big Bird Peak to the top. From here you will have expansive views of the spectacular Deadman Canyon, Cloud Canyon, and Big Bird Lake far below.

The ski back to Pear Lake Hut is one of the finest intermediate descents in the Sierra Nevada. Depending on the route you take, you can expect a continuous run of 3–4 miles over wonderful and varied terrain.

Another favorite ski descent near the Pear Lake Hut is to ski Winter Alta and the bowl below Alta Peak. This north-facing cirque, rimmed by Alta Peak and the high ridge that extends from Alta Peak to Winter Alta, holds excellent skiing opportunities. Alta Peak is about 1 mile south of Pear Lake, and Winter Alta is located about 0.7 mile northeast of Alta Peak.

Mount Kaweah ★

Height: 13,802 feet	
Route: South Ridge	
Best time to go: March through early May	
Trip duration: 7 days or more	
Mileage: About 24 miles to the summit	
Elevation gain: About 9,600 feet	
Effort factor: 23.6	
Level of difficulty: Advanced (Black Diamond)	
Snowboards: Not recommended; extremely long approach	
Maps: Lodgepole, Triple Divide Peak, Mount Kaweah, Mount Brewer, Sphinx Lakes	

The circumnavigation of the Kaweahs takes the ski mountaineer over the western portion of the High Sierra Route, a classic trans-Sierra traverse (see also Summit 46 for a description of the route). This may be the most demanding multiday trip in the guide, but it has everything—great ski descents, superb alpine scenery, rugged terrain, extreme remoteness, and a summit seldom visited in the summer, let alone the winter or spring. After the first day of your

*Mount Kaweah with the Kaweah Range on the right, as seen from the summit of
Mount Whitney*

trip there is a good chance you will not see anyone for the rest of this mini-
expedition.

The trip begins at the Pear Lake trailhead, located near the Wolverton Ski
Area; follow the Summit 47 map and route description for the route into Pear
Lake Hut, Table Meadow, and the terrain along the south face of the Tableland
toward Big Bird Peak.

As with the previous trip, from Pear Lake Hut ski up the Marble Fork Kaweah
River to the beautiful Table Meadow and the two upper tarns near 10,800 feet.
Continue in a southeasterly direction near the 11,000-foot level, crossing a
10,800-foot pass in a prominent spur ridge jutting south off of the main crest.
Traverse into the basin and the unnamed lake at 10,800 feet nestled in the
basin just south of Big Bird Peak (now see the map for Summit 48). Ski over the
pass due south of Big Bird Peak (11,300 feet) into the upper glacial cirque of
Deadman Canyon. Make the traverse across the top of the canyon and over
the next small pass that divides Deadman Canyon from Cloud Canyon. The
impressive west ridge of Triple Divide Peak is in full view. These high traverses
are spectacular and give a sense of extreme height and exposure as the clouds
rise from the valleys below. Ski to the head of Cloud Canyon and over the
small notch (11,600 feet) located directly above Lion Lake. Descend to the area
around Lion Lake, which is an excellent place to camp.

As you ski from lake to lake in the Nine Lake Basin and start down the Big Arroyo, you will pass Lion Rock, Mount Stewart, and Kaweah Gap on the right, and the Kaweah Ridge and the impressive Black Kaweah, Red Kaweah, and Mount Kaweah on the left. Black Kaweah is one of the great peaks of the Sierra Nevada—high, remote, visually impressive, and seldom climbed. Since the first ascent in 1920, fewer than a hundred climbers have reached its summit.

Continue to the south of Mount Kaweah. Ski up the south slopes to the

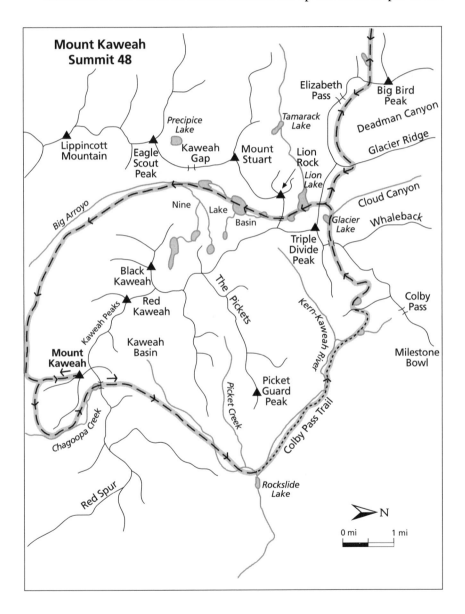

summit, a climb of more than 3,000 feet. From the top there are wonderful views in all directions, especially of the Whitney group just 12 miles to the east.

The ski descent from the summit is breathtaking—a 3,000-foot blast. Continue down and around the base of Mount Kaweah to Chagoopa Creek. Head north up the creek to the lake just below Kaweah Pass at 12,400 feet. Cross the pass and ski into the Kaweah Basin. This is as remote as it gets. You are now 4 or 5 days out with another 3 days to get back to civilization. Ski down the basin to Rockslide Lake and the Kern-Kaweah River below. An alternate route would be to stay high and ski across the Kaweah Basin, crossing a minor pass at 10,900 feet into Picket Creek, then through the 11,900-foot pass between The Pickets and Picket Guard Peak.

From Rockslide Lake turn left (west) up the Kern-Kaweah River and follow the Colby Pass Trail north toward Colby Pass. Stop short of Colby Pass and turn east-southeast at 11,200 feet and climb the steep shoulder (12,000 feet) located about 0.5 mile south of Colby Pass. Traverse into a small lake basin, dropping to near 11,300 feet before climbing up to Triple Divide Pass (12,200 feet), and drop into upper Cloud Canyon to Glacier Lake. Ski around and below the steep bluff to the west of Glacier Lake and traverse across the top of Cloud Canyon and Deadman Canyon, returning to the Tableland, Pear Lake, and the starting point at the Wolverton Ski Area.

The descent of the Tableland, from its 11,400-plus-foot crest, down to Pear Lake Hut is one of the best intermediate runs in the Sierra.

49
Sawtooth Peak

Height: 12,343 feet	
Route: Monarch Lake	
Best time to go: February through May	
Trip duration: 1 day	
Mileage: 5 miles	
Elevation gain: 4,543 feet to the summit	
Effort factor: 7.0	
Level of difficulty: Intermediate	
Snowboards: Recommended; steep terrain with short approach	
Map: Mineral King	

The Monarch Lakes are nestled in a beautiful lake basin just below Sawtooth and Mineral Peaks at an elevation of 10,400 feet. Sawtooth Peak is a favorite of

The spectacular North Face of Sawtooth Peak. Skiers can ascend either the left or right skyline. Photo by Guy McClure

summer climbers and is equally enjoyable to the ski mountaineer or snow-boarder in the early spring. Empire Mountain, 1.5 miles northwest of Sawtooth Peak and Glacier Pass, is also a wonderful ski destination. Since these slopes face south and west, the skiing is best early in the season.

From Visalia on Highway 99, drive east on Highway 198 to the town of Three Rivers. Just beyond Three Rivers and about 2 miles before the Sequoia National Park entrance, turn right onto Mineral King Road. This road is not

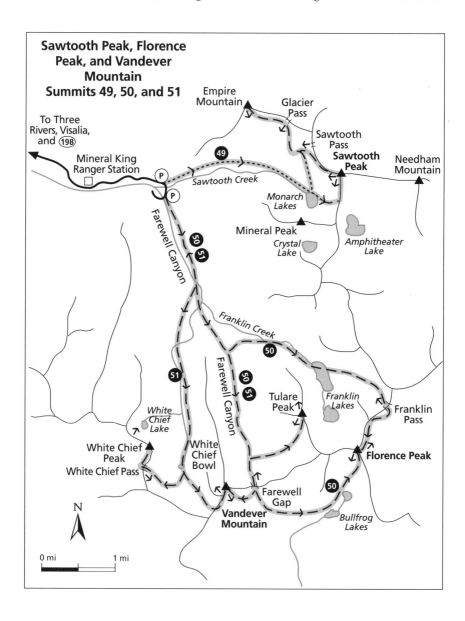

Sawtooth Peak, Florence Peak, and Vandever Mountain
Summits 49, 50, and 51

open in the winter but is usually open by the last week in May. It is long, narrow, and winding (698 curves), and the drive to the trailhead will take at least 90 minutes. After 18.2 miles you'll pass the gate that closes the road in winter and spring; Silver City at 21.7 miles; and the Mineral King Ranger Station at 24.4 miles. Drive 0.9 mile beyond the ranger station to the Sawtooth Peak parking area (7,800 feet).

Follow the route of the summer trail to Lower Monarch Lake. If there is plenty of snow coverage in the basin above 8,800 feet, leave the trail and follow the valley and the route of the stream to the Monarch Lakes. From Lower Monarch Lake climb to the upper lake and the pass at 11,400 feet, south of Sawtooth Peak leading to Amphitheater Lake to the southeast. From the pass, climb to the summit. Alternatively, follow the route of the summer trail north toward Glacier Pass (11,100 feet) and then switchback up to Sawtooth Pass (11,600 feet) and follow the ridge to the summit. The upper slopes of both these routes may have inadequate snow coverage due to the southerly exposure.

Sawtooth Peak, Empire Mountain, and Glacier Pass can be skied or snowboarded in a single day. However, this compact area makes for an excellent multiday trip as well. A base camp at the Monarch Lakes provides the opportunity to explore the area, with side trips to Spring Lake, Columbine Lake, or Amphitheater Lake. These lakes are located on the far (east) side of the ridge crest.

If a trip is planned before the road is opened in May, add about 7 miles to the distances above. Plan to start walking/skiing at around mile 18.2 (at the gate) on Mineral King Road. The skiing in the winter and early spring before the road is opened is worth the added effort.

50
Florence Peak

Height: 12,432 feet	
Routes: Franklin Pass, Northeast Slopes	
Best time to go: March through May	
Trip duration: 1 or 2 days	
Mileage: 6 miles to the summit	
Elevation gain: 4,632 feet	
Effort factor: 7.6	
Level of difficulty: Advanced (Black Diamond)	
Snowboards: Recommended; short approach and steep terrain	
Map: Mineral King	

Florence Peak is the tallest peak in the ring of summits high above Mineral King Valley and has two fine ascent and descent routes from its summit. One route is via Farewell Gap and the Bullfrog Lakes, and the other is by way of Franklin Pass and the upper northeast slopes of the summit. In addition, there are numerous other skiing opportunities in the immediate area, including the impressive northwest bowl above the Franklin Lakes and below Florence Peak and the east- or west-facing slopes of Tulare Peak. A base camp at 9,200 feet in Farewell Canyon would allow excellent access to the trips described below and those of Vandever Mountain (Summit 51).

To reach the start for either route, follow the directions in the previous description (Summit 49) to the Mineral King Ranger Station near the end of Mineral King Road. Drive 1.2 miles beyond the office to the parking area near the road to the pack station (7,800 feet).

From the end of Mineral King Road, ski up Farewell Canyon for about 2 miles. The route is relatively flat and gains only 600 feet. Leave Farewell Canyon (near 8,400 feet) and ascend the creek that drains the Franklin Lakes; the

The view of the Franklin Lakes Bowl and the Northwest Face of Florence Peak (on the left) from Rainbow Peak. Tulare Peak is on the right. Photo by Guy McClure

route steepens and climbs nearly 2,000 feet. From the upper lake climb another 1,400 feet to Franklin Pass (11,700 feet) and up the northeast slopes to the summit of Florence Peak.

The view from the top is impressive. Not only do you see Vandever Mountain, Tulare Peak, White Chief Peak, and Sawtooth Peak, but there are some exceptional views of the Kaweahs and the Whitney Group—Mount Langley, Mount LeConte, and Mount Whitney.

The skiing off the summit to the northeast is on moderately steep terrain. As you descend Franklin Pass, the slopes steepen considerably for about 600 feet; use caution, as they avalanche and a fall would be difficult to arrest. The slopes on this route, facing predominantly north, hold the snow late into the season. An alternate route to the summit of Florence Peak would be to ski up Farewell Canyon and over Farewell Gap (10,600+ feet). From the gap, complete a high traverse to Bullfrog Lakes and climb the south-southwest bowl to the summit. The snow on these south-facing slopes melts more quickly.

Tulare Peak can be approached from either Farewell Canyon or the upper Franklin Lake and can be skied on either side. The south- and west-facing slopes will be better early in the morning and early in the season, and the north and east slopes will hold the snow longer. A ski down the east side of Tulare Peak will take you into the Franklin Lakes bowl below the impressive and inspiring northeast face of Florence Peak.

If a trip is planned before the road is opened in May, add about 7 miles to the distances above. Plan to start walking/skiing at around mile 18.2 (at the gate) on Mineral King Road. The skiing in the winter and early spring before the road is opened is worth the added effort.

51
Vandever Mountain

Height: 11,947 feet	
Route: Farewell Gap	
Best time to go: February through early June	
Trip duration: 1 day	
Mileage: 5 miles to the summit	
Elevation gain: 4,147 feet	
Effort factor: 6.6	
Level of difficulty: Intermediate	
Snowboards: Recommended	
Map: Mineral King	

The glacial cirque between Vandever Mountain and White Chief Peak contains excellent skiing. This north-facing cirque holds the snow the longest of

Vandever Peak and the White Chief Bowl. The White Chief Bowl has the best late-season skiing in the Mineral King area. Photo by Guy McClure

any of the routes in the Mineral King area. There was adequate snow in mid-July 1998 to ski White Chief Pass and the large bowl between White Chief Peak and Vandever Peak. Granted, 1998 was a heavy snow year, but this example illustrates that this is a likely place to find late-season skiing.

To reach the start for this route, follow the directions for Sawtooth Peak (Summit 49) to the Mineral King Ranger Station near the end of Mineral King Road. Drive 1.2 miles beyond the office to the parking area near the road to the pack station.

From the end of Mineral King Road, ski up Farewell Canyon to Farewell Gap (10,600 feet), a climb of 2,800 feet over about 4 miles. Climb the southeast slopes of Vandever Mountain to the summit. From here you can descend your ascent route or take an alternate route into White Chief Bowl. To ski into White Chief Bowl, ski or snowboard off the summit to the southwest, dropping about 400 feet to near the 11,600-foot level. Turn to the north-northwest and ski down the spur ridge that divides the northwest face. You can follow the ridge some distance, or peel off the ridge to either the left into White Chief Bowl or to the right and down the couloir between the main north ridge and the north-northwest spur.

An alternate approach is to ski up Farewell Canyon to around 9,000 feet (about a quarter mile below the creek junction) and traverse west into the valley and stream that drains the White Chief Bowl. Cross the route of the summer trail near 9,300 feet and climb into White Chief Bowl—the large glacial cirque between White Chief Peak and Vandever Mountain. Climb either Vandever Mountain or White Chief Peak via White Chief Pass. There is also good skiing from the pass between White Chief Peak and Eagle Crest to White Chief Lake.

If a trip is planned before the road is opened in May, add about 7 miles to the distances above. Plan to start walking/skiing at around mile 18.2 (at the gate) on Mineral King Road. The skiing in the winter and early spring before the road is opened is worth the added effort.

The Last Run—Appendices
Appendix 1: The Best of the Classics

SKI MOUNTAINEER'S PEAKS ★

The Ski Mountaineer's Peak designation (★), used in this guide to identify the twenty finest snowboard and ski mountaineer summits in California, is awarded based on the total ski experience—the approach, the climb, and the ski descent. Factors that were considered include the quality of the skiing, the length of the ski descent, aesthetics of the mountain and route, the peak's elevation and dominance in the region, and the inaccessibility (remoteness) of the summit. Many peaks with this designation may require a high level of mountaineering skill, including experience with ice axe and crampons, and a few may require the use of a rope. The Ski Mountaineer's Peaks are, from north to south:

Mount Shasta (Summits 1, 2, and 3)	Mount Goddard (Summit 33)
Lassen Peak (Summit 5)	North Palisade (Summit 34)
Matterhorn Peak (Summit 18)	Mount Sill (Summit 36)
Mount Lyell (Summit 22)	The Thumb (Summit 37)
Mount Ritter (Summit 23)	Birch Mountain (Summit 38)
Red Slate Mountain (Summit 25)	University Peak (Summit 41)
Mount Dade (Summit 26)	Mount Williamson (Summit 42)
Mount Tom (Summit 28)	Mount Whitney (Summit 43)
Mount Humpherys (Summit 30)	Mount Brewer (Summit 46)
Mount Darwin (Summit 32)	Mount Kaweah (Summit 48)

THE SNOWBOARD CHALLENGE

The best snowboard summits are those with short, direct access and continuous, steep terrain. Following is a selection of the summits meeting these criteria. Many of these peaks can be done in a single day. These summits are equally challenging and appropriate for the free-heel (tele) and fixed-heel (randonnée) skier.

Mount Shasta ★ (Summits 2 and 3)	Bloody Mountain (Summit 24)
Lassen Peak (Summit 6)	Mount Tom ★ (Summit 28)
Mount Tallac (Summit 10)	Basin Mountain (Summit 29)
Pyramid Peak (Summit 11)	Mount Humphreys ★ (Summit 30)
Red Lake Peak (Summit 13)	North Palisade ★ (Summit 34)
Mount Walt (Summit 16)	Birch Mountain ★ (Summit 38)
Cleaver Peak (Summit 17)	University Peak ★ (Summit 41)
Matterhorn Peak ★ (Summit 18)	Mount Whitney ★ (Summit 43)
Mount Dana (Summit 20)	

Backcountry snowboarding in the Sierra Nevada Photo by John Moynier

SINGLE-DAY GEMS

The following excellent peaks can be skied or snowboarded in a single day.

Mount Shasta ★ (Summit 3)
Shastina (Summit 4)
Lassen Peak ★ (Summits 5 and 6)
Mount Diller (Summit 7)
Mount Rose (Summit 8)
Mount Tallac (Summit 10)
Pyramid Peak (Summit 11)
Ralston Peak (Summit 12)
Red Lake Peak (Summit 13)
Leavitt Peak (Summit 15)
Mount Walt (Summit 16)
Cleaver Peak (Summit 17)
Matterhorn Peak ★ (Summit 18)

Dunderberg Peak (Summit 19)
Mount Dana (Summit 20)
Koip Peak (Summit 21)
Bloody Mountain (Summit 24)
Mount Tom ★ (Summit 28)
Basin Mountain (Summit 29)
Mount Lamarck (Summit 31)
Birch Mountain ★ (Summit 38)
Mount Gould (Summit 40)
Sawtooth Peak or Empire
   Mountain (Summit 49)
Vandever Mountain or White
   Chief Bowl (Summit 51)

Appendix 2: The Fifty Classics Listed by Level of Difficulty

The three tables that follow list each summit described in this guide. The trips are grouped by the level of skiing ability required—intermediate, advanced (Black Diamond), or expert (Double Black Diamond). Within each table, the peaks are arranged by the effort required for each summit climb (effort factor). As explained in Chapter 1, "Ascent and Descent Ratings," the effort factor rating measures the amount of effort necessary to climb each peak by combining the number of miles with the amount of elevation gain.

Skiing near Treasure Lakes (Summit 26) Photo by John Moynier

INTERMEDIATE SKI TERRAIN

Summit Number	Peak Name	Peak Elevation	Region	Route	Miles	Elev. Gain (in feet)	Effort Factor
13	Red Lake Peak	10,061	Tahoe	Northeast Bowl	3	1,561	3.1
9	Signal Peak	7,841	Tahoe	Fordyce Road	2.5	2,140	3.4
9	Castle Peak	9,103	Tahoe	West Ridge	3	2,000	3.5
12	Ralston Peak	9,235	Tahoe	South Slope	2	2,735	3.7
7	Mount Diller	9,087	Lassen	Ridge Lakes	3	2,287	3.8
40	Kearsarge Peak	12,618	Whitney	Sardine Canyon	3	3,418	4.9
10	Mount Tallac	9,735	Tahoe	South Ramp	4	3,300	5.3
20	Mount Dana	13,057	Yosemite	West Slopes	4	3,407	5.4
11	Pyramid Peak	9,983	Tahoe	South Ridge	3	3,983	5.5
51	White Chief Peak	11,040	Sequoia	White Chief Pass	5	3,240	5.7
50	Tulare Peak	11,588	Sequoia	Franklin Lakes	4	3,788	5.8
49	Empire Mountain	11,509	Sequoia	South Face	5	3,709	6.2
51	Vandever Peak	11,947	Sequoia	Farewell Gap	5	4,147	6.6
49	Sawtooth Peak	12,343	Sequoia	Monarch Lakes	5	4,543	7.0
14	Tryon Peak	9,920	Yosemite	Northeast Bowl	8	3,120	7.1
17	Cleaver Peak	11,760	Yosemite	Northeast Face	5	4,660	7.2
19	Dunderberg Peak	12,374	Yosemite	Northeast Ridge	7	4,236	7.7
19	Dunderberg Peak	12,374	Yosemite	Southeast Gully #2	7	4,236	7.7
47	Winter Alta	11,200	Sequoia	Pear Lake Hut	8	3,900	7.9
31	Mount Lamarck	13,417	Bishop	Lamarck Col	7	4,917	8.4
15	Leavitt Peak	11,570	Yosemite	East Ridge	8	4,370	8.4
27	Mount Morgan (South)	13,748	Mammoth	North Ridge	8	4,848	8.9
47	Tableland	11,485	Sequoia	Pear Lake Hut	10	4,425	9.5
39	Striped Mountain	13,120	Palisades	Northeast Bowl	8	7,779	11.8
22	Mount Lyell ★	13,114	Yosemite	Lyell Glacier	12	6,500	12.5
33	Black Giant	13,330	Bishop	Northwest Face	13	6,400	12.9
36	Mount Sill ★	14,153	Palisades	Glacier Creek Cirque	16	9,300	17.3

ADVANCED (BLACK DIAMOND) SKI TERRAIN

Summit Number	Peak Name	Peak Elevation	Region	Route	Miles	Elev. Gain (in feet)	Effort Factor
6	Lassen Peak	10,457	Lassen	Northeast Face	2	2,000	3.0
9	Castle Peak	9,103	Tahoe	East Gully	3	2,000	3.5
10	Mount Tallac	9,735	Tahoe	Northeast Bowl	3	3,300	4.8
8	Mount Rose	10,776	Tahoe	Galena Creek	5	2,676	5.2
29	Basin Mountain	13,181	Bishop	Basin Couloir	2	4,800	5.8
13	Ralston Peak	9,235	Tahoe	Northeast Gullies	3	4,335	5.8
16	Mount Walt	11,480	Yosemite	North Ridge Ramp	4	4,380	6.4
27	Mount Morgan (North)	13,005	Mammoth	Esha Canyon	4	5,200	7.2
12	Price Peak	9,974	Tahoe	East Face	5	4,774	7.3
50	Florence Peak	12,432	Sequoia	Franklin Pass	6	4,632	7.6
19	Dunderberg Peak	12,374	Yosemite	North Couloir	7	4,236	7.7
19	Dunderberg Peak	12,374	Yosemite	Southeast Gully #1	7	4,236	7.7
47	Mount Alta	11,200	Sequoia	Pear Lake Hut	8	3,900	7.9
5	Lassen Peak ★	10,457	Lassen	Summit Traverse	7	4,600	8.1
21	Koip Peak	12,979	Yosemite	East Ridge	6	5,079	8.1
4	Shastina	12,330	Mount Shasta	Cascade Gulch	6	5,470	8.5
25	Red Slate Mountain ★	13,163	Mammoth	Northwest Couloir	6	5,583	8.6
44	Mount Irvine	13,779	Whitney	Meysan Lake Cirque	6	5,779	8.8
44	Mount LeConte	13,845	Whitney	North Face Gullies	6	5,845	8.8
27	Mount Morgan (South)	13,748	Mammoth	Headwall Gullies	8	4,848	8.9
26	Mount Dade ★	13,600	Mammoth	Hourglass Couloir	10	4,700+	9.7
35	Mount Sill	14,153	Palisades	L-Shaped Couloir	7	6,200	9.7
35	Mount Sill	14,153	Palisades	Northwest Couloir	7	6,200	9.7
40	Mount Gould	13,005	Whitney	East Bowl	8	5,805	9.8
28	Mount Tom ★	13,652	Bishop	Elderberry Canyon	5	7,352	9.9
3	Mount Shasta ★	14,162	Mount Shasta	Hotlum-Wintun Rdge	6	7,000	10.0
2	Mount Shasta ★	14,162	Mount Shasta	Bolam-Hotlum Ridge	6	7,162	10.2
38	Birch Mountain ★	13,665	Palisades	Southeast Face	6	7,165	10.2
37	The Thumb ★	13,388	Palisades	Southeast Ramp	7	6,888	10.4

Summit Number	Peak Name	Peak Elevation	Region	Route	Miles	Elev. Gain (in feet)	Effort Factor
41	University Peak ★	13,589	Whitney	Southeast Couloir	9	6,389	10.9
41	University Peak ★	13,589	Whitney	University Pass	9	6,389	10.9
38	Birch Mountain ★	13,665	Palisades	Birch Lake Glacier	8	7.165	11.2
23	Mount Ritter ★	13,157	Mammoth	Southeast Glacier	12	5,432	11.4
42	Mount Williamson ★	14,375	Whitney	North Fork Bairs Creek	7	8,175	11.7
45	Mount Pickering	13,474	Whitney	North Couloir	9	7,600	12.1
33	Mount Goddard ★	13,568	Bishop	North Ridge	16	7000	15.0
46	Mount Brewer ★	13,570	Sequoia	South Face	14	9,035	16.0
48	Mount Kaweah ★	13,802	Sequoia	South Ridge	24	9,600	23.6

EXPERT (DOUBLE BLACK DIAMOND) AND EXTREME SKI TERRAIN

Summit Number	Peak Name	Peak Elevation	Region	Route	Miles	Elev. Gain (in feet)	Effort Factor
24	Bloody Mountain	12,544	Mammoth	Bloody Couloir	3	3,544	5.0
20	North Peak	12,242	Yosemite	North Couloir	5	2,800	5.3
20	Mount Dana	13,057	Yosemite	Dana Couloir	4	3,407	5.4
20	Mount Dana	13,057	Yosemite	Solstice Couloir	4	3,407	5.4
20	Mount Dana	13,057	Yosemite	Ellery Bowl	4	3,407	5.4
18	Matterhorn Peak ★	12,279	Yosemite	East Couloir	5	5,179	7.7
18	Matterhorn Peak ★	12,279	Yosemite	East Ridge Ramp	5	5,179	7.7
30	Mount Humphreys ★	13,986	Bishop	Humphreys Couloir	5	5,586	8.1
25	Red Slate Mountain ★	13,163	Mammoth	Red Slate Couloir	6	5,583	8.6
43	Mount Whitney ★	14,491	Whitney	Mountaineers Route	6	6,191	9.2
34	North Palisade ★	14,242	Palisades	U-Notch	7	6,200	9.7
34	North Palisade ★	14,242	Palisades	V-Notch	7	6,200	9.7
34	Thunderbolt Peak	14,003	Palisades	North Couloir	7	6,200	9.7
28	Mount Tom ★	13,652	Bishop	Headwall Gullies	5	7,352	9.9
43	Mount Whitney ★	14,491	Whitney	North Face	8	6,191	10.2
41	University Peak ★	13,589	Whitney	North Couloir	9	6,389	10.9
32	Mount Darwin ★	13,381	Bishop	Darwin Glacier	9	6,917	11.4
39	Cardinal Mountain	13,396	Palisades	South Gullies	8	7,996	12.0
1	Mount Shasta ★	14,162	Mount Shasta	Whitney Glacier	8	8,662	12.7

Appendix 3: California's Hundred Highest Peaks

The following list was compiled using data from Steve Roper's *The Climber's Guide to the High Sierra*, R. J. Secor's *The High Sierra*, and the newly photo-revised USGS 7.5-minute topos. The revised topos adjust, up or down, many elevations from the older 15-minute maps due to more accurate mapping techniques available today. The 100 peaks are arranged in descending order of elevation, measured in feet.

Determining which peaks to include in a list of the 100 highest peaks in California seems simple enough. However, it is not always readily apparent whether a given high point is a peak or merely a point or pinnacle on the ridge leading to the main summit. To minimize subjectivity, I followed several guidelines: To qualify for the list, a peak must project conspicuously above its surroundings, rising at least 400 feet above the land bridge (col or pass) connecting it with the nearest peak and be at least 0.5 mile from its neighbor. Also it must be named on the USGS maps or have a commonly used name.

THE CALIFORNIA 100

Rank	Peak Name	Elevation	Region
1.	Mount Whitney	14,491	Mount Whitney
2.	Mount Williamson	14,370+	Mount Whitney
3.	White Mountain	14,246	White Mountains
4.	North Palisade	14,242	Palisades
5.	Mount Shasta	14,162	Mount Shasta
6.	Mount Sill	14,153	Palisades
7.	Mount Russell	14,088	Mount Whitney
8.	Split Mountain	14,042	Palisades
9.	Mount Langley	14,022	Mount Whitney
10.	Tyndall	14,019	Mount Whitney
11.	Middle Palisade	14,012	Palisades
12.	Mount Muir	14,012	Mount Whitney
13.	Thunderbolt Peak	14,003	Palisades
14.	Mount Barnard	13,989	Mount Whitney
15.	Mount Humphreys	13,986	Bishop
16.	Mount Keith	13,976	Mount Whitney
17.	Mount Stanford	13,973	Mount Whitney
18.	Trojan Peak	13,947	Mount Whitney
19.	Disappointment Peak	13,917	Palisades
20.	Mount Agassiz	13,893	Palisades
21.	Norman Clyde Peak	13,855	Palisades
22.	Junction Peak	13,845+	Mount Whitney
23.	Mount LeConte	13,845+	Mount Whitney
24.	Mount Mallory	13,845	Mount Whitney

25.	Caltech Peak	13,832	Mount Whitney
26.	Mount Darwin	13,831	Bishop
27.	Mount Kaweah	13,802+	Sequoia
28.	Mount McAdie	13,799	Mount Whitney
29.	Mount Irvine	13,779+	Mount Whitney
30.	Mount Winchell	13,775	Palisades
31.	Mount Morgan	13,748	Mammoth Lakes
32.	Mount Gabb	13,741	Mammoth Lakes
33.	Bear Creek Spire	13,720+	Mammoth Lakes
34.	Red Kaweah	13,720+	Sequoia
35.	Mount Mendel	13,710	Bishop
36.	Mount Abbot	13,704	Mammoth Lakes
37.	Black Kaweah	13,680+	Sequoia
38.	Midway Mountain	13,665	Mount Whitney
39.	Mount Tom	13,652	Bishop
40.	Milestone Mountain	13,638	Mount Whitney
41.	Table Mountain	13,632	Mount Whitney
42.	Second Kaweah	13,602	Sequoia
43.	Birch Mountain	13,602	Palisades
44.	Mount Dade	13,600+	Mammoth Lakes
45.	University Peak	13,589	Mount Whitney
46.	Mount Brewer	13,570	Sequoia
47.	Mount Goddard	13,568	Bishop
48.	Tunnabora Peak	13,563	Mount Whitney
49.	Mount Dubois	13,559	White Mountains
50.	Cloudripper	13,525	Palisades
51.	Mount Carillon	13,517+	Mount Whitney
52.	Mount Ericsson	13,517+	Mount Whitney
53.	Thunder Mountain	13,517+	Mount Whitney
54.	Mount Galey	13,510	Palisades
55.	Mount Fiske	13,503	Bishop
56.	Mount Hale	13,494	Mount Whitney
57.	Mount Pinchot	13,494	Palisades
58.	Mount Thompson	13,494	Bishop
59.	Mount Bolton Brown	13,491	Palisades
60.	Jumpoff	13,484	White Mountains
61.	Mount Pickering	13,474	Mount Whitney
62.	Mount Prater	13,471	Palisades
63.	Mount Versteeg	13,451+	Mount Whitney
64.	Mount Mills	13,451	Mammoth Lakes
65.	Montgomery Peak	13,441	White Mountains
66.	Mount Newcomb	13,422	Mount Whitney
67.	Mount Haeckel	13,418	Bishop
68.	Mount Lamarck	13,417	Bishop

69.	Cardinal Mountain	13,396	Palisades
70.	Mount Jepson	13,389	Palisades
71.	Kaweah Queen	13,382	Sequoia
72.	Mount Wallace	13,377	Bishop
73.	Mount Hilgard	13,361	Mammoth Lakes
74.	Mount Powell	13,360+	Bishop
75.	The Thumb	13,356	Palisades
76.	Black Giant	13,330	Bishop
77.	Mount Jordan	13,320+	Mount Whitney
78.	Black Mountain	13,291	Palisades
79.	Mount McDuffie	13,282	Bishop
80.	Deerhorn Mountain	13,281	Mount Whitney
81.	Royce Peak	13,280+	Mammoth Lakes
82.	Picture Puzzle Peak	13,280	Palisades
83.	Mount Bradley	13,264	Mount Whitney
84.	Mount Goethe	13,264	Bishop
85.	Feather Peak	13,240+	Mammoth Lakes
86.	South Guard	13,231	Sequoia
87.	Mount Heller	13,225	Mount Whitney
88.	North Guard	13,209	Sequoia
89.	Mount Warlow	13,206	Bishop
90.	Mount Emerson	13,204	Bishop
91.	Mount Julius Caesar	13,200+	Bishop
92.	Red Spur Peak	13,186	Sequoia
93.	Acrodectes	13,183	Palisades
94.	Basin Mountain	13,181	Bishop
95.	Striped Mountain	13,179	Palisades
96.	Mount Ritter	13,143	Mammoth Lakes
97.	Mount Baxter	13,136	Palisades
98.	Diamond Peak	13,126	Palisades
99.	Red Slate Mountain	13,123+	Mammoth Lakes
100.	Mount Lyell	13,114	Yosemite

Appendix 4: Wilderness Permits and Maps

All overnight trips in California's national parks and national forests require wilderness permits. Day trips do not require permits, except for the Mount Whitney Trail and trails in the Mount Whitney Zone. Securing a permit in advance is not necessary for any of the ski trips described in this guide, *provided the trip occurs before the start of the wilderness permit quota season.* Currently, each national forest or national park establishes its own wilderness permit quota levels and quota periods. Generally, quotas are applied from the middle of June through September 15. Mount Whitney's quota period runs from May 1 through November 1 each year. Check with the appropriate national forest or national park to find out its respective quota period.

To secure a wilderness permit, contact the appropriate national forest district office or national park office listed below. Many of the national forest district offices and national park offices provide for self-registration after normal working hours. Forest and trail maps also can be purchased at the offices below.

NATIONAL FORESTS

Website links to all U.S. and California national forests:
www.fs.fed.us/links/nfs.htm
www.r5.fs.fed.us/

Mount Shasta Ranger District
204 West Alma Street
Mount Shasta City, CA 96067
Phone: 530-926-4511
www.r5.fs.fed.us/shastatrinity/

Tahoe National Forest
Truckee Ranger District
10342 Highway 89 North
Truckee, CA 95734
Phone: 530-587-3558
www.r5.fs.fed.us/tahoe/

Eldorado National Forest
3070 Camino Heights Drive
Camino, CA 95709
Phone: 530-644-6048
www.r5.fs.fed.us/eldorado/

Lake Tahoe Visitor Center, Eldorado National Forest
Highway 89, South Lake Tahoe
Camino, CA 95709
Phone: 530-573-2674

Toiyabe National Forest
Bridgeport Ranger District
P.O. Box 595 (Highway 395)
Bridgeport, CA 93517
Phone: 760-932-7070
www.fs.fed.us/htnf/

Inyo National Forest
Mono Basin Scenic Area Visitor Center
P.O. Box 429
Lee Vining, CA 93541
Phone: 760-647-3044

Inyo National Forest
Mammoth Ranger District
P.O. Box 148 (Highway 203)
Mammoth Lakes, CA 93546
Phone: 760-924-5500

Inyo National Forest
White Mountain Ranger District
798 North Main Street (Highway 395)
Bishop, CA 93514
Phone: 760-873-2500, 760-873-2483

Inyo National Forest
Mount Whitney Ranger District
P.O. Box 8 (640 South Main)
Lone Pine, CA 93545
Phone: 760-876-6200
www.r5.fs.fed.us/inyo/

NATIONAL PARKS
Website links to all national parks:
www.nps.gov/parks

Lassen Volcanic National Park
P.O. Box 100, Mineral, CA 96063
Phone: 530-595-4444
www.nps.gov/lavo/

Yosemite National Park
P.O. Box 577
Yosemite, CA 95389
Phone: 209-372-0740 or 209-372-0200
www.nps.gov/yose/

Sequoia and Kings Canyon National Parks
Three Rivers, CA 93271
Phone: 559-565-3708 or 559-565-3134
www.nps.gov/seki/

Appendix 5: Contacts and Resources

MOUNTAIN GUIDES AND SCHOOLS

Adventure to the Edge
Jean Pavillard and Bela Vadasz
Phone: 800-349-5219
atedge@crestedbutte.net
www.atedge.com
Custom-designed tours in the Colorado Rockies, Sierra Nevada,
European Alps, Mexican volcanoes, South America, and beyond.

Alpine Skills International
Bela and Mimi Vadasz
P.O. Box 8, Norden, CA 95724
Phone: 530-426-9108 or 800-916-PEAK
ASI@alpineskills.com
www.alpineskills.com
Complete guide service and climbing school providing ski moun-
taineering courses, telemark and randonnée ski instruction, guided
ski descents, and avalanche training.

American Mountain Guides Association (AMGA)
www.amga.com
Complete list of AMGA-certified guides.

Backcountry_Resource_Center
Paul Richins, Jr.
http://pweb.jps.net/~prichins/backcountry_ resource_center.htm
Information for backcountry skiers, climbers, and hikers interested in
exploring the mountains of California, the United States, Canada, and
beyond.

Bardini Foundation
Phone: 760-872-1665
bardini@telis.org
Mountain guide and instructional services.

Cosley and Houston Alpine Guides
Kathy Cosley and Mark Houston
Bishop, CA 93514
Phone: 760-872-3811
CosleyHouston@telis.org
www.cosleyhouston.com

John Fischer
P.O. Box 694
Bishop, CA 93515
Phone: 760-873-5037 or 760-873-9128
Guide services.

Mountain Adventure Seminars
Phone: 800-36-CLIMB or 209-753-6556
mail@mtadventure.com
www.mtadventure.com
Ski school, avalanche courses, guided ski tours, mountaineering;
located in Bear Valley, California.

Moving Over Stone
Doug Robinson
Phone: 650-938-1086
drobinson@movingoverstone.com
www.movingoverstone.com/
Sierra rock climbs and backcountry skiing.

John Moynier
P.O. Box 597
Mammoth Lakes, CA 93546
Phone: 760-934-2596, ext. 251
jmoynier@mcwd.dst.ca.us
Ski mountaineering guide and professional avalanche instructor.

Doug Nidever
Phone: 760-648-7221
nidever@qnet.com
www.themountainguide.com
Mountain guide and instructional services.

Shasta Mountain Guides
Andy Selters and Michael Zanger
1928 Hill Road
Mount Shasta, CA 96067
Phone: 530-926-3117
guides@macshasta.com
www.shastaguides.com

Sierra Guides Alliance
P.O. Box 650

El Portal, CA 95318
Phone: 209-379-2231
or toll free 877-425-3366
sierraguides@hotmail.com
www.guidesalliance.com
Specializing in backcountry snowboarding and skiing adventures in
the Sierra Nevada.

Sierra Mountain Center
Todd Vogel and S. P. Parker
P.O. Box 95, Bishop, CA 93514
Phone: 760-873-8526
sierramc@earthlink.net
www.sierramountaincenter.com
Mountain trips with a special emphasis on ski mountaineering.

Sierra Wilderness Seminars
Timothy Keating
369-B Third Street, San Rafael, CA 94901
Phone: 415-455-9358
SWSInc@aol.com; www.swsmtns.com

Tim Villanueva
P.O. Box 1733, Bishop, CA 93515
Phone: 760-872-4413
Guide services.

Yosemite Mountaineering School
Yosemite National Park
P.O. Box 577 Yosemite, CA 95389
Phone: 209-372-1244 or 209-372-8344

MOUNTAINEERING CLUBS
American Alpine Club
710 Tenth Street, Suite 15
Golden, CO 80401
Phone: 303-384-0112
www.americanalpineclub.org
Sierra Nevada Section: www.alpineclub.org

California Mountaineering Club (CMC)
P.O. Box 5623, Pasadena, CA 91117-0623
www.mountaineer.com

Sierra Club
1414 K Street, Suite 300
Sacramento, CA 95814
Phone: 916-557-1108
or
730 Polk Street
San Francisco, CA 94109
www.sierraclub.org
Sierra Club Chapters in California and the United States:
www.sierraclub.org/chapters/

SKI MOUNTAINEERING STORES
(a select few near the trailheads)
Alpenglow
North Lake Blvd. (Highway 28)
Tahoe City, CA 96145
Phone: 530-583-6917

The Backcountry
255 North Lake Blvd. (Highway 28)
Tahoe City, CA 96145
Phone: 530-581-5861

The Backcountry
11400 Donner Pass Road
Truckee, CA
Phone: 530-582-0909
www.thebackcountry.net

The Fifth Season
Mount Shasta City, CA 96067
Phone: 530-926-3606

Kitteridge Sports
3218 Main Street (Highway 203)
P.O. Box 598, Mammoth Lakes, CA 93546
Phone: 760-934-7566
www.kittredgesports.com

Mammoth Mountaineering Supply
3189 Main Street
Mammoth Lakes, CA 93546
Phone: 760-934-4191
www.mammothgear.com

Wilson Eastside Sports
Highway 395
Bishop, CA
Phone: 760-873-7520
www.eastsidesports.com

ROAD CONDITIONS AND SNO-PARK INFORMATION

Sno-Park permits can be purchased at local ski shops, mountaineering stores, and other establishments. Sno-Parks are snow-cleared parking areas, with sanitation facilities, that provide direct access to popular cross-country ski trails, snowmobile routes, and snow play areas. There are about twenty Sno-Parks in northern California. (Failure to display a valid Sno-Park permit may result in a $75 fine!)

California Department of Parks and Recreation
P.O. Box 942896
Sacramento, CA 94296
Phone: 916-324-1222
Sno-Park locations and map.

Caltrans
Phone (within California): 800-427-ROAD (7623)
Phone (from outside California): 916-445-ROAD (7623)
Statewide road conditions, including dates of road openings in spring.

Caltrans Maintenance Stations—for expected dates when closed roads will open in the spring

Woodfords (Highway 4, Ebbetts Pass)
Phone: 530-694-2241

Sonora Junction (Highway 108, Sonora Pass)
Phone: 760-932-7261

Bridgeport (Virigina Lakes Road and Highway 108, Sonora Pass)
Phone: 760-872-0705

Lee Vining (Highway 120, Tioga Pass)
Phone: 760-647-6391

Crestview (Highway 203, Mammoth Lakes and Rock Creek Road)
Phone: 760-648-7508

Bishop (for all highways)
Phone: 760-872-0601 or 872-0615

Mount Shasta (various access roads)

Fifth Season
Mount Shasta City
Phone: 530-926-3606 or 530-926-5555
or
Mount Shasta Ranger District
204 West Alma Street
Mount Shasta City, CA 96067
Phone: 530-926-4511
www.r5.fs.fed.us/shastatrinity/

National Park Road Conditions

Lassen Volcanic National Park (Lassen Loop Road)
Phone: 530-595-4444

Sequoia and Kings Canyon National Parks (Highways 180,
198, and Mineral King Road)
Phone: 559-565-3708 or 559-565-3134
(or Caltrans; see above)

Yosemite National Park (Tioga Pass Road)
Phone: 209-372-0740 or 209-372-0200
(or Caltrans; see above)

WEATHER AND AVALANCHE CONDITIONS

Mount Shasta
Phone: 530-926-5555
www.r5.fs.fed.us/shastatrinity/mtshasta/

Central California and Tahoe
Phone: 916-646-2000, 530-587-2158, or 800-795-5988

Central and South Sierra Nevada
Phone: 760-873-3213

Cyberspace Snow and Avalanche Center (CSAC)
www.csac.org/
For avalanche forecasts, see www.csac.org/Bulletins/

National Weather Service
www.nws.noaa.gov/

CNN Weather
www.cnn.com/WEATHER/
Forecasts for 7,200 cities worldwide.

The Weather Channel
www.weather.com/twc/homepage.twc
Five-day forecast for any city.

CROSS-COUNTRY SKI LODGES AND BACKCOUNTRY HUTS
Benson Hut
Reservations c/o Clair Tappaan Lodge (see address below)
Sierra backcountry hut located in the Donner Pass/Lake Tahoe
region. It is a half- to full-day ski in to the hut.

Bradley Hut
Reservations c/o Clair Tappaan Lodge (see address below)
Sierra backcountry hut located in the Donner Pass/Lake Tahoe
region. It is a half- to full-day ski in to the hut.

Camp Richardson Resort
South Lake Tahoe, CA 96158
Phone 800-766-4670
Located on Highway 89 north of South Lake Tahoe; you can
drive to the resort.

Clair Tappaan Lodge
19940 Donner Pass Road (Old Highway 40)
P.O. Box 36
Norden, CA 95724
Phone: 530-426-3632
www.sierraclub.org/outings/lodges/huts
You can drive to the lodge.

Coopins Meadow Lodge
P.O. Box 294
Sierraville, CA 96126
Phone: 530-837-3104
Located 15 miles north of Truckee. Park near Little Truckee
Summit (Highway 89) and ski in to the lodge.

Ludlow Hut
Reservations c/o Clair Tappaan Lodge (see address above)

Sierra backcountry hut located in the Donner Pass/Lake Tahoe region. It is a half- to full-day ski in to the hut.

Pear Lake Hut
Sequoia National Park, Natural History Association
HCR 89 Box 10
Three Rivers, CA 93271
Phone: 559-565-3759
www.sequoiahistory.org
It is a full-day ski in to the hut.

Peter Grubb Hut
Reservations c/o Clair Tappaan Lodge (see address above)
Sierra backcountry hut located in the Donner Pass/Lake Tahoe region. It is a 1- to 2-hour ski in to the hut.

Rock Creek Winter Lodge
Route 1, Box 12
Mammoth Lakes, CA 93546
Phone: 760-935-4170
It is a short 2-mile ski on a groomed road to the lodge.

Sorensen's Resort
14255 Highway 88
Hope Valley, CA 96120
Phone: 800-423-9949 or 530-694-2203
You can drive to the resort.

Tamarack Lodge
P.O. Box 69
Mammoth Lakes, CA 93546
Phone: 760-934-2442
www.tamaracklodge.com
You can drive to the lodge.

Tioga Pass Resort
Tioga Pass Road
P.O. Box 307
Lee Vining, CA 93541
Phone: 209-372-4471 (October 15 through May 1)
www.tiogapassresort.com
It is a half- to full-day walk and ski to the resort.

Appendix 6: Equipment Checklist

CLOTHING AND PERSONAL ITEMS

Map and compass
Internal-frame pack
Sleeping bag rated to 0–10 degrees
Therm-a-Rest® sleeping pad
Skis, boots, and poles (avalanche probe type) or Snowboard, boots, snowshoes, poles
Climbing skins
Wax kit and scraper
Gaiters
Weatherproof gloves/mitts
Light pair of gloves
Midweight thermal turtleneck
Lightweight thermal short-sleeved tee-shirt

Powerstretch or micro-fleece vest
Lightweight nylon windbreaker
Fleece jacket with hood
Gore-Tex® parka with hood
Powerstretch tights
Baggy nylon shorts
Gore-Tex® pants or bibs with full-length zippers
Extra pair of wool-blend socks
Down/fleece booties or Gore-Tex® socks
Hat with sun visor
Warm hat and neck gaiter or balaclava
Sunglasses and goggles

PERSONAL EQUIPMENT

Plastic measuring cup (2-cup size) and spoon
Two widemouth water bottles (1 liter each)

Water purification tablets
Headlamp or flashlight
Extra batteries
Inexpensive watch

TOILETRIES

Sunblock SPF-50
Lip balm
Aloe vera gel
Toilet paper
Moist towelettes

Antibacterial waterless soap
Toothbrush and toothpaste
Bandanna
Retractable scissors

GROUP EQUIPMENT

Food and cookware
Bibler® hanging stove
Two or three lighters
Extra pair of sunglasses or goggles
Fuel canisters

Free-standing (three- or four-pole) tent
Snow shovel
Repair kit (see list below)
First-aid kit (see Appendix 7)

REPAIR KIT

Duct tape
Ski binding repair tools

Tent-pole and ski-pole splints
Spare basket

Pocket knife with leather punch	Epoxy
Pliers	Steel wool
Screwdriver	Hacksaw blade for metal
Wire	Sewing kit
Vise-grips	

OPTIONAL ITEMS

(Some of the following are necessary for certain difficult routes.)

Ice axe	Cellular phone
Crampons including wrench	Gore-tex® bivy sack
Rope, 7–8 mm	Down jacket or down vest
Avalanche transceivers	Fleece pants with full-length zipper
Camera and film	Snow saw
Altimeter	Thermometer
GPS receiver	Water filter

Appendix 7: Contents of a Wilderness First-Aid Kit

by Colin Fuller, M.D.

This first-aid kit has been developed for use on backcountry wilderness trips of 3 to 10 days; the number of items can be pared back for shorter trips. The kit is not as comprehensive as one that might be used on a major expedition, but is a compromise, considering that a complete first-aid kit would entail considerable weight.

First Aid Item	Application
Ibuprofen—Motrin/Advil, 200 mg	for aches, minor pain, joint/muscle stiffness, headache, fever
Personal medications	for asthma, diabetes, allergies, etc.
Codeine	for severe pain
Antibiotics (Septra DS)	for bronchitis and urinary-tract infections (women)
Sulfacetamide 10 percent solution	for an inflamed, purulent eye
Diamox 125 mg	for altitude sickness
Antacid tablets	for nausea and upset stomach
Antidiarrheal agents (Immodium A-D)	for diarrhea or loose bowels
Metronidazole (Flagyl)	for severe, prolonged diarrhea when *Giardia* is suspected
Decongestants	for congestion and hay fever
Moleskin	for blisters
Band-Aids and 2 x 4.5-inch adhesive bandages	to cover and protect cuts and lacerations
Butterfly bandages	to close lacerations
Sterile 4-inch gauze pads	to cover and protect wounds

Stretch gauze, 2-inch roll	for hard-to-bandage areas
Adhesive cloth tape, 2-inch roll	to wrap sprains, secure dressings
Self-adhesive elastic bandage, 3-inch	for sprains, joint dislocations
Mild antiseptic soap or hydrogen peroxide	for cleaning abrasions and wounds
Topical antibiotic ointment (Neosporin)	for minor abrasions and wounds
Hydrocortisone ointment (1 percent)	for rashes, burns, and severe sunburn
Scissors (part of Swiss Army knife)	to cut bandages, moleskin, tape, dressings
First-aid field manual	for reference and guidance

Appendix 8: Selected Bibliography

Beck, David. *Ski Touring in California.* Berkeley, CA: Wilderness Press, 1980.

Brower, David, editor. *The Sierra Club Manual of Ski Mountaineering.* New York: Ballantine Books, 1969.

Browning, Peter. *Places Names of the Sierra Nevada: From Abbot to Zumwalt.* Berkeley, CA: Wilderness Press, 1986.

Burhenne, H. J. *Sierra Spring Ski-Touring.* San Francisco: Mountain Press, 1971.

Carline, Dr. Jan D., Dr. Steven C. McDonald, and Dr. Martha J. Lentz. *Mountaineering First Aid: A Guide to Accident Response and First Aid Care.* Seattle: The Mountaineers, 1996.

Crapsey, Malinee, editor. *The Sequoia Bark*, a newspaper published by the Sequoia Natural History Association, National Park Service, and Kings Canyon Park Service.

Daffern, Tony. *Avalanche Safety for Skiers and Climbers*, 2nd Ed. Seattle: The Mountaineers, 1999.

Dwyer, Richard A., and Richard E. Lingenfelter. "Snowshoe Thompson," *Dan De Quille, the Washoe Giant: A Biography and Anthology.* Reno and Las Vegas: University of Nevada Press, 1990, pp 73–99.

Farquhar, Francis P. *History of the Sierra Nevada.* Berkeley: University of California Press, 1969.

Fleming, June. *Staying Found: The Complete Map and Compass Handbook.* Seattle: The Mountaineers, 1994.

Graydon, Don, and Kurt Hanson, eds. *Mountaineering: The Freedom of the Hills*, 6th Ed. Seattle: The Mountaineers, 1997.

Harris, Stephen L. *Fire and Ice: The Cascade Volcanoes.* Seattle: The Mountaineers, 1980.

Heacox, Kim. *California State Parks.* California Geographic Series Number Two. Helena, MT: Falcon Press, 1987.

Hill, Russell B. *California Mountain Ranges.* California Geographic Series Number One. Helena, MT: Falcon Press, 1986.

King, Clarence. *Mountaineering in the Sierra Nevada*. Lincoln, NE: University of Nebraska Press, 1971.

Letham, Lawrence. *GPS Made Easy: Using Global Positioning Systems in the Outdoors*. Seattle: The Mountaineers, 1998.

McClung, David, and Peter Schaerer. *The Avalanche Handbook*. Seattle: The Mountaineers, 1993.

Moynier, John. *Avalanche Aware: Safe Travel in Avalanche Country*. Helena, MT: Falcon Press, 1998.

_____. *Backcountry Skiing in the High Sierra*, 2nd Ed. Helena, MT: Falcon Press, 1997.

_____, and Claude Fiddler. *Sierra Classics: 100 Best Climbs in the High Sierra*. Helena, MT: Falcon Press, 1993.

Muir, John. *John Muir: The Eight Wilderness-Discovery Books*. Seattle: The Mountaineers, 1995.

_____, ed. *West of the Rocky Mountains*. (Originally published as *Picturesque California* in 1888.) Philadelphia: Running Press, 1976.

Muir, John, Exhibit. Website edited and maintained by Harold Wood and Harvey Chinn. www.sierraclub.org/john_muir_exhibit/

National Park Service. *Lassen Volcanic National Park Official Map and Guide*. U.S. Department of the Interior.

_____. *Sequoia and Kings Canyon National Parks Official Guide and Map*. U.S. Department of the Interior.

_____. *Yosemite National Park Official Guide and Map*. U.S. Department of the Interior.

Parker, Paul. *Free-Heel Skiing: Telemark and Parallel Techniques for All Conditions*. Seattle: The Mountaineers, 1995.

Reid, Robert Leonard. *Treasury of the Sierra Nevada*. Berkeley, CA: Wilderness Press, 1983.

Roper, Steve. *The Climber's Guide to the High Sierra*. San Francisco: Sierra Club Books, 1976.

Rebuffat, Gaston. *Between Heaven and Earth*. New York: Oxford University Press, 1965.

_____. *On Snow and Rock*. New York: Oxford University Press, 1968.

Secor, R. J. *The High Sierra: Peaks, Passes, and Trails,* 2nd Ed. Seattle: The Mountaineers, 1999.

Selters, Andy. *Glacier Travel and Crevasse Rescue,* 2nd Ed. Seattle: The Mountaineers, 1999.

Index

About the Author

Paul Richins has over thirty years of wilderness and ski mountaineering experience. A longtime member of the American Alpine Club and the Sierra Club, he has participated in major expeditions to Alaska, Canada, Norway, Tibet, and Argentina. He has made numerous ski traverses of the Sierra Nevada and Lassen Volcanic National Park, and has skied across the Lyngen Alps in Norway, the length of the Teton Mountain Range in Wyoming, and nearly the 300-mile length of the Sierra Nevada. Paul has climbed and/or skied hundreds of other peaks in France, Norway, Canada, Argentina, Ecuador, and the western United States as well as each peak featured in this guidebook.

Through his Backcountry_Resource_Center website http://pweb.jps.net/~prichins/backcountry_ resource_center.htm, Paul provides free information for backcountry skiers, climbers, and hikers interested in exploring the mountains of California, the United States, Canada, and beyond.

By profession, Paul is an economist and project manager responsible for overseeing a team of engineers, planners, economists, and environmental scientists at the California Energy Commission. He is also the author of *Mount Whitney: The Complete Trailhead-to-Summit Hiking Guide*. He lives in El Dorado Hills, California, with his daughter, Sierra Nicole Richins.

Paul Richins and Prince at base camp on Mount Humphreys Photo by Ann Gimpel

THE MOUNTAINEERS, founded in 1906, is a nonprofit outdoor activity and conservation club, whose mission is "to explore, study, preserve, and enjoy the natural beauty of the outdoors. . . . " Based in Seattle, Washington, the club is now the third-largest such organization in the United States, with 15,000 members and five branches throughout Washington State.

The Mountaineers sponsors both classes and year-round outdoor activities in the Pacific Northwest, which include hiking, mountain climbing, ski-touring, snowshoeing, bicycling, camping, kayaking and canoeing, nature study, sailing, and adventure travel. The club's conservation division supports environmental causes through educational activities, sponsoring legislation, and presenting informational programs. All club activities are led by skilled, experienced volunteers, who are dedicated to promoting safe and responsible enjoyment and preservation of the outdoors.

If you would like to participate in these organized outdoor activities or the club's programs, consider a membership in The Mountaineers. For information and an application, write or call The Mountaineers, Club Headquarters, 300 Third Avenue West, Seattle, Washington 98119; (206) 284-6310.

The Mountaineers Books, an active, nonprofit publishing program of the club, produces guidebooks, instructional texts, historical works, natural history guides, and works on environmental conservation. All books produced by The Mountaineers are aimed at fulfilling the club's mission.

Send or call for our catalog of more than 300 outdoor titles:
The Mountaineers Books
1001 SW Klickitat Way, Suite 201
Seattle, WA 98134
1-800-553-4453
mbooks@mountaineers.org
www.mountaineersbooks.org